Original Christian Ethics Today

Original Christian Ethics Today

Relating Early and Today's Christianity

David W. T. Brattston

WIPF & STOCK · Eugene, Oregon

ORIGINAL CHRISTIAN ETHICS TODAY
Relating Early and Today's Christianity

Copyright © 2019 David W. T. Brattston. All rights reserved. Except for brief quotations in critical publications or reviews, no part of this book may be reproduced in any manner without prior written permission from the publisher. Write: Permissions, Wipf and Stock Publishers, 199 W. 8th Ave., Suite 3, Eugene, OR 97401.

Wipf & Stock
An Imprint of Wipf and Stock Publishers
199 W. 8th Ave., Suite 3
Eugene, OR 97401

www.wipfandstock.com

PAPERBACK ISBN: 978-1-5326-9806-4
HARDCOVER ISBN: 978-1-5326-9807-1
EBOOK ISBN: 978-1-5326-9808-8

Manufactured in the U.S.A.   OCTOBER 21, 2019

Except where otherwise indicated, all Bible quotations are from the Authorized (King James) version.

Scripture quotations marked (NIV) are taken from the Holy Bible, New International Version®, NIV®. Copyright © 1973, 1978, 1984, 2011 by Biblica, Inc.™ Used by permission of Zondervan. All rights reserved worldwide. www.zondervan.com

Except where otherwise indicated, all patristic quotations are as translated in *The Ante-Nicene Fathers: Translations of the Writings of the Fathers Down to A.D. 325* ed. Alexander Roberts and James Donaldson. American Reprint of the Edinburgh edition by A. Cleveland Coxe (Buffalo, NY: Christian Literature, 1885–96; continuously reprinted Edinburgh: T. & T. Clark; Grand Rapids: Eerdmans; Peabody, MA: Hendrickson). Herein cited as "ANF."

Dedicated to

Gary W. Yemen, MD
Calgary, Alberta

who suggested this collection

Contents

Preface | ix

Chapter 1   Anger | 1
Chapter 2   Anxiety | 4
Chapter 3   Bible Study as Intended | 6
Chapter 4   Bible Study Groups | 13
Chapter 5   Business and Commerce | 16
Chapter 6   Chastity—Meaning | 18
Chapter 7   Chastity—Reasons | 23
Chapter 8   Chastity—Scope | 27
Chapter 9   Church Buildings: Good or Bad? | 32
Chapter 10   Common Property or Common Fund? | 37
Chapter 11   Contentment | 40
Chapter 12   Corruption, Including Bribery | 43
Chapter 13   Encouragement | 47
Chapter 14   Enemies | 50
Chapter 15   Envy | 60
Chapter 16   Fasting | 64

Chapter 17   Food | 77
Chapter 18   Gambling | 80
Chapter 19   Gluttony | 84
Chapter 20   Gossip! | 87
Chapter 21   Greed | 91
Chapter 22   Hate Commandment | 96
Chapter 23   The Homeless | 98
Chapter 24   Homosexuality | 100
Chapter 25   Honor Your Parents | 104
Chapter 26   Hospitality | 111
Chapter 27   Humor in the Christian Life | 114
Chapter 28   The Husband's Role and His Duties | 118
Chapter 29   Imitate | 123
Chapter 30   Immigrants and Racism | 127
Chapter 31   Jealousy | 130
Chapter 32   Judging Christians, Then and Now | 132
Chapter 33   Keep Your Word Before AD 200 | 135

Chapter 34   The Medicine of
             Immortality | 138
Chapter 35   Modesty in Dress
             and Appearance | 142
Chapter 36   Mutilate Yourself (Matt
             18:8–9) | 150
Chapter 37   Nighttime Activities | 153
Chapter 38   Patience | 157
Chapter 39   Praying Without
             Ceasing | 160
Chapter 40   Pride | 162
Chapter 41   Renewal | 165
Chapter 42   Second Coming | 167
Chapter 43   Self-Correction | 170
Chapter 44   The Sick | 173

Chapter 45   Silence | 176
Chapter 46   Sloth | 179
Chapter 47   Suicide and Assisted
             Suicide | 182
Chapter 48   Taxes | 187
Chapter 49   Temptation and
             1 Corinthians 10:13 | 193
Chapter 50   Tithing | 196
Chapter 51   Trust and Distrust | 200
Chapter 52   Usury | 203
Chapter 53   Veiling of Christian
             Women | 206
Chapter 54   Wifely Submission | 210

Bibliography | 217

Preface

THE following book is an edited selection of my magazine and website articles about Christian ethics and behavior prior to the middle of the third century AD, and their relevance today. It uses the original drafts I submitted to editors between 1993 and 2019.

These articles originated in my search for how I, as a Christian, ought to behave in order to love God and my neighbor in action. As a lawyer and judge on minor tribunals, I learned that what to do in order to love one's neighbor is not always clear, nor does it necessarily follow a direct route. There can be valid doubts and uncertainties about which course of action best helps a neighbor, and perplexities can often arise concerning which of two neighbors to favor or love more when their legitimate interests conflict.

My first response was to turn to the Bible. I found the Bible and systems of biblical ethics to be insufficient, or at least unclear and subject to myriad interpretations, each claiming exclusive validity for itself. I felt it needed a supplement or method of interpretation that was unassailable on objective grounds.

Dissatisfied with the contending claims to conformity with the Scriptures, and the lack of a means of objectively verifying them free of denominational presuppositions (no matter how inadvertent), I looked for a source that could not be duplicated or fabricated. Anybody can claim a latter-day revelation, unique guidance by the Holy Spirit, or correct method of interpretation. Even descent through a line of ordinations stretching back to the apostles is suspect because there are conflicting allegations as to which modern-day denomination most closely represents the collectivity of the ancient church, and succession cannot be proved in most cases. I wanted something unique, something that could not be invented or asserted by just anyone while remaining unsupported by unassailable evidence.

PREFACE

So I went to the literature of the earliest age of Christianity, before medieval and modern differences as to the Scriptures' pronouncements on morality came about. Unlike claims to recent revelation, unique guidance by the Holy Spirit, or faultless hermeneutics, this method cannot be falsely raised because there is only one body of primitive Christian writings and, unlike modern pretensions to possession of direct divine guidance, it cannot be contrived or asserted without being liable to falsification by a definite body of universally accepted data.

At length, I composed a finding guide of over 1,600 pages for the study of Christian ethics before the devastating epidemic and mass apostasy of AD 249–251. I have used it to resolve moral issues not sufficiently answered by any authors or present-day church pronouncements.

Most of the articles began as guidance for myself. I usually wrote a piece for my own edification, and only later looked for a magazine or website to publish it in case other Christians were facing the same problem. Using the finding list, I searched New Testament and other early Christian literature and tried to produce a written consolidation of the consensus of all the ancient teaching on a topic to guide my own actions. Often I did not know which way I would conclude on a specific issue until the second or third draft. Then I searched for a periodical or website that I believed would be receptive. The result is articles that are nondenominational, or, better, predenominational, because I draw on sources that predate the division into separate modern ecclesiastical organizations. The ancient writings are the common inheritance of all Christendom. As a result, many of the following articles have been published by more than one denomination.

I realize that there is much repetition from chapter to chapter, especially as to details about the ancient authors, and the citation systems are not uniform from article to article. This is because each is self-contained, with the hope that readers can choose any chapter at random and be fully informed from it as to the sources, like a collection of stand-alone meditations or sermonettes for all occasions.

A final note: except for chapter 10 of book 2 of the *Paedagogus*, the present book employs the English translation in ANF. For 2.10, which is not in English in ANF, this book uses the English translation at pages 164–78 of Simon P. Wood's *Clement of Alexandria: Christ the Educator* (New York: Fathers of the Church, 1954). It is divided into paragraphs as well as pages; the paragraph number in Wood appears in parentheses as the last element in a citation of the *Paedagogus*.

PREFACE

Except for book 3 of the *Stromata*, the present book employs the English translation in ANF. For book 3, which is not in English in ANF, this book uses the English translation of the *Stromata* at pages 40–92 of *Alexandrian Christianity: Selected Translations* by John Ernest Leonard Oulton and Henry Chadwick (London: SCM, 1954). It is divided into paragraphs as well as pages; the paragraph number in Oulton and Chadwick appears in parentheses as the last element in a citation of Clement's *Stromata*.

Chapter 1

Anger

"Be Angry But Do Not Sin"

ANGER poses a puzzle for students of the ageless gospel. In some places, the New Testament and other early Christian writings oppose it, while in others it is allowed, perhaps even considered godly. This article will examine the writings of the earliest Christians on the subject to see if they can be harmonized, or whether Jesus' first followers contradicted themselves and each other.

Jesus was against "everyone who is angry with his brother" (Matt 5:22). Paul's letters especially discountenance anger. In Ephesians 4:31, Colossians 3:8, and 2 Corinthians 12:20 he classifies it with slander. The first two also lump it together with malice. The third considers it to be in the same category as jealousy and selfishness. Galatians 5:19–21 includes it in the same class not only with jealousy and selfishness, but also with sexual immorality, idolatry, drunkenness, orgies, and hatred. James 1:20 states "the anger of a man does not work the righteousness of God." *The First Letter of Clement* and *The Pastor of Hermas*, very early Christian books that for centuries the church fathers recommended as edifying spiritual reading, contain ten separate negative comments against anger. Including "wrath" and "rage," the New Testament and other Christian literature before AD 250 contain about 100 disapprovals of anger.

Yet anger is a naturally occurring emotion that comes upon a person whether s/he wants it to or not, and is usually sudden and unplanned. It is often unavoidable, and was experienced by the best and most exemplary of Bible personages. In the Acts of the Apostles, Paul appears to have been angered by some Jews and pagans on his missionary journeys, while his Epistles indicate a similar feeling toward some of his congregations. Hebrews 3:10, 11, and 17 depict God himself as angry, as does much of the Old Testament. Mark 3:5 states point-blank that Christ was angry, while some people today believe he was angry when casting the money-changers out of the Temple (Mark 11:15–18 and parallels). The prominent Bible scholar Origen, the leading preacher of the first half of the third century, conceded that even "the perfect"[1] among us experience anger without forethought on their part. He even saw it as beneficial and necessary when it leads to restraining sin, restoring righteousness, and reproaching, correcting, and disciplining sinners. In the early period of Origen's labors, Tertullian, a prominent North African minister, wrote that being unjustly angry and allowing the sun to set on one's anger were daily and usually unavoidable occurrences.

The New Testament must be interpreted in context, both within its own pages and within the Christian culture that grew up alongside it. I include the earliest nonbiblical Christian writings as part of the latter. When taking all these sources as a whole, it appears that what early Christianity taught was that anger should be controlled and dampened down, and that Christians should not allow the involuntary emotion to control their actions or attitudes.

The earliest Christians recognized not so much an outright ban on anger, but restrictions and limits so that it would not harm anyone. James 1:19 counsels Christians to be "slow to anger"; it does not forbid it entirely. First Corinthians 13:5 (NIV) states that love "is not *easily* angered," not that love is never angered. Ephesians 4:26 is particularly informative: (1) "Be angry but do not sin" indicates that anger itself is not a sin, but merely may bring a person closer toward sin, and (2) "do not let the sun go down on your anger" called forth comments from early authors. Origen instructed Christians to abandon anger before it causes the sunshine of faith to set upon us and bring spiritual darkness to our souls. A few years earlier, his teacher, Clement of Alexandria, praised this verse as a prime example of the apostles' wholesome teaching. Tertullian's comment is stated above.

The ancient use of adjectives also suggests that what was condemned was not the involuntary emotion itself, but anger that has become unjust, furious (both Tertullian), boiling, unmanageable (both Clement of

---

1. Origen, *Commentary on Ephesians* 4.26a, 193–94.

Alexandria), uncontrolled, flaming, irrational, or brutal (all Origen). Origen also opposed being drunk with anger or enslaved by it. *The Didache*, a church manual dating from the first century, discountenanced "hot" anger. Titus 1:7 indicates that a bishop in particular is not to be "quick-tempered."

The fact that some early authors imposed parameters and limits indicate that, while they did not approve of anger, they nevertheless did not regard it as an automatic sin. It is like alcohol and tobacco today: the existence of secular government regulations implies that the government tolerates them, though it disapproves of them.

We are to avoid acting under the influence of anger because it may impair our judgment and self-control. Origen counselled Christians to conquer anger in ourselves, chasten ourselves to remove incentives to it, and soften it—say, by moderation and meditation. About the same era, a book of testimonies proving that Christianity is superior to Judaism instructs people to overcome anger (*Three Books of Testimonies Against the Jews*).

The consensus among Christian writers before AD 250 appears to be that, while we might be unable to avoid becoming angry, we should make efforts to damp it down and control it. If this does not work, we should avoid acting under its influence. We must not be *prone* to anger or be quick-tempered (Titus 1:7, *Didache*, and Origen). Still less should we provoke it in other people (Eph 6:4, Clement of Alexandria, Origen), pray under its influence (1 Tim 2:8, Origen), or reprove someone in anger (*Didache*).

As in so many other ways, Jesus' actions in cleansing the temple are a model of behavior when angry. His calmness and deliberation show he was not controlled or enslaved by anger. Nor did he prolong the emotion or allow it to interfere with his relationships with other people. In Matthew's account (21:12–14), he immediately returned to his usual healing ministry, while in John 2:13–21, he at once engaged in teaching and a peaceful conversation.

Except in the one instance indicated, all Scripture quotations are from the Revised Standard Version of the Bible, copyright 1946, 1952, 1971 by the Division of Christian Education of the National Council of the Churches of Christ in the USA. Used by permission.

Chapter 2

Anxiety

"Be not soon shaken in mind, or be troubled, neither by spirit, nor by word, nor by letter as from us"

—2 Thessalonians 2:2

Documents from the church's foundational period encourage Christians not to be anxious or troubled. Among the more familiar are Matthew 6:25 ("Take no thought for your life, what ye shall eat, or what ye shall drink; nor yet for your body, what ye shall put on. Is not the life more than meat, and the body than raiment?"), Matthew 24:6 ("ye shall hear of wars and rumors of wars; see that ye be not troubled"), John 14:1 ("Let not your heart be troubled: ye believe in God, believe also in me"), and John 14:27 ("Peace I leave with you, my peace I give unto you: not as the world giveth, give I unto you. Let not your heart be troubled, neither let it be afraid.").

This sentiment was reinforced in apostolic times outside the present Bible in a letter from the church at Rome to the church at Corinth: "let us give up vain and fruitless cares."[1] In the 190s AD, the dean of Christianity's foremost school wrote that the proper Christian "is not disturbed by anything which happens; nor does he suspect those things which, through divine arrangement, take place for good."[2] On the subject of persons with money, he wrote that the Master, "bids him banish from his soul his notions

---

1. 1 Clement 7.2 (ANF 1:7).
2. Clement of Alexandria, *Stromata* 7.13 (ANF 2:547).

about wealth, his excitement and morbid feeling about it, the anxieties, which are the thorns of existence, which choke the seed of life."[3] Traveling Christians in the early third century were to exhort local believers "to please God in everything, and abound and go forward in good works, and be free from anxious care in everything, as is fit and right for the people of God."[4]

The same literature provides alternatives and remedies for anxiety. Matthew 6:25–33 reminds us that just as God provides the necessities of life and some of its luxuries to birds, flowers, and grass, so also he cares for every human being and will supply each with all the food, drink, and clothing we need. Verse 33 assures: "seek ye first the kingdom of God, and his righteousness; and all these things shall be added unto you." About AD 200, readers were exhorted to trust Christ "and to esteem Him our Nourisher, Father, Teacher, Counsellor, Healer, our Wisdom, Light, Honor, Glory, Power and Life, so that we should not be anxious concerning clothing and food."[5] First Peter 5:7 exhorts us to cast all our cares upon the Lord "for He careth for you." The letter from Rome to Corinth completes its above thought by saying "let us give up vain and fruitless cares, and approach to the glorious and venerable rule of our holy calling. Let us attend to what is good, pleasing, and acceptable in the sight of Him who formed us."[6]

---

3. Clement of Alexandria, *Quis Dives Salvetur* 11, (ANF 2:594).
4. *Two Letters on Virginity* 2.1 (ANF 8:61).
5. *Two Letters on Virginity* 2.1 (ANF 8:61).
6. *1 Clement* 7.2–3 (ANF 1:7).

Chapter 3

Bible Study as Intended

BIBLE study should never be considered a light pastime to be pursued half-heartedly while partially distracted by other activities. It was never meant to be. The first readers and hearers of the New Testament regarded engaging with the Scriptures as a serious and intense endeavor that requires concentration, exertion, much time and labor, and a proper attitude. These first readers and hearers were the Christians who lived and taught their faith prior to the mass apostasy of AD 249–251; before it, unwritten biblical interpretations and instructions of Jesus and the apostles about how to deal with the Scriptures were still fresh in Christian memories, a time when most Christians today consider the Holy Spirit to have been still guiding the church.

Our Main Author

The constant effort, vigilant attention, intense study, work, and approach practiced and taught by these first heirs of the gospel are described for us mainly by Origen (a church father of the first half of the third century) if for no other reason than that more of his works have survived than of all other authors. Dean of the foremost Christian educational institution of the period, he later established what has been called "the first Christian university."[1] He wrote more about the Bible and Christian faith than anyone else before Martin Luther. Unlike Luther, he never married, and thus devoted more of his time to studying and teaching the word of God. In fact, Origen considered the correct exposition of Scripture as his main mission

---

1. McGuckin, *Westminster Handbook to Origen*, 1.

in life. Origen even produced a massive 6,000-page version of the Old Testament with the Hebrew original and various Greek versions in parallel columns. He preached or wrote commentaries on almost every book of the Bible. He possessed a wider acquaintance with the Christianity of his day than other writers and preachers, for he traveled widely in order to collect religious books, to hear other teachers, and to act as a theological consultant at the request of pastor-bishops throughout the eastern Mediterranean as well as government officials who wished to learn about Christianity. His sermons reveal that he had memorized an astounding amount of Scripture and could recall and compare exact wordings of many passages, all in a time before concordances were in existence. He died prematurely from torture inflicted while he had been imprisoned for the faith.

Read the Bible

Origen and other early Christians commended reading the Bible as a first step, and only as a first step. Origen preached that true conversion entails reading the Old Testament to see who became righteous and to imitate them, reading the New Testament, and writing the words of both into one's heart.[2] He exhorted that the Bible be read and understood correctly to avoid falling into false teachings.[3] He advised reading the Bible every day.[4] The *Didascalia*, a Syrian church manual finalized at about Origen's time, instructed Christians with free time to form a Bible study group, but also, if this was not possible locally, to read widely in the Scriptures.[5] Another writer in the first half of the third century noted that Christian male travelers who stay overnight in a community read the Bible aloud to the Christian women there.[6]

Search the Scriptures

However, this was not mere cursory reading. What Origen intended was devoting oneself to diligent reading of the whole Bible, and engaging

---

2. Origen, *Homilies on Jeremiah* 4.6.3.
3. Origen, *On First Principles* 4.7.
4. Origen, *Commentary on Romans* 9.1.12.
5. Connolly, *Didascalia apostolorum*, 2.
6. *Two Letters on Virginity* 2.4.

oneself busily with the precepts of the New Testament.[7] In fact, Christ never commanded people to merely read the Scriptures; what he mandated was that we *search* them, which requires more effort than just reading. "Search the Scriptures; for in them ye think ye have eternal life: and they are them which testify of me," records John 5:39. Origen referred to this verse three times in writings of which I am aware. Once was to prove that benefits from one's involvement with and understanding of the Scriptures come only through humble and faithful enquiry, and not "fleetingly" reading or listening to them.[8] He indicated that the Bible is not to be read "carelessly" or "as if in passing."[9] On another occasion, he quoted John 5:39 in commending "those who know how to ascend from a simple faith and to investigate the meaning which lies in the divine Scriptures, agreeably to the injunctions of Jesus, who said 'Search the Scriptures.'"[10] Another time, he phrased the quotation as "Thoroughly examine the Scriptures" when exhorting his congregation to devote themselves wholly to God's law and meditate on it through reading or hearing.[11] The Bible itself approvingly states that Paul's listeners in Berea "were more noble than those in Thessalonica, in that they received the word with all readiness of mind, and searched the Scriptures daily" (Acts 17:11).

Intense Study

Thorough examination is required, as noted in the above extract about not reading "carelessly" or "as if in passing,"[12] while another sermon of Origen's exhorted his listeners to examine God's word "very carefully."[13] In still another sermon he promised that thorough study renders difficult and obscure passages easier to understand.[14] He encouraged his congregation to investigate the Scriptures read at public worship with each other and to draw comparisons with other parts of the Bible.[15] He also encouraged

---

7. Origen, *Homilies on Psalm 36* 3.6.
8. Origen, *Commentary on Romans* 7.17.4.
9. Origen, *Homilies on Joshua* 1.4; Origen, *Homilies on Genesis* 5.6.
10. Origen, *Against Celsus* 3.33 (ANF 4:477).
11. Origen, *Homilies on Joshua* 19.4.
12. Origen, *Homilies on Joshua* 31.
13. Origen, *Homilies on Genesis* 3.3.
14. Origen, *Homilies on Numbers* 27.1.
15. Origen, *Homilies on Exodus* 12.2.

vigilance in Bible study.[16] He preached that through devoting themselves to Bible study and perseverance in meditation on Scripture his hearers would understand it and would truly receive spiritual manna.[17] His *Commentary on Ephesians* exhorted his readers to "persevere" in the acquisition of the riches of the word of God in order to enrich others, especially through their prayers.[18] Zeal to learn the Scriptures was and is required, as is prayer that the reader will understand the Scriptures.[19] Zeal for going to church for a Bible study was mandated by another church manual, written in AD 217 and ascribed to Hippolytus, a pastor-bishop in central Italy, in order to equip both clergy and layfolk to make sure the church continued the practices and teachings of the apostles.[20]

Search the Scriptures Daily and Meditate

Hippolytus assumed local churches would hold Bible studies every morning to equip Christians to avoid the evil of the day.[21] All were urged to attend and, if they could not, or if there was no study at church that day, they should read Scripture passages at home.[22] On the same frequency, remember that the Bereans searched the Old Testament every day (Acts 17:11). Origen preached that Christians should meditate and pray day and night that Christ open the meaning and understanding of the Scriptures to them/us,[23] which is reminiscent of the Israelites under Joshua (Josh 1:8) and the psalmist (Ps 1:2) meditating on God's law day and night.

Such meditation was important in early Christianity. Around AD 100, a letter bearing the name of an apostle stated:

> we ought to join ourselves to those that fear the Lord, those who meditate in their heart on the commandment which they have received, those who utter the judgments of the Lord and observe

---

16. Origen, *Homilies on Exodus* 5.5.
17. Origen, *Homilies on Psalm 36* 3.10.
18. Origen, *Commentary on Ephesians* 6:17b–19a.
19. Origen, *Homilies on Exodus* 12.2, 12.4; Origen, *Homilies on Luke*, 125.
20. Hippolytus, *Apostolic Tradition* 35.3.
21. Hippolytus, *Apostolic Tradition* 35.2.
22. Hippolytus, *Apostolic Tradition* 36.1.
23. Origen, *Homilies on Exodus* 12.4; Origen, *Homilies on Isaiah* 5.1; Origen, *Homilies on Leviticus* 12.4.1; Origen, *Homilies on Luke*, 125.

them, those who know that meditation is a work of gladness, and who ruminate upon the word of the Lord.[24]

One purpose the *Didascalia* related for privately organized Bible study groups was so its members could meditate on the Scriptures. Origen recommended "continual meditation on the divine word."[25] Along with prayer, it helps combat the devil.[26] Meditating on God's law was deemed particularly appropriate for clergy.[27] Full understanding of Holy Writ, said Origen, comes through meditating on it,[28] again a daily process.[29]

Undivided Attention

Bible study cannot be carried out while simultaneously sharing time with other activities. Origen rebuked his congregation more than once for their divided attention or lack of attention while the Scriptures were being read in public worship. Some persons present ignored the Bible readings in favor of discussing secular matters such as money, business profits, possessions, children, clothing, and household matters, with the result that some were not even aware that the Scriptures were being read.[30] Another author of the same period condemned Christians who "gad about among the houses of virgin brethren or sisters, on pretense of visiting them, or reading the Scriptures to them, or exorcising them,"[31] and stated that it was inappropriate to read the Scriptures as entertainment at banquets where alcohol is served.[32]

The degree of concentration and effort required also precludes multitasking. Origen called upon his congregation to be "totally intent," "watchful," and to "give attention carefully" to the Scripture readings in church.[33] He regarded "Search the scriptures" as necessitating "constant effort and

---

24. *Letter of Barnabas* 10.11 (ANF 1:144).
25. Origen, *Homilies on Joshua* 1.7.
26. Origen, *Homilies on Joshua* 16.5.
27. Origen, *Homilies on Joshua* 17.3.
28. Origen, *Homilies on Genesis* 10.5.
29. Origen, *Homilies on Exodus* 12.2; Origen, *Homilies on Joshua* 17.3, 19.4; Origen, *Homilies on Psalm 36* 3.10.
30. Origen, *Homilies on Genesis* 10.1; Origen, *Homilies on Exodus* 12.2; 13.3.
31. *Two Letters on Virginity* 1.10 (ANF 8:58).
32. *Two Letters on Virginity* 2.6.
33. Origen, *Homilies on Exodus* 13.3.

uninterrupted nightly vigils"[34] and despaired for any person who is lazy as regards Scripture study.[35]

In a major section titled "On the Inspiration of Holy Scripture" in the first-ever Christian handbook of systematic theology, Origen wrote that giving oneself to "labor and toil" was necessary in studying the Scriptures[36] and that it was imperative to "endure the fatigue of" such studying,[37] that "great pains and labor are to be employed, until every reader reverentially understand that he is dealing with divine and not human words inserted in sacred books."[38] Origen also held out the promise that

> he who should devote himself with all chastity, and sobriety, and watchfulness, to studies of this kind, might be able by this means to trace out the meaning of the Spirit of God.[39]

Attitude

So far, you will have gleaned some information about the proper inward disposition toward the Bible and the study of it. Do not read cursorily, but be prepared to exert labor and toil and bear up under fatigue in order to "reverentially understand," pursue it with zeal, give it your undivided attention, and practice sobriety and watchfulness while so engaged. In addition, Origen pronounced that "great attention must be bestowed by the cautious reader on the divine books, as being divine writings."[40] He encouraged "an upright and sincere heart" while searching the Scriptures.[41] He further stated that divine knowledge ought to be sought after "in a religious and holy spirit, and in the hope that many points will be opened up by the revelation of God."[42] He warned that "divine things are brought down somewhat slowly to the comprehension of man, and elude the view in proportion as one is either skeptical or unworthy."[43]

34. Origen, *Commentary on Romans* 7.17.4.
35. Origen, *Commentary on Romans* 9.1.12.
36. Origen, *On First Principles,* 4.14 (ANF 4:363), Latin.
37. Origen, *On First Principles,* 4.14 (ANF 4:363), Greek.
38. Origen, *On First Principles,* 4.19 (ANF 4:68), Greek.
39. Origen, *On First Principles,* 4.14 (ANF 4:362), Latin.
40. Origen, *On First Principles* 4.20 (ANF 4:369), Greek.
41. Origen, *Commentary on Romans* 7.17.4.
42. Origen, *On First Principles,* 4.9 (ANF 4:358), Latin.
43. Origen, *On First Principles,* 4.7 (ANF 4:354), Latin.

Three earlier authors had already commented on the proper approach to Bible study. Second Peter 3:16 spoke against unlearned and unstable men that wrest the Scriptures to their own destruction. Acts 17:11 spoke highly of the Bereans for their "readiness of mind." Hippolytus deprecated heretics who lack simplicity of spirit toward the Scriptures.[44]

Such an approach is only to be expected from people who believed, as Origen expressed it:

> If any one, moreover, consider the words of the prophets with all the zeal and reverence which they deserve, it is certain that, in the perusal and careful examination thus given them, he will feel his mind and senses touched by a divine breath, and will acknowledge that the words which he reads were no human utterances, but the language of God; and from his own emotions he will feel that these books were the composition of no human skill, nor of any mortal eloquence, but, so to speak, of a style that is divine.[45]

Application to the Twenty-first Century

How can we apply the ancient insights to our lives today? Should we even try? On the one hand, we might look at who the above writers were. Most or all of them were clergy whose daily bread came in large part from engagement with the Scriptures. Hippolytus and the author of the *Didascalia* were pastor-bishops who were so familiar with the Bible and the church around them that they could write manuals. Origen was the most intense Scripture scholar prior to the Reformation, perhaps of all time. Can we laypeople, who must work for a living, possess the time and opportunity to follow the above sentiments?

On the other hand, we live in an era where the workday is much shorter, and our free waking hours are greatly extended by electric lights. Nothing the early Christian writers said is inapplicable today. We can all concentrate more, correct bad study habits, search diligently instead of casually perusing a text, meditate on what we read, pay attention to the Bible readings in church, and be more intentional and focused in our private study of the word of God. Many of us can join or form a Bible study group. If we do not fully understand a passage the first time we read it, we can read it again and use one of the many Bible study aids freely available to compare it with other passages, which is to search the Scriptures as Jesus commanded.

---

44. Hippolytus, *Blessings of Moses*, ch. Levi.
45. Origen, *On First Principles* 4.6 (ANF 4:354), Latin.

Chapter 4

Bible Study Groups

Not a Modern Invention

BIBLE study groups are not a modern invention. They were well established among believers by the early third century AD, and possibly by the first. By "Bible study group" this article means likeminded Christians gathering together at a time other than Sunday public worship to collectively learn from and discuss Scripture passages.

According to the New Testament, Jewish worship included laypeople's commentary on the Old Testament. Luke 4:16–22 depict Jesus, with no formal theological degrees or office in the synagogue, as reading from the book of Isaiah in a synagogue service, just as Jews take turns reading their Scriptures in the twenty-first century. The difference is that he commented on them, which is not the present Jewish custom for the unqualified. Thus, the scene was more like a Christian Bible study than a formal worship service.

The scene is similar in Acts 13:14–15. There the leaders of the synagogue asked two strangers in town to speak to the congregation even though they were not officiating clergy.

A Bible study group fully within our conventional sense appears in Acts 17:11. There the Jews in the town of Berea searched the Scriptures every day, not just on the Sabbath, to determine whether they supported the teachings of Paul and Silas. Given the community rifts and debates that accompanied Paul's preaching elsewhere in Acts, the Bereans most certainly had discussions among themselves, on all days of the week.

Hippolytus was a bishop (at that time the term for a parish or town pastor) in central Italy who was martyred around AD 235. He was very zealous that Christians keep to the practices and institutions that had been handed down from the apostles. Fearing them eroded or corrupted in his own day, in AD 217 he wrote a book describing them as they existed at that time or a few decades earlier so that both clergy and laity would have a ready resource that would enable them to detect and resist new and unauthorized changes.

In his *Apostolic Tradition* 35, Hippolytus described the preparations for the Christian workday. Both males and females were to wash their hands and pray immediately after rising in the morning. Then they were to attend a local Bible study if one was being held that day, so that they could hear God through the instructor and enable the group's prayers to protect them from whatever evil might threaten them while at work. Hippolytus also wrote that attendance at a Bible study group would help the (Christian) attendees to learn what responsibilities they had at home. Then they were to go about their workday.

Christians, wrote Hippolytus, should be eager to go to the church for such Bible study, and consider it a great loss if they could not.

In the first third or first half of the second century, roughly the time of Hippolytus, a church manual called the *Didascalia* was compiled in Syria, setting out the duties and rights of husbands, wives, children, pastor-bishops, deacons, and other roles and situations in which Christians find themselves. It also deals with modesty, secular work, church discipline, backsliders, and repentant sinners. It is much longer than Hippolytus's *Apostolic Tradition*, but could serve the same purpose: a ready reference for Christian clergy and laity for keeping to apostolic norms and practices.

The *Didascalia* 2 opposes idleness and straying aimlessly around the streets. It exhorts layfolk to work diligently at their trades or other work. If a Christian is wealthy enough to live without working, s/he is to be constant in seeking out likeminded Christians in order to learn and meditate collectively on the Scriptures. This manual goes a step further than the *Apostolic Tradition*, for it places a requirement on the individual to organize a Bible study group and not merely attend one that is already established at the local church.

Besides demonstrating that studying the Bible in groups was an ancient activity, the examples of Jesus, the Bereans, Hippolytus, and the *Didascalia* also disclose that such groups were composed of sincere believers, and were not academic, value-neutral classes for educational credits in which believers, nonbelievers, and the indifferent all had an equal say. In fact, one source in the first half of the third century discountenanced Bible study or Bible reading so ecumenical that scoffers and the indifferent could participate equally with Christians who were diligently seeking direction from the Scriptures as to how to conduct their lives:

> We do not cast that which is holy before dogs, nor pearls before swine; but with all possible *self*-restraint, and with all discretion, and with all fear of God, and with earnestness of mind we praise God. For we do not minister where heathens are drinking and blaspheming in their feasts with words of impurity, because of their wickedness. Therefore do we not sing *psalms* to the heathens, nor do we read to them the Scriptures . . . . Do not so, my brethren; we beseech you, my brethren, let not these deeds be done among you; but put away those who choose thus to behave themselves with infamy and disgrace. It is not proper, my brethren, that these things should be so. [1]

Now go and study with your likeminded Christian brothers and sisters, seeking them out and organizing a Bible study group if there is none already in your community.

---

1. *Two Letters on Virginity* 2.6 (ANF 8:63); italics theirs.

Chapter 5

Business and Commerce

CHRISTIAN literature in its first 200 years has much to say to people in business, both then and now. Predating the mass apostasy of AD 249–251 and well before the division into modem denominations, this literature is the property of all Christendom and speaks to every believer.

First, we are not to wander idly in the streets but are to work at our livelihoods and actually earn our livings, says 2 Thessalonians 3:10–12. This exhortation to be diligent in our means of support was repeated almost two centuries later in a Syrian church manual and guide to Christian behavior.

Next, we must be honest in the conduct of our businesses. The oldest Christian document that has come down to us, 1 Thessalonians 4:1–6, states that to live rightly and please God, Christians are to abstain from extramarital sex, giving in to passion, and defrauding our brothers and sisters in business transactions. Justin, who was martyred for the faith about AD 165, noted that many pagans had been converted through being impressed by the honesty of Christians with whom they had commercial dealings. Origen, the greatest Bible scholar, commentator, preacher, and all-round churchman of his time and for centuries afterward, wrote against stealing in the course of buying and selling and other commercial transactions. His writings referred to in the present chapter date from between AD 232 and 244.

According to 2 Thessalonians 3:12, Christians are to be peaceful and quiet in business. A collection of Christian ethics dating from the first or early second century added that we are to exercise patience in it.

Being a Christian businessperson entails other constraints. We are to study business habits and conduct instead of being idle or inactive, wrote

Tertullian, a prominent lawyer who after conversion became a clergyman and prolific author on Christian topics. In the first decades of the third century, Tertullian forbade Christian merchants and tradespeople to make, sell, or supply objects they knew were intended to be used for sinful purposes. The examples he had in mind were idolatry, prostitution, and fight-to-the-death gladiatorial battles, but I imagine he would also forbid objects that can be used only for abortion or multipurpose ones intended for the same function. He dismissed arguments that providing goods for sinful purposes was permissible because it was part of the supplier's means of support, and that trade in sinful merchandise was more profitable than for morally neutral items.

Total preoccupation with business affairs at the expense of one's spiritual life was condemned in the 190s AD by Origen's teacher, and later by Origen himself. Both men had been deans of the world's foremost educational institution. In describing the ideal Christian concerns and lifestyle, Clement (the teacher) counselled his readers to consider themselves defrauded when distracted from Bible study and other spiritual exercises by the need to attend to business or otherwise secure the necessities of life. Origen disapproved of people so consumed by the world that they are always thinking about their livelihood, always speaking about it, always setting their hope on it, always involved in earthly commerce, and even suing at law because of earthly concerns. God calls us from daily business to serve him more, preached Origen.

Origen's most frequent targets were members of his congregation who were so wrapped in commerce, buying, selling, and profits that they failed to attend church or pay attention there. In sermons, he railed against people missing Sunday worship because they were occupied with their businesses. Even those who did come, he grumbled, concerned themselves about commercial dealings, money, and profits during the sermon or reading of the Scriptures. As if this were not objectionable enough to the frustrated and ignored preacher, some businesspeople who did attend promptly forgot what they heard during the service as soon as they left, and resumed or continued their preoccupation with commerce.

The message of the New Testament and earliest church fathers is clear: be always occupied in something useful, be upright in your livelihood, but do not let it divert you from other service to God and church.

Chapter 6

Chastity—Meaning

The Original Meaning of Christian Chastity

Did Jesus and the Bible writers really require marriage before sex? Were the church's present rules on sexual restraint late in coming and in contradiction to the original Christian faith?

For answers to such questions, let us look at the writings of the earliest Christians, those before the middle of the third century, long before the church became wedded to the state or even tolerated under the law of the land, a time when the unwritten oral teachings and Bible interpretations of Jesus and his first followers were still fresh in Christian memories. How these early writers recorded and understood Jesus and the New Testament is an indication of how he and its writers meant them to be understood, for postbiblical writers before AD 250 shared their culture, milieu, and mindset.

Chastity is Required

Polycarp was a pastor-bishop who had known the apostle John in his youth and may have been "the angel of the church in Smyrna" addressed in Revelation 2:8. In a letter to church leaders in the early second century he wrote:

> I exhort you . . . that ye be chaste and truthful. "Abstain from every form of evil." For if a man cannot govern himself in such matters, how shall he enjoin them on others?[1]

---

1. Polycarp, *Letter to the Philippians* 11.1 (ANF 1:35).

CHASTITY—MEANING

In the middle of the same century, Hermas, a married brother of a bishop of Rome, claimed to have received revelations regarding the Christian life, among them:

> Put away from you all wicked desire, and clothe yourself with good and chaste desire; for clothed with this desire you will hate wicked desire, and will rein yourself in even as you wish.[2]

and:

> "I charge you," said he, "to guard your chastity, and let no thought enter your heart of another man's wife, or of fornication, or of similar iniquities; for by doing this you commit a great sin."[3]

Clement of Alexandria was dean of the world's foremost Christian educational institution between AD 192 and 202, when he wrote in favor of "constant chastity" and against "fornication" and "the deeds of the flesh."[4] He warned that Christians who did not keep their bodies chaste destroy the temple of God and shall themselves be destroyed.[5] Addressing himself to various categories of Christians while they were repenting from each category of sin, he instructed adulterers to no longer burn with passion, and "Fornicator, live for the future chastely."[6] Clement considered fornication and lack of chastity as "diabolical passions," but would allow sexual intercourse within "a controlled marriage" between loving spouses rather than simply for the sake of indulging in lust.[7]

in AD 203, Hippolytus, a pastor-bishop in central Italy, counseled his readers to be chaste and pure even in speech.[8] Both men and women, he wrote, are to imitate the chastity of Susannah, the beautiful married lady in Daniel 13 who was willing to be put to death rather than have sexual intercourse with two elders of Israel.[9]

Tertullian was a prominent Roman lawyer before being converted and becoming the father of Latin Christian literature. Between AD 198 and

---

2. Herm. Mand. 12.1.1 (ANF 2:28).
3. Herm. Mand. 4.1.1 (ANF 2:21).
4. Clement of Alexandria, *Paedagogus* 2.10(100), 176–77.
5. Clement of Alexandria, *Quis Dives Salvetur* 18.
6. Clement of Alexandria, *Quis Dives Salvetur* 40 (ANF 2:602).
7. Clement of Alexandria, *Stromata* 3.7(58); *Stromata* 3.12(81), 78.
8. Hippolytus, *Commentary on Daniel* 1.10.
9. Hippolytus, *Commentary on Daniel* 1.22.

202—within a decade of his conversion—he wrote against "unlawful lovers" and "loving of pleasing by carnal means."[10]

Clement's successor as dean was Origen, the most outstanding Bible scholar, interpreter, and preacher of the first half of the third century. He wrote more about Christianity than any individual before the Reformation, almost twelve centuries later. Often traveling as a consultant to bishops throughout the eastern Mediterranean, he possessed the best overview of Christian ethics in his day.

Between AD 238 and 250 Origen's *Commentary on Romans* and various sermons commended chastity and discountenanced unchastity, both in isolation in a text and in lists of vices and virtues. These moral qualities appear without elaboration in some individual passages,[11] while other passages expound that the person who lives a chaste life conquers the spirit of fornication,[12] that unchastity should be put to death so that the soul will live eternally,[13] and that Christians should live in chastity and holiness of body and heart.[14]

In addition to commending chastity alone, some ancient writers mentioned it in lists with other virtues, inclusion therein implying that all listed items were held in the same high regard. Tertullian considered chastity akin to compassion, helping the needy, martyrdom, temperance, truth, wisdom,[15] endurance, justice, and refraining from theft.[16] Origen classified it with concord, curbing desires, examination of conscience, faith, fasting, good works, honesty, humility of soul, knowledgeable, mercy, openness to correction, prudence, patience, peace, respect for justice, self-control, sobriety, struggling against evil forces, subduing vices, temperance, truth, uprightness, watchfulness, wisdom—and especially gentleness, justice, and piety.[17] Theophilus, pastor-bishop of Antioch in the third quarter of

---

10. Tertullian, *On the Apparel of Women* 1.2 (ANF 4:15).
11. E.g. Origen, *Homilies on Psalm 36* 3.11.
12. Origen, *Homilies on Joshua* 15.6.
13. Origen, *Commentary on Romans* 6.14.4.
14. Origen, *Commentary on Romans* 2.14.14.
15. Tertullian, *Ad Nationes* 1.4.
16. Tertullian, *On the Soul* 40.
17. Origen, *Commentary on Romans* 2.7.5, 6.3.9, 6.5.3, 6.14.4, 10.37.4; Origen, *On First Principles* 3.1.5; Origen, *Homilies on Ezekiel* 6.3.34; Origen, *Homilies on Joshua* 8.6; Origen, *Homilies on Leviticus* 9.8.2; Origen, *Homilies on Luke* Rauer's Fragment 195; Origen, *Homilies on Numbers* 23.2, 25.4; Origen, *Homilies on Psalm 36* 2.8; Origen, *Homilies on Psalm 37* 1.2, 1.6.

the second century, put it on a par with justice, monogamy, peace, self-restraint, temperance, truth, wisdom, worship, and acknowledging God.[18]

Hermas considered chastity to be in the same ethical category as faith, gentleness, glorious virtue, guilelessness, intelligence, justice, love, meekness, peacefulness, purity, and self-restraint,[19] which he contrasted with bitterness, drunken revels, foolishness, hankering after women, overreaching, pride, and wrathfulness.[20] He said that chastity arises from guilelessness, and that intelligence arises from chastity. He indicated that the virtues of chastity, faith, guilelessness, intelligence, love, self-restraint, and simplicity are closely interrelated, and work symbiotically.[21]

Actual Christian Practice

A wide range of early authors indicate that chastity was actually practiced by the rank-and-file, to the extent that it was an emblem of Christian identity.

Later martyred for the faith in the middle of the second century, Justin, in a defense and description of Christian practices and mores, wrote: "And many, both men and women, who have been Christ's disciples from childhood, remain pure at the age of sixty or seventy years."[22]

Writing of Christianity from the outside, the famous pagan physician Galen, around AD 180, noted as well known about Christians that many, both men and women, abstained from sex their entire lives.[23]

About the same time as Galen, Justin's former student Tatian produced an *apologia,* or book like Justin's, in which he criticized the debaucheries recorded in Greek myths about their goddesses, whom pagans worshipped even though the same sexual license was unacceptable for human women in Greco-Roman society. In contrast to the goddesses, Tatian wrote of Christians: "all our women are chaste" and called upon pagan worshippers not to scoff at female Christians when their female deities are unchaste, even by the pagans' own standards.[24]

Also in Galen's time, Theophilus, in his own *apologia,* recorded:

18. Theophilus, *To Autolycus* 3.15.
19. Herm. Vis. 3.8.5, Herm. Mand. 6.2.3.
20. Herm. Mand. 6.2.4.
21. Herm. Vis. 3.8.3–5.
22. Justin Martyr, *1 Apology* 15 (ANF 1:167).
23. Walzer, *Galen on Jews and Christians,* Reference 6.
24. Tatian, *Address to the Greeks* 33 (ANF 2:78–79).

But far be it from Christians to conceive any such deeds; for with them temperance dwells, self-restraint is practised, monogamy is observed, chastity is guarded, iniquity exterminated, sin extirpated, righteousness exercised, law administered, worship performed, God acknowledged.[25]

Tertullian's *apologia* noted that, upon conversion to Christianity, previously adulterous wives were known to become chaste.[26] He contrasted pagan morals with Christian, mentioning as well known that, although Christians share earthly goods with each other, they do not share or swap wives.[27] Tertullian pointed out that after Christians conclude their public worship and go their separate ways, they "have as much care for our modesty and chastity as if we had been at a school of virtue rather than a banquet."[28]

Among Origen's students was Potamiaena. She was martyred sometime around AD 205 while "she was blooming in the perfection of her mind and physical graces."[29] She endured torture, verbal and physical abuse, and martyrdom rather than surrender her chastity and virginity.

Origen touted as manifestations of God's power in coverts to Christianity that people who had indulged in

> licentiousness and injustice and covetousness . . . have become in some way meeker, and more religious, and more consistent, so that certain among them, from a desire of exceeding chastity, and a wish to worship God with greater purity, abstain even from the permitted indulgences of (lawful) love.[30]

This was no pious hope for consumption only by Christians. The quoted words appear in a book that deals with the allegations of an anti-Christian philosopher who regarded Christianity as a deception and harmful to human beings. The book repeats comments about Christianity voiced by its pagan opponents, and as much as possible deals with the pagans' own observations of the behaviors of Christians. Even contemporary pagans acknowledged these changes of character as typical of Christian conversion.

---

25. Theophilus, *To Autolycus* 3.15 (ANF 2:115).
26. Tertullian, *Apology* 3.
27. Tertullian, *Apology* 39 (ANF 3:46).
28. Tertullian, *Apology* 39 (ANF 3:47).
29. *Martyrdom of Potamiaena and Basilides*, 1:253.
30. Origen, *Against Celsus* 26 (ANF 4.407).

Chapter 7

Chastity—Reasons

Reasons for Traditional Sexual Ethics

CHRISTIANITY'S restrictions on sexual activities did not originate as arbitrary, purposeless rules such as are found in the finer points of writing style or table etiquette. Although a commentator himself on nonsexual social manners and decorous behavior, Clement of Alexandria, dean of Christendom's foremost school in the 190s AD, gave reasons for the church's rules on chastity, as did other Christian writers in the period before the Decian Persecution of AD 249–251.

The value of consulting Clement and other postbiblical Christian writers before these dates is that the Bible interpretations and oral teachings of Jesus, the apostles, and other New Testament writers were still fresh in their memories and they preserve Christian teaching as it was understood by Christians—or Christians not many generations earlier—who knew Bible writers personally, and hence the way in which Jesus had meant the Bible to be understood. The year AD 250 also marks the two hundredth anniversary of the beginning of distinctively Christian literature, and also the first quarter-millennium of our era. This was long before the church became wedded to the state or even legal under the law of the land. Dating from before the division into modern-day denominations, such writings are the common inheritance of all Christians.

An additional reason for reading Clement in particular is that his main writings considered in this chapter discuss both Christian and pagan sources, such as ancient philosophers and Greco-Roman classics. His appeals to philosophers' conceptions of natural laws and reason are cogent in our largely post-Christian age. They render Clement's expositions both Christian and universal.

Violations of Christian sexual ethics are to be avoided, Clement wrote, because anyone who contravenes them injures themselves more than other people, for s/he loses community respect if his/her affairs become publicly known.[1] Even in the twenty-first century, fornicators and adulterers try to hide their dalliances by committing them in the dark, which Clement commented was in the hope that other human beings will not see and God will not remember. Clement called them "most wretched" because they fear only human beings and think they can hide from God.[2]

Another reason Clement gave for abstaining from extramarital affairs was the harm that came from violation of the laws of nature either (1) through begetting unwanted children outside the family circle and protection, and/or (2) through homosexual affairs and heterosexual "safe-sex" that put semen to a use nature never intended.[3] Abstinence from unregulated intercourse also enables Christians to obey the Bible's commandment "make no provision for the flesh to gratify its desires."[4] Stability of the family unit without needing to be concerned about biological children outside it also gives spouses the necessary freedom to control all things within the family.[5] In the days when it was customary for bishops to be drawn from older men who had raised legitimate offspring,[6] successful family management equipped fathers to better oversee the church.[7] In the same vein was Bishop Polycarp's observation around AD 107 that Christians, especially clergy, are hard pressed to encourage other people to practice high sexual ethics if they cannot govern their own bodies.[8] Polycarp was a pastor-bishop who had known the apostle John in his youth and may have been "the angel of the church in Smyrna" addressed in Revelation 2:8.

Clement put forward another reason: chastity is God's command for using the body as a temple of the Holy Spirit, and God will destroy

1. Clement of Alexandria, *Paedagogus* 2.10(100).
2. Clement of Alexandria, *Paedagogus* 2.10(99).
3. Clement of Alexandria, *Paedagogus* 2.10(90–91).
4. Clement of Alexandria, *Stromata* 3.7(58); Rom 13:14.
5. Clement of Alexandria, *Stromata* 3.12(79).
6. 1 Tim 3:2–5; Titus 1:6.
7. Clement of Alexandria, *Stromata* 3.12(79).
8. Polycarp, *Letter to the Philippians* 11.2.

whoever mars his/her body through unchastity.[9] The *Didascalia*, a church manual dating from the first three decades of the third century (being the first three decades after Clement), says that a chaste woman receives praise from God.[10]

Origen remarked that when chastity puts unchastity to death, the soul will live eternally,[11] and that—along with sobriety and watchfulness—chastity is a necessary aid for studying the Bible.[12] Origen was Clement's successor as dean and became the leading Bible scholar, teacher, and preacher of the first half of the third century. He wrote more about Christianity than anyone else before the sixteenth-century Reformation. Often traveling as a consultant at the invitation of bishops throughout the eastern Mediterranean, he possessed the best overview of the Christian ethics of his day.

Lastly, we must consider that the first heirs of Christ's teaching did not regard sexual morality in isolation, but as a virtue to be exercised in conjunction with the others.[13] The ancients seldom mentioned chastity in isolation but usually in lists that included a number of other commendable qualities. Origen stated outright that virtues such as wisdom, piety, and respect for the property and lives of other people do not stand alone, nor can they be practiced in isolation from one another.[14] Throughout the very long chapter 10 of his *Paedagogus* (*Christ as Instructor*) Clement stressed moderation and restraint not only in sex, but also in food and other good gifts from God that can be harmful in excess or when not properly applied.

In the first half of the first century, Hermas, a married brother of a bishop-elder of Rome, claimed to have received revelations regarding the Christian life, among them that some virtues are in a continuum and work symbiotically: "from Faith arises Self-restraint; from Self-restraint, Simplicity, from Simplicity, Guilelessness; from Guilelessness, Chastity; from Chastity, Intelligence; and from Intelligence, Love."[15] All of them lead to and are led from other virtues.

Dating from the 160s AD, a collection was compiled of alleged statements and activities of the apostle Paul not recorded in the Bible. It attributes

---

9. Clement of Alexandria, *Quis Dives Salvetur* 18.
10. Connolly, *Didascalia apostolorum,* 3.
11. Origen, *Commentary on Romans* 6.14.4.
12. Origen, *On First Principles* 4.1.14 Latin.
13. Origen, *Commentary on Romans* 6.4.2.
14. Origen, *Commentary on Romans* 6.3.9, 6.4.2, 6.5.3.
15. Herm. Vis. 3.8.7 (ANF 2:16).

to him the statement that those who keep their bodies chaste shall become temples of God and that God will speak with continent people.[16] The book actually condemns all sex, even between spouses. Like many New Testament apocrypha with the same theme, the collection was later branded as heretical, but it nevertheless remained very popular and widely circulated, thus showing that many who dissented from the Catholic church of the time were much stricter, not more permissive, than what we today think of as classical Christian traditional teaching on sex. Indeed, much of Book 3 of Clement's *Stromata* is a point-by-point and in-depth rebuttal of heretical disdain for sex and marriage, which was usually motivated by general hatred for the flesh and the body as evil in themselves. The mainstream church represented a happy balance and golden mean between ascetic heretics who condemned all sex for everyone and the entrenched excessive debauchery of the surrounding pagans.

---

16. *Acts of Paul and Thecla* 5.

Chapter 8

Chastity—Scope

Scope of Prohibited Sexuality

IN the Bible and Christian literature before the middle of the third century AD, the concepts of adultery and other sexual impurities were not confined to merely engaging in the sex act with persons other than one's lawful spouse in a monogamous marriage. By today's popular standards, chastity in the earliest church severely restricted Christians in their day-to-day lives and thoughts. This early literature was composed long before the church became linked to the state or even became legal, a time when the unwritten oral teachings and Bible interpretations of Jesus and his first followers were still fresh in Christian memories. How these early writers recorded and understood Jesus and the New Testament is an indication of how they meant them to be understood, because postbiblical writers before AD 250 shared their culture, milieu, and mindset.

The first indication is in the words of Jesus: "You shall not commit adultery. But I say to you that every one who looks at a woman lustfully has already committed adultery with her in his heart" (Matt 5:27–28). The first heirs of the gospel, postbiblical authors before AD 250, applied this prohibition in its full literal sense, and did not teach that it possessed some different, laxer, purely spiritual meaning. It was regarded as binding in the full force of its words by Clement of Alexandria,[1] Origen,[2] Tertullian,[3] and another Christian teacher, who was martyred around AD 165.[4] A married man in Egypt, Clement was rector of Christendom's leading institute of learning in the 190s AD. He was very conversant with the Bible, church tradition, and the Greek and Latin classics and philosophy. His student, the lifelong celibate Origen, concentrated more on purely Christian studies. Origen was the foremost Bible scholar, teacher, and preacher of the first half of the second century. Bishops throughout the eastern Mediterranean basin often requested his presence as a theological consultant, he traveled much, and learned more about Christianity wherever he could. He was thus more knowledgeable about the consensus of Christian teaching and practice than other authors.

A husband himself, Tertullian had been a prominent lawyer at Rome before his conversion, return to north Africa, and ordination. His writings in this chapter date from AD 197 to 220. He provides double value for the study of early Christian ethics because he wrote first as a member of the mainstream church, and later as member of a sect which was antagonistic toward it. Bishop Theophilus of Antioch, in the third quarter of the second century, expressed the collective thought succinctly: "And concerning chastity, the holy word teaches us not only not to sin in act, but not even in thought, not even in the heart to think of any evil, nor look on another man's wife with our eyes to lust after her."[5]

Marriage to a divorced person or remarriage after one's own divorce was out of the question, according to the New Testament,[6] Clement,[7] Tertullian,[8] and Theophilus.[9] Surprisingly, for an author who expounded at length and in many books on almost every other spiritual topic, Origen confined his comments on remarriage after divorce to three chapters of one

---

1. Clement of Alexandria, *Stromata* 3.6(46), 3.14(94).

2. Origen, *On First Principles* 3.1.6 Latin, 4.1.19 Latin; Origen, *Commentary on Romans* 3.9.7, 9.31.2; Origen, *Homilies on Genesis* 1.8, 3.6; Origen, *Homilies on Joshua* 9.3.

3. Tertullian, *On Idolatry*, ch. 2; Tertullian, *On the Soul*, chs. 40, 58.

4. Justin Martyr, *1 Apology* 15.

5. Theophilus, *To Autolycus* 3.13 (ANF 2:115).

6. Matt 5:32, 19:9; Mark 10:11–12; Luke 16:18; Rom 7:2–3; 1 Cor 7:10–11, 27.

7. Clement of Alexandria, *Stromata* 3.12(83), 3.15(97).

8. Tertullian, *Against Marcion* 4.34, 5.7; Tertullian, *On Modesty* 16; Tertullian, *On Monogamy* 9; Tertullian, *To His Wife* 2.2.

9. Theophilus, *To Autolycus* 3.13 (ANF 2:115).

book,[10] and even then put them forward as thoughts to mull over rather than as formal presentations of official church teaching. He indicated that in his time the church had permitted remarriage in individual cases,[11] but perhaps he was mistaking divorce for annulment.

Even the consent of the spouse for a specific occasion, or with a specific person, or for an open-marriage arrangement, did not nullify the sinfulness of unchastity. Tertullian contrasted pagan and Christian values and practices in his day:

> All things are common among us but our wives. We give up our community where it is practised alone by others, who not only take possession of the wives of their friends, but most tolerantly also accommodate their friends with theirs, following the example, I believe, of those wise men of ancient times, the Greek Socrates and the Roman Cato, who shared with their friends the wives whom they had married, it seems for the sake of progeny both to themselves and to others; whether in this acting against their partners' wishes, I am not able to say. Why should they have any care over their chastity, when their husbands so readily bestowed it away?[12]

This would rule out one aspect of the hospitality of certain Inuits, as well as that of some Kenyans.

The apostle's prohibition in Ephesians 5:1–11 was understood by Clement of Alexandria to command chastity in speech,[13] which the Bible passage itself clearly shows. Similar restraints against dirty jokes and other verbal unchastity are found in Colossians 3:8, Clement,[14] Tertullian,[15] and Origen.[16] Origen extended this to cover "lewd songs."[17] In the middle of the second century, the church father Tatian extended it not only to songs but also to art.[18] The same general thought was voiced by Hippolytus, a bishop

---

10. *Commentary on Matthew* 14:22–24.

11. *Commentary on Matthew* 14:23.

12. Tertullian, *Apology* 39 (ANF 3:46–47).

13. Clement of Alexandria, *Paedagogus* 2.6, Clement of Alexandria, *Stromata* 3.4(28).

14. Clement of Alexandria, *Paedagogus* 2.10(98), Clement of Alexandria, *Stromata* 3.5(43).

15. Tertullian, *De Spectaculis* 17.

16. Origen, *Commentary on Romans* 2.13.25, 3.3.3, 6.4.2; Origen, *Homilies on Ezekiel* 3.3.40–44.

17. Origen, *Homilies on Genesis* 3.5, 96.

18. Tatian, *Address to the Greeks* 22.

in central Italy in AD 203;[19] the *Didache*, a church manual and guide for daily Christian living written in Egypt or Syria in the late first or early second century;[20] and the *Didascalia*, a Syrian manual of church organization and morals dating from the first three decades of the third century.[21]

Women at least were to dress in a modest and chaste manner in public, not because failure to do so diminished their own chastity, but for the effect on adult males. Sometime between AD 198 and 202, Tertullian instructed that women's clothing was to be chaste, and that they were not to excessively daub themselves with cosmetics. They were not to clothe themselves in a manner that attracted "unlawful lovers," or that suggested they were open to "pleasing by carnal means."[22] Facilitating lust by immodest dress was itself a violation of the commandment.

Chapter 3 of the *Didascalia* was more specific. A Christian wife was not to adorn herself in a manner that pleased men other than her husband, lest these other men lust after her in their hearts or otherwise think impure thoughts about her. She was not to wear the type of clothing or shoes that resembled those of prostitutes, nor dress her hair in the manner they favored. The *Didascalia* even went so far as to recommend that she cover her head with her robe in public, lest she look pleasing to a man other than her husband.

I suppose that today this means that if a woman must use curlers in her hair, she should do so when she is out in public rather than only at home. Some women wear them only in their homes, looking beautiful for everyone but their husbands. The ancient counsel would prompt her to wear them any place but at home so that she looks beautiful only for him. If a man lusts after a woman because she does not obey these strictures, she also is guilty of his sin.[23]

Even at the grassroots level, there was widespread belief that adultery included not only "actual fleshly contact," but also kisses and embraces with the wrong person.[24]

Unless a Christian is careful, there can even be adultery or fornication between spouses within a lawful marriage. A husband is to love his

19. Hippolytus, *Commentary on Daniel* 1.10.
20. *Didache* 3.3, 5.1.
21. Connolly, *Didascalia apostolorum* 21.
22. Tertullian, *On the Apparel of Women* 1.2 (ANF 4:15).
23. Connolly, *Didascalia apostolorum* 3.
24. Tertullian, *On Idolatry* 2 (ANF 3:62).

wife more than sexual pleasure, and is to exercise self-control so that his purpose and activity are directed by love rather than physical lust. He must intend only loving aspects in the sex act, including the conception of a child or at least being open to the transmission of life, as cooperating with God in the ongoing process of creation. Clement warned that if a husband does not keep within these parameters and seeks only sexual pleasure, the marriage becomes "fornication."[25] "Adultery" is the word used for the same situation by the *Sentences of Sextus*, a popular collection of sayings and instructions for the Christian life compiled in the second century.[26]

In the 160s AD, a collection was produced of alleged statements and activities of the apostle which are not recorded in the Bible. The collection reported Paul as saying that those who keep their bodies chaste shall become temples of God and that God will speak with continent people.[27] The book actually condemns all sex, even between spouses, which merits Tertullian later branding it as heretical; this shows that those who dissented from the mainstream church of the time were much stricter, not more permissive, than what have become classical traditional teachings on sex.

---

25. Clement of Alexandria, *Paedagogus* 2.10(99), 175–176.
26. *Sentences of Sextus*, 43.
27. *Acts of Paul and Thecla* 5.

Chapter 9

Church Buildings: Good or Bad?

"A House Not Made with Hands" (2 Cor 5:1)

THE reason God does not provide a lot of money to many Christian congregations is that they spend it in a way he has not told them to. In addition to a general obsession with money in churches as a whole, there runs rampant an idolatry surrounding local houses of worship, on which many congregations lavish money that God wants put to other uses. To grow more in grace, they should devote their funds to institutions that help the truly needy, rather than on erecting or maintaining expensive buildings. Indeed, some Christians are so fixated on physical structures that they often mistakenly apply the word "church" exclusively to an edifice of brick, stone, or wood, in contradiction to the way the word was used at the time the foundations of the Christian faith were laid.

The authors of the New Testament and other Christian literature before the middle of the third century AD would be shocked and disgusted at present Christian attitudes to money and buildings. Erecting and maintaining a special building for Christian worship services was alien, if not repulsive, to Christ's apostles and their early followers. In the earliest days of the faith, Christians met and even celebrated Holy Communion in the Jewish Temple and private homes (Acts 2:46; 5:42). All the local churches greeted in the Epistles bearing the name of the apostle Paul (Rom 16:5; 1 Cor 16:19; Col 4:15 and Phlm 2) were gatherings of flesh-and-blood believers in private homes, not material edifices designated solely for public worship. Not one of the 109 instances of "church" in the Revised Standard Version of the Bible refers to a physical structure.

The New Testament Epistles further exclude the thought that a Christian temple is a structure of wood, bricks, stones, or concrete. First Corinthians 3:16 plainly teaches that it is a believer's body that is the temple of the Holy Spirit. Chapter 6 verse 19 is even plainer, saying that "your body is a temple of the Holy Spirit" while the context (vv. 13–20) totally put out of question that the Christian temple is anything other than flesh, blood, and spirit. In its description of the worldwide church, Ephesians 2:19–22 speaks of the Christian temple as being founded on Christ, the apostles, and the prophets, with no mention of a stone foundation or wooden superstructure. Both passages are notable in applying the word "temple" to flesh-and-blood Christians rather than a material edifice. In this they agree with the four greetings to churches in homes (citations above). In 1 Peter 2:4–6, the "stones" on which the church is built are not granite or some other construction material, but are Christ and believers, i.e., people.

In the 190s AD, Clement of Alexandria was dean of the world's foremost Christian educational institution. He possessed an intimate knowledge of both the Bible and also of Greek philosophers and literature. He considered the best of philosophy to have copied its ideas from the Hebrew Scriptures, and was thus of divine origin. Clement cited Isaiah 66:1, Acts 17:24–25, Plato, and other philosophers when he wrote against the very notion of using a temple or other physical structure to worship God, speaking as if it was out of the question for Christians.[1]

Even as late as the first half of the third century AD, Christians regarded the concept of distinctive religious buildings as the mark of Jewish or pagan idolatry. Observe the following quotations from Clement's former student Origen, who was a seminary professor, the founder of systematic theology, the most important writer of the early Greek church, and the greatest preacher of his day. In *Against Celsus,* he wrote that one of the distinctive traits of Christians was that we do not honor the deity by means of temples, because such buildings "are adapted rather to demons, which are somehow fixed in a certain place which they prefer to any other, or which take up their dwelling . . . after . . . certain rites and incantations."[2] Quoting the founder of Stoic philosophy, Origen presented the view of the church of his day: "And there will be no need to build temples, for nothing ought to be

---

1. Clement of Alexandria, *Stromata* 5.11.74–76.
2. Origen, *Against Celsus* 3.34 (ANF 4:477–78.).

regarded as sacred, or of much value, or holy, which is the work of builders and of mean men."[3]

The earliest-known building given over exclusively to Christian worship was not erected until after AD 240. Even then, it was a modest affair, a renovated private dwelling, not an imposing cathedral such as many Christian assemblies today regard as essential to the preaching and practice of Christianity. Granted, older Christian writings contain three instances in which Christians worshipped outside private homes, but none of them is a precedent for the magnificent and costly houses of worship that many Christians now build or maintain. One such edifice was "the hall of Tyrannus" in Acts 19:9; the note in the Oxford Annotated RSV Bible implies that this structure was not the property of the church, or even used exclusively for its worship, but was available only by the grace of its owner and then only because he had no use for it at that time of day. Another reference is to a barn or warehouse in the late second-century *Acts of Paul*. It is unclear whether or not it was owned by Christians for their exclusive use, but even if it was, it was nevertheless just a stable. Last but not least are the instances of the apostles frequenting the Jerusalem Temple (Acts 2:46; 3:1; 5:20; 22:17). Both the biblical context and our knowledge from other sources indicate that this sumptuous edifice was far from being the property of Christians, but was a public place owned and maintained by unconverted Jews.

Now that the Jerusalem Temple is mentioned, believers who enjoy financing lavish houses of worship might point to the Old Testament requirements for the tabernacle and temple as an argument that God delights in gargantuan and costly buildings. However, even if we were to accept this aspect of Jewish law as binding on Christians, a calculation of the dimensions of these structures shows them to have been of modest proportions indeed. With two biblical cubits equaling one yard, it can be seen that they were quite tiny in comparison to many modern worship structures.

A similar study of the Old Testament also reveals an occurrence in the construction of the tabernacle that would be unheard-of today: Moses turned away donations when the building fund was sufficient, and he commanded the Israelites to refrain from making further contributions to it (Exod 36:6–7).

The New Testament does mention collections of money and even contains appeals for donations similar to those common in church circles today (e.g. Acts 11:28–29, Rom 15:25–27, 1 Cor 16:1–3, 2 Cor 8–9, and Gal 2:10). However, the purpose of such collections was not for the erection,

---

3. Origen, *Against Celsus* 1.5 (ANF 4:398, quoting Zeno of Citium, *Polity*).

maintenance, or enlargement of houses of worship. The solicited money was for the relief of needy Christians, especially those in Jerusalem.

According to the Gospel writers, Jesus taught that helping the poverty-stricken is a Christian duty (Matt 19.21; Mark 10:21; Luke 14:13–14, 18:22). Other early Christian writers concurred, as 1 John 3:17 and Origen's *Homilies on Exodus* 7.6 condemn people—especially Christians—who possess money but close their hearts against brothers and sisters in need, while chapter 2 of the Epistle of James is particularly concerned for the welfare of the less fortunate. Indeed, James 2:15–17 says that a Christian's faith is dead if not accompanied by works to relieve poverty.

The command to help the needy was repeated (1) by Origen in his *Commentary on the Epistle to the Romans* 10.6.3, (2) by Justin, who was martyred for the faith around AD 165 (*1 Apology* 67.2), (3) in a first-century letter from the church at Rome to that at Corinth (*1 Clem.* 38.2), and (4) repeatedly in *The Shepherd of Hermas*, a lengthy instruction in Christian life and conduct dating from the first half or middle of the second century. The latter two writings were once so popular and highly regarded that they were included in some early editions of the New Testament.

The repetition of the command to assist the needy in so many sources of such early date shows how highly the command was regarded by Christian writers who knew not only the words of Jesus' teaching, but also how they were practiced and applied under the supervision of the apostles and their first successors. Yet these same Christians never commended the erection of a cathedral or other palace of worship. Hermas in particular counseled Christians to buy souls instead of lands, and not to accumulate lands and buildings. He made no exception for land on which to erect a chapel.

Particularly relevant to the present article is *The Acts of Thomas*, an account of the missionary efforts of the apostle Thomas in India. Compiled around AD 200, the second of these acts narrates that he was not only a carpenter, but also a master architect and all-round construction contractor. As such, he was retained by a king to build a magnificent palace. The story turns on two differences in meaning—one by Thomas, one by the king—as to what this palace would be and the best use of the money the king intended to spend on it. His majesty was surprised when the apostle told him that Thomas could erect it at any time of year and was not dependent on the seasons. This had one meaning for Thomas but another for the king.

The king did not supervise the project, but sent Thomas off to build it some distance from his residence. The king also sent installment payments without seeing how they were applied. The apostle did indeed provide him with a sumptuous new home, but not in the sense the king had thought or intended. Thomas spent his majesty's money by giving it to the poor, the sick, orphans, and widows—without a physical building being involved. According to Thomas, such use of the king's money and the type of people it benefited would provide his majesty—and us today—with a beautiful home and palace in heaven. When the king learned how his money had been spent on disadvantaged people instead of stone, bricks, mortar, and superstructure, he became very angry and imprisoned Thomas. He was unimpressed by the apostle's explanation that the king could not see the splendid palace in this life but only after death, in heaven. Severe punishment loomed for Thomas until the king's brother had a near-death experience in which he viewed the wonderful place waiting in heaven for those who spend their money on the poor and afflicted instead of on material buildings. When the brother recovered, he reported his vision to the king, and they both saw the proper use of money, and converted to Christianity.

This ancient account, dating from only a century after the last apostle, illustrates the attitude of the primitive church and its first successors toward how Christians should spend their money. Indeed, they all considered helping the poverty-stricken as a top priority, not as an afterthought to be attended to only after a sumptuous palace of worship was provided for.

Christ himself spoke some apropos words for Christians in this regard: we are not to accumulate treasures on earth, but to store up treasures in heaven (Matt 6:20) by feeding the hungry, providing clothes to the needy, and welcoming strangers (Matt 25:34–46). In fact, Matthew 7:21–23 states that we will be blessed at the last judgment only for doing what God has specifically commanded; all other mighty works and activities done in his name—no matter how great or well-intentioned—count for nothing in the kingdom of heaven. God has specifically commanded us to assist orphans, widows, and other poor, but he never told us to build even a small chapel, let alone spend money on a huge cathedral.

In summary, Christians should spend their and their church's money on what God said he wants. Instead of lavishing it on a house of worship, "let us do good to all men, especially to those who are of the household of faith" (Gal 6:10). "For if the earthly tent we live in is destroyed, we have a building from God, a house not made with hands, eternal in the heavens" (2 Cor 5:1).

Chapter 10

Common Property or Common Fund?

As described in the first few chapters of Luke's Acts of the Apostles, the very earliest Jerusalem Christians sold their property and distributed the proceeds among the poor in the Christian community (Acts 2:44–45; 4:34–35). For instance, the apostle Barnabas sold his land and paid the proceeds into church coffers, as did others (4:36—5:11). In the earliest days of the Jerusalem church, this was the routine course for propertied Christians. Because many early believers were wealthy enough to travel (2:5, 8–11) and settled in Jerusalem only unexpectedly, there was both a large reservoir of wealth to draw upon and a present and sudden need.

Community ownership and control of such liquidated assets continued until local funds were exhausted. Then the church at Antioch needed to bail out the Judean community (Acts 11:29–30). A recurrent theme in Paul's letters to congregations was fundraising to help the Jerusalem commune (Rom 15:26; 1 Cor 16:2–3; 2 Cor 8:1—9.5).

The economic experiment was apparently not implemented elsewhere. Christian attitudes toward wealth and possessions did indeed continue Jesus' anti-materialism, but relief of unfortunates came through a common congregational fund maintained by voluntary periodic contributions from individual property holders who retained ownership and control over the rest of their assets.

The earliest evidence of this other method of church finance is in the Corinthian Epistles. There Paul exhorts private Christians to voluntarily put aside money every Lord's Day for poor relief (1 Cor 16:2–3). "Each man should give what he has decided in his heart to give, not reluctantly or under compulsion" (2 Cor 9:7).

Second-century writers provide more details. Justin Martyr had traveled widely throughout the eastern Mediterranean and settled at Rome where he became a Christian teacher until martyred around AD 165. Justin described the maintenance, purposes, and administration of the common fund:

> And they who are well to do, and willing, give what each thinks fit; and what is collected is deposited with the president, who succors the orphans and widows, and those who, through sickness or any other cause, are in want, and those who are in bonds, and the strangers sojourning among us, and in a word takes care of all who are in need.[1]

Here the recipients are travelers and persons in needy circumstances instead of members of the Christian community as a whole.

A few years after Justin, a pagan satire tells of an adventurer who became a Christian leader for a short time. The book describes Christian treatment of him when pagans jailed him on religious charges. Gifts of money flowed to him from many congregations, and he soon acquired much wealth as a result of imprisonment for the faith. This led the author to exclaim that any conman can acquire a fortune by pretending to be a Christian in adverse circumstances.[2]

Tertullian wrote in more detail and at greater length. A prominent Roman lawyer before conversion, he became a prolific author on Christian subjects. In AD 197, Tertullian elaborated:

> Though we have our treasure-chest, it is not made up of purchase-money, as of a religion that has its price. On the monthly day, if he likes, each puts in a small donation; but only if it be his pleasure, and only if he be able: for there is no compulsion; all is voluntary. These gifts are, as it were, piety's deposit fund. For they are not taken thence and spent on feasts, and drinking-bouts, and eating-houses, but to support and bury poor people, to supply the wants of boys and girls destitute of means and parents, and of old persons confined now to the house; such, too, as have suffered shipwreck; and if there happen to be any in the mines, or banished to the islands, or shut up in the prisons, for nothing but their fidelity

---

1. Justin Martyr, *1 Apology* 67.6 (ANF 1:186).
2. Lucian of Samosata, "Passing of Peregrinus," 5:13.

to the cause of God's Church, they become the nurslings of their confession.[3]

Here the intended beneficiaries are generally the same as in Justin, except that Tertullian includes only people who are in distressed circumstances involuntarily, e.g. Tertullian does not include travelers who are not shipwrecked. He also indicates that, unlike the believers in the early chapters of Acts, the money is not spent for meals for the whole Christian community.

In a way, the Jerusalem Christians were all poor and needy because they had given all their property to the Christian assembly. Later, outside Judea, the common fund was only for the truly unfortunate who could not help themselves. As recorded in 2 Corinthians 9:7, Justin, and Tertullian, contributions were not a matter of course by all Christians, but entirely voluntary. A disproportionate share came from the rich, who nevertheless kept rights of ownership and of disposition over the rest of their property. The fact that the donors had money to give voluntarily indicates that they possessed a store of wealth which was not already part of the common fund.

---

3. Tertullian, *Apology* 39 (ANF 3:46.).

Chapter 11

Contentment

"Godliness with contentment is great gain."

—1 Timothy 6:6

Contentment in the New Testament sense is not merely a warm fuzzy feeling that comes of its own accord, but must be pursued and requires effort. This appears from the New Testament itself as interpreted through other Christian writings of the next century and a half.

The writings of early Christians help to uncover the original meanings of New Testament texts now in doubt because of variations in manuscripts, just as the Dead Sea Scrolls do for our canonical Old Testament. These postbiblical writings form a larger context for the New Testament: Scripture scholars of almost all denominations work on the basis that a Bible passage or book should be interpreted in context, drawing on one part of the context to better interpret another so that the resultant interpretation will be that of a harmonious whole. Anglo-American courts do the same with statutes. Early Christian literature also gives us a better idea of the meaning or the most accurate meaning of New Testament parables and events because it reveals the presuppositions shared by the New Testament personages and their original hearers, and thus disclose the interpretation and lessons that persons contemporaneous with the biblical writers were intended to draw from them. In this way, the ancient sources help inform us of biblical concepts (which are sometimes quite different from ours) and help supply the Bible's conceptual framework. In any endeavor, knowledge of the thought and events of an era is most accurately obtained from contemporaries of it or—as second best—from material dating from neighboring times and neighboring geographical regions, i.e., with people who were acquainted with the language, culture, thought processes, and actions of the personages whose thoughts and deeds are being studied. Reliable information can be obtained about the events in the New Testament and the thought of its writers by consulting ancient people who spoke the same language and shared the same culture and were familiar with—or shared—their way of looking at and evaluating the world.

The first source to consult for ascertaining the Bible meaning of contentment is the Bible itself. Hebrews 13:5 urges Christians to "be without covetousness; and be content with such things as ye have." Here contentment with one's present belongings is contrasted with covetousness. To attain the former, we must rid ourselves of the latter, which requires effort.

The antithesis between contentment and covetousness appeared in *The First Letter of Clement* only a short time after 1 Timothy and Hebrews. *First Clement* may even predate them, depending on where we place its date between the probable ones of AD 70 or 97. In any event, it comes from apostolic times and was included in some early versions of the New Testament. Chapter 2.1 praises the recipients' abstinence from coveting others' status and privileges, being "content with the provision which God had made for you."

Covetousness is contrasted as the opposite of contentment in three authors of the second century. The middle of the century saw the finalization of the Christian version of *The Sibylline Oracles* 2.56–57, a book ascribed to a pagan prophetess as another witness to the coming of Jesus, into which believers had inserted Christian teachings. The *Oracles* forbid making money unjustly, commanded abstinence from other people's property, and counselled being "satisfied with what is available."

Hermas was a Christian prophet or recipient of divine revelations. A brother of a bishop of Rome, Hermas produced a book on ethical behavior sometime in the first half of the second century. On testing Christian prophets, God, through Hermas, wrote that they must be content with "fewer wants than those of other men" and free from "vain desire."[1] In another passage, contentment is listed among such good traits as righteousness, chastity, purity, good works, and great virtues. Like *First Clement*, Hermas's book was in some early Bibles.

---

1. Herm. Mand. 11.8 (ANF 2:27).

A later Clement, Clement of Alexandria in Egypt, was more explicit. Rector of Christendom's leading religious school in the 190s AD, he wrote that covetousness is fornication "because it is opposed to contentment with what one possesses."[2]

A few years after the Egyptian Clement came *The Acts of Thomas* in eastern Syria. It contrasted contentment with one's own possessions, not only against fornication, but also against adultery, pederasty, hypocrisy, and theft.

The Christian authors who commented on contentment before the mass apostasy of AD 249–251 were unanimous that it was the opposite of covetousness. We can fall into covetousness by accident or inattention, but not so with contentment in the biblical use of the word. To be content, a person must make the effort of deflecting his/her attention from the coveted thing, counting one's blessings, and reviewing the ample provision God has already made for them. A mental and spiritual effort, but an effort nonetheless.

---

2. Clement of Alexandria, *Stromata* 3.12(89).

Chapter 12

Corruption, Including Bribery

Pity and Pray

"We meet together as an assembly and congregation, so that, offering up prayer to God as with united force, we may wrestle with Him in our supplications. This violence God delights in. We pray, too, for the emperors, for their ministers and for all in authority."

—Tertullian *Apology* 39

So runs part of a description of Christian worship around AD 200, with the subjects of prayer dating back to the apostle Paul: "I urge first of all that prayers, supplications, intercessions and thanksgiving be made for all people, for kings and for all who are in authority and high positions" (1 Tim 2:1–2).

Similarly early Christian sources also indicate what sort of rulers these people in authority and high position should try to be. A Christian martyred for his faith at government hands around AD 165 wrote that Christians pray that their rulers exercise "judgment."[1] About the same era, another Christian said they are forbidden to be tyrants.[2] Like all people, those in authority are to be firmly virtuous, not only that they not be corrupted, but

---

1. Justin Martyr, *1 Apology* 17 (ANF 1:168).
2. *Acts of John,* 36.

also that they not even be effectively tempted.[3] They are not to allow themselves to become corrupted by material prosperity.[4] Writing between AD 192 and 202, Clement was dean of the world's foremost Christian school.

The latest source for the present chapter was Clement's successor of dean, and the most influential Bible scholar, teacher, and preacher of the first half of the third century. Origen wrote that the reason Christ divested himself of his glory, took the form of a servant, restored the laws of rule and government, and subdued all enemies was in order to teach rulers to exercise moderation in government.[5]

Surveying the scene in the world today, we notice that some public officials have more need of prayers than others if they want to live up to the high ideals God has set for them and which the early authors mentioned. Origen had this sort in mind when he encouraged friends in Egypt to have pity and pray for wrongdoers among rulers.

One church father who is particularly valuable for our topic is Irenaeus of Lyons in France. His Christian training had been in Turkey by the earliest disciples of the apostles. One of these teachers was probably "the angel of the church in Smyrna" addressed in Revelation 2:8. In the 180s AD, Irenaeus wrote the longest passage on the limits on secular government before Christianity became legal in the fourth century:

> For since man, by departing from God, reached such a pitch of fury as even to look upon his brother as his enemy, and engaged without fear in every kind of restless conduct, and murder, and avarice; God imposed upon mankind the fear of man, as they did not acknowledge the fear of God, in order that, being subjected to the authority of men, and kept under restraint by their laws, they might attain to some degree of justice, and exercise mutual forbearance through dread of the sword suspended full in their view, as the apostle says: "For he beareth not the sword in vain; for he is the minister of God, the avenger for wrath upon him who does evil." And for this reason too, magistrates themselves, having laws as a clothing of righteousness whenever they act in a just and legitimate manner, shall not be called in question for their conduct, nor be liable to punishment. But whatsoever they do to the subversion of justice, iniquitously, and impiously, and illegally, and tyrannically, in all these things shall they also perish; for the

---

3. Clement of Alexandria, *Stromata*, 7.7.
4. Clement of Alexandria, *Stromata*, 5.11.
5. Origen, *On First Principles*, 3.5.6.

just judgment of God comes equally upon all, and in no case is defective.[6]

Like all early Christian writers, Irenaeus taught that we must obey civil governments in all matters that do not infringe on our religion—at least we should not participate in tumults and tax fraud—but here he outlined God's parameters on secular authorities. They must not subvert justice nor act sinfully nor illegally. They must not be dictators. If they offend, God will deal with them. Today, in democracies, God acts through citizens exercising the peaceful and guaranteed restraints provided by the same secular laws, even if this is only by exercising one's freedom of speech in exposing political and bureaucratic corruption.

One form of wrongdoing among corrupt politicians and other officeholders is bribery. This was firmly condemned by the church in its early, foundational period, when the oral teachings of Christ were still echoing in Christian ears. Bribery was condemned by Clement in *Paedagogus* 3.12 and a few years earlier by Theophilus, bishop of Antioch,[7] and earlier still, in the middle of the second century, by the *Epistle of the Apostles* 37. Even in the New Testament, a Roman governor expected Saint Paul to try to bribe him, but the apostle did not do so (Acts 24:26).

Rank-and-file Christians were forbidden to so much as *offer* a bribe, even if it might save their lives. Remember the example of Paul gave us. The above church fathers wrote in a time when the church was being persecuted. Certain death was the penalty for failing to participate in pagan worship, which Christians rightly considered to be idolatry and a betrayal of the lordship of Christ. Some frightened believers found a third alternative: bribe the relevant government officials to obtain an untrue government certificate that they had participated, soothing their consciences that they had not actually done so in fact. This was condemned by Christian authors around AD 211. Tertullian, who wrote at greater length, pointed out that such a Christian's life would be saved not by the Lord but by money.[8] Recipients of such bribes would not be the heavenly treasury but such low fellows as "an informer, a soldier, or some paltry thief of a ruler."[9] Relying on a bribe to escape undesirable consequences would be to rely on

---

6. Irenaeus, *Against Heresies*, 5.24.2 (ANF 1:552).
7. Theophilus, *To Autolycus* 3.9.
8. Tertullian, *On Flight in Persecution*, 12.
9. Tertullian, *On Flight in Persecution* 12 (ANF 4:123).

Mammon, the god of money, which Jesus expressly forbade in Matthew 6:24 and Luke 16:13.

What lessons can ordinary citizens learn from writings dating from so early that there was no time or opportunity for errors to predominate in the church? The first is: do not participate in governmental corruption, even if the outcome would be extremely favorable to you. The other is, as Origen exhorted, to pity and pray for wrongdoers among rulers. Of course, in democracies, the people, either collectively or as individuals, have legal means at their disposal to call erring and corrupt public servants to account, and in doing so will implement the restraints on bureaucrats and politicians that Irenaeus envisioned.

Chapter 13

Encouragement

IN honor of his services to the church, the twelve apostles conferred the title "Son of Encouragement" on Joses the Levite of Cyprus (Acts 4:36). He later encouraged Paul to enter church work (Acts 11:25–26), and became one of his companions as a missionary. He was one of Paul's colleagues that often encouraged him during his apostolate (Col 4:11; Phlm 7).

Paul himself was a frequent encourager. He encouraged the new Christian community at Philippi in Macedonia (Acts 16:40), the churches at Colossae (Col 4:8), Thessalonica (1 Thess 2:11–12), and Laodicea (Col 2:3), and the people along the route of his evangelistic tour in Acts 20:1–2.

Paul wrote of encouragement as a spiritual gift or grace that holders are obliged to use repeatedly for the benefit of the whole church, along with prophecy, ministry, teaching, leadership, and donating (Rom 12:6–8). Even the gift of prophecy was given, say 1 Corinthians 14:3 and 31, to strengthen, build up, and encourage listeners.

Other ancient Christians shared this approach. First Peter was written for the purpose of encouraging readers (1 Pet 5:12). When Paul landed in Italy, the church at Rome encouraged him by sending a welcoming committee many miles to meet him (Acts 28:15). The eighth mandate of *The Shepherd of Hermas*, a series of visions compiled by a brother of a bishop of Rome in the first half of the second century, ranked "encouraging those who are sick in soul"[1] among such good works as love, concord, patience, helping widows, caring for orphans, hospitality, respect for the elderly, providing the necessaries of life to the needy, and mercy on debtors. In the 180s AD, the bishop of Lyons in France wrote that the universal church practiced

---

1. Herm. Mand. 8.10 (ANF 2:25).

the virtues of sympathy, compassion, steadfastness, truth, and charity "for the aid and encouragement of mankind."[2] Including "encourage," some of Hermas's list appears in a similar teaching of Clement of Alexandria, the leading Christian scholar and writer of the 190s AD.[3] In the early third century, whenever traveling missionaries stayed overnight in a town or village where there were Christian males, they would speak words of encouragement to them, and encourage them to please God, and do good works.[4]

The New Testament encourages all Christians to encourage one another (Rom 1:12; 2 Cor 13:11; 1 Thess 5:11), hopefully on a daily basis (Heb 3:13), especially about the second coming (1 Thess 4:18), and to attend church (Heb 10:24–25).

Encouragement takes the form of a command in other passages. First Thessalonians 4:13 mandates encouraging the faint-hearted or feeble-minded, along with warning the idle and unruly, supporting the weak, and being patient with all.

This applies even more to clergy, for 2 Timothy 4:2 commands them to preach, correct, rebuke, and encourage. Pastor-bishops are also to exhort orthodox Christians as against heretics (Titus 1:9), to encourage young men (Titus 2:6), and to encourage Christians generally (Titus 2:15). In the early third century, bishops had the duty of encouraging forerunners of nuns that conducted themselves properly amid the self-seeking of their lax sisters.[5]

The pagan writer Lucian of Samosata recorded in the 160s AD that Christians were so enthusiastic in encouraging those of their number that were imprisoned for their faith that they sent generous support from distant towns. Lucian noted that such behavior was so widespread and regular that an impostor or charlatan could easily acquire much money by pretending to be a Christian in need of help or encouragement.[6]

Christian leaders encouraged their people in various attitudes and actions. One was Christian unity (Rom 15:5; 2 Cor 13:11). Another was to keep the faith (Acts 14:22). There were also encouragements to work quietly and earn an honest living (2 Thess 3:12), to correct one's behavior as a member in the local congregation (1 Tim 5:1), to be sober-minded,

---

2. Irenaeus, *Against Heresies*, 2.31.3 (ANF 1:407).
3. Clement of Alexandria, *Stromata* 7.12.
4. *Two Letters on Virginity*, 2.1.
5. Connolly, *Didascalia apostolorum*, 13.
6. Lucian of Samosata, "Passing of Peregrinus," 5:13.

self-controlled or sensible (Titus 2:6), to attend public worship (Heb 10:25), and generally to behave in a manner worthy of God (1 Thess 2:12).

A Christian need not be personally present in order to encourage others. The twelve apostles and the rest of the Jerusalem church encouraged the Christians at Antioch by sending a delegation with a written message (Acts 15:32). Paul similarly sent Timothy and other colleagues to distant towns and cities (Eph 6:21–22; Col 4:7–8; 1 Thess 3:2). Chapters 1 and 2 of the Letter to Titus give details of the encouragement such co-workers were to give.

In sum, practicing of the gift of encouragement was a recurrent theme in Christian literature before AD 250, with clergy frequently encouraging their flocks and fellow shepherds, and all church members were to encourage one another, preferably daily.

Chapter 14

Enemies

Overview

Hatred, opposition, unpopularity, and persecution in one form or another come with the territory of being a Christian, and did so at the very beginnings of our religion. Predictions of such adverse behavior are attributed to Jesus in the four Gospels and in other Christian documents written while the oral teachings and Bible interpretations of the New Testament writers were still fresh in Christians' memories. All of them cited in this chapter were written so early that there was no time for the Christian message to have been corrupted. The early biblical and nonbiblical literature also contains instructions as to how Christians are to respond to such abuse, and gives reasons why we should respond in this manner. The following is not just one possible interpretation of the Bible among many, but was handed down by people—or Christians not many generations later—who knew Christ or the apostles in the flesh and could ask them to explain what they had said and how they interpreted the Scriptures.

Expect Trouble

The most direct warning for people who would count the cost of following Jesus before deciding to do so is at Matthew 10.22: "you will be hated by all for my name's sake." The probability of adverse reaction by non-Christians is expressed elsewhere to be a blessing. Yes, Christians who are hated, opposed, unpopular, and persecuted for their discipleship are in some way in a blessed or enviable position:

1. Matthew 5:10: "Blessed are those who are persecuted for righteousness' sake, for theirs is the kingdom of heaven."
2. Matthew 5:11: "Blessed are you when men revile you and persecute you and utter all kinds of evil against you falsely on my account."
3. Luke 6:22: "Blessed are you when men hate you, and they exclude you and revile you, and cast out your name as evil, on account of the Son of man!"
4. Polycarp of Smyrna, near Ephesus, a pastor who had frequently associated with the apostles, similarly wrote in the first half of the second century that heaven blesses "those that are persecuted for righteousness' sake."[1] Polycarp may have been "the angel of the church in Smyrna" addressed in Revelation 2:8.
5. *Diatessaron* 8.35: "Blessed are ye when men shall hate you, and separate you from them, and persecute you, and reproach you and shall speak against you with all evil talk, for my sake, falsely."[2] Dating from the mid-second century AD, the *Diatessaron* is a harmonized interweaving of the four Gospels and another early recollection of Jesus' sayings. It was the standard text of the gospel in Syria until the fifth century. It gives us a supplementary and more coordinated view of Jesus' teachings as they were perceived by early believers, the people to whom they were originally directed.
6. In the *Epistle of the Apostles*, also mid-second century, Jesus is credited with a fuller description of Christians who rebuke and warn other people, who speak out against religious doubting, confusions, divisions, jealousy, envy, hatred, fault-finding, and respect of sinners. Such Christians shall be hated, mocked, despised, persecuted, thrust aside, and ostracized.[3]

Love Your Enemies

The ways in which Christians are to respond to such treatment are contrary to natural human inclination and its instinct to reply in kind. First, the

---

1. Polycarp, *Letter to the Philippians* 2.3 (ANF 1:33).
2. *Diatessaron*, ANF 10:56.
3. *Epistle of the Apostles* 50.

teaching of the earliest Christian authors is that we are to love our enemies and those who hate us:

1. Matthew 5:44: "Love your enemies."
2. Luke 6:27: "Love your enemies, and do good to those who hate you."
3. Luke 6:35: "love your enemies, and do good."
4. *Epistle of the Apostles* 18 says the same as Matthew 5:44.
5. *Diatessaron* 9.18 expresses the same thought as Luke.[4]
6. Love for those who hate them was described as a characteristic of Christian behavior by Justin, a philosopher and teacher who was martyred for the faith around AD 165.[5]
7. Irenaeus, a disciple of Polycarp and later a pastor-bishop in France, repeated the statement about love for enemies in the 180s AD,[6] and explained that in giving this command Christ extended the law of Moses, even to loving our enemies in addition to family and neighbors.[7]
8. In the closing years of the second century, the church father Tertullian observed that because we Christians are to love our enemies, then we cannot hate anyone at all, not even persecutors.[8] Tertullian was a prominent Roman lawyer who became a minister in Carthage in what is today Tunisia. He was the most prolific Christian author in the Latin language before Augustine.
9. About the same time as Tertullian, the *Letter to Diognetus*, in describing Christians' relations with the world, compares them to the soul, and the (unfriendly) world to the flesh of a body: "The soul loves the flesh that hates it, and [loves also] the members; Christians likewise love those that hate them. The soul is imprisoned in the body, yet preserves that very body."[9]

---

4. ANF 10:58.
5. Justin Martyr, *1 Apology* 15 (ANF 1:167).
6. Irenaeus, *Against Heresies* 2.32.1 (ANF 1:408).
7. Irenaeus, *Against Heresies* 4.13.3 (ANF 1:477–78).
8. Tertullian, *Apology* 37 (ANF 3:45).
9. *Letter to Diognetus* 6.6–7 (ANF 1:27).

10. A summary of these sentiments can be found in the *Didache*, a church manual dating from the first or early second century. It counsels: "love them that hate you; and ye shall not have an enemy."[10]

Pray for Your Enemies

A spiritual application of such love is to pray for one's enemies and for those who hate, abuse, slander, persecute, exhibit violence to, and despitefully use a Christian:

1. Matthew 5:44: "pray for those who persecute you."

2. Luke 6:28: "pray for those who abuse you."

3. Around AD 125, the Christian philosopher Aristides of Athens described the Christians' response to slanders of Greek pagans against them:

   > But the Christians are just and good, and the truth is set before their eyes, and their spirit is long-suffering; and, therefore, though they know the error of these (the Greeks), and are persecuted by them, they bear and endure it; and for the most part they have compassion on them, as men who are destitute of knowledge. And on their side, they offer prayer that these may repent of their error.[11]

4. Polycarp exhorted the Philippian Christians to "Pray for all the saints," kings, princes, and "for those that persecute and hate you, and for the enemies of the cross."[12]

5. *Didache* 1.3: "Pray for your enemies, and fast for them that persecute you."[13]

6. The *Sentences of Sextus,* in the first half of the second century, counselled Christians to consider nobody to be their enemy[14] and to pray that they might do good to whatever enemy they still might have.[15]

---

10. *Didache* 1.3 (ANF 7:377).
11. Aristides, *Apology* 17 (ANF 10:279).
12. Polycarp, *Letter to the Philippians* 12.3 (ANF 1:36).
13. *Didache* 1.3 ANF 7:377.
14. *Sentences of Sextus* 105.
15. *Sentences of Sextus* 213.

7. Justin Martyr, quoting the Gospels, wrote that it is standard Christian practice to "Pray for our enemies"[16] and to "pray for them that despitefully use you."[17]

8. *Diatessaron* 9.13: "pray for those that curse you . . . pray for those who take you with violence and persecute you."[18]

9. Irenaeus, *Against Heresies*, 2.32.1 is to the same effect, and adds that by such prayer and other Christianly response we can avoid imitating the "arrogance, lust, and pride of others."[19]

10. Clement of Alexandria in Egypt was dean of the foremost Christian educational institution of the day. In the 190s AD, he taught that the purpose of Exodus 23:4–5 and Deuteronomy 22:1–4 is "in order to teach those who are trained in these things to pray for their enemies."[20] Other types and figures of the Old Testament, he said, also teach this principle.

11. In exegeting 1 Corinthians 6:1–6, Clement noted that "the Lord expressly enjoined 'to pray for enemies,'"[21] as did Paul. Looking at the other side of the coin, Clement said of Paul in this passage: "he teaches that he [the model Christian] is not mindful of injuries, and does not allow him even to pray against the man who has done him wrong."[22] Clement's thrust in this commentary is that praying for those who have done them wrong, as well as complete forgiveness of them, substantially contributes to a Christian becoming long-suffering and loving toward all people, which is what God wants.

12. Quoting an earlier source, Tertullian enjoined Christians to "Love your enemies, and bless those which hate you, and pray for them which calumniate you."[23]

---

16. Justin Martyr, *1 Apology* 15 (ANF 1:167).
17. Justin Martyr, *1 Apology* 15 (ANF 1:167).
18. *Diatessaron*, ANF 10:57–58.
19. Irenaeus, *Against Heresies* (ANF 1:408).
20. Clement of Alexandria, *Stromata* 2.18 (ANF 2:367).
21. Clement of Alexandria, *Stromata* 7.14 (ANF 2:548).
22. Clement of Alexandria, *Stromata* 7.14 (ANF 2:548).
23. Tertullian, *Against Marcion* 4.16 (ANF 3:370).

Bless Your Enemies

Akin to praying for someone is to bless them. The earliest Christian literature exhorts us to bless even people who hate, slander, curse, or persecute us:

1. Luke 6:28: "bless those who curse you."
2. Romans 12:14: "Bless those who persecute you; bless and do not curse them."
3. *Didache* 1.3 is to the same effect, as is Justin Martyr, *1 Apology*, 15.
4. Tertullian also repeated Christ's command to bless people who hate a Christian in a passage showing that Jesus was teaching a new and more thoroughgoing kind of patience.[24]

Do Good to Your Enemies

In addition to these purely spiritual manifestations of love and forgiveness, various writers admonished Christians to render practical good works of love to their enemies and to people who hate and persecute them. The gospel that is lived is more effective than a gospel that is merely preached or confined to the spiritual dimension:

1. Luke 6:27: "do good to those who hate you."
2. Luke 6:35: "love your enemies, and do good, and lend, and expect nothing in return."
3. Romans 12:20, quoting Proverbs 25:21: "if your enemy is hungry, feed him; if he is thirsty, give him drink."
4. Artistides, in a chapter on the characteristic behavior of Christians: "their oppressors they appease (lit.: comfort) and make them their friends; they do good to their enemies."[25]
5. *Diatessaron* 9.13: "deal well with those that hate you."[26]
6. *Diatessaron* 9.18: "love your enemies, and do good to them, and lend, and cut not off the hope of any man."[27]

---

24. Tertullian, *Against Marcion* 4.16 (ANF 3:370).
25. Aristides, *Apology* 15 (ANF 10:276).
26. *Diatessaron*, ANF 10:57–58.
27. *Diatessaron*, ANF 10:58.

7. Clement of Alexadnria, *Stromata*, 7.12, describing the model Christian:

> Certainly, he relieves the afflicted, helping him with consolations, encouragements, and the necessaries of life; giving to all that need, though not similarly, but justly, according to desert; furthermore, to him who persecutes and hates, even if he need it; caring little for those who say to him that he has given out of fear; if it is not out of fear that he does so, but to give help.[28]

Call Your Enemies Your Brothers

So great was this love, long-suffering, and magnanimity that Theophilus, a pastor-bishop of Antioch in Syria in the third quarter of the second century, indicated that Christians applied and practiced Isaiah 66:5: "Say to those that hate you, and that cast you out, 'Ye are our brethren.'"[29] Also considering Isaiah 66.5, Tertullian added:

> if they who are our enemies, and hate us, and speak evil of us, and calumniate us, are to be called our brethren, surely He did in effect bid us bless them that hate us, and pray for them who calumniate us, when he instructed us to reckon them as brethren.[30]

Clement's more encompassing comment was "if all are not yet brethren to us, they ought to be regarded in that light."[31]

Joy at Persecution

In the topsy-turvy world of Christ's kingdom, where radical uncompromising love overturns natural human inclinations, our internal reaction to hatred, ostracism, and slander on account of the name is just as surprising:

1. Matthew 5:12: "Rejoice and be glad, for your reward is great in heaven, for so men persecuted the prophets who were before you."

---

28. Clement of Alexandria, *Stromata* 7.12 (ANF 2:542).
29. Theophilus, *To Autolycus* 3.14 (ANF 2:115).
30. Tertullian, *Against Marcion* 4.16 (ANF 3:370).
31. Clement of Alexandria, *Stromata* 7.14 (ANF 2:548).

2. Luke 6:23: "Rejoice . . . and leap for joy, for behold, your reward is great in heaven; for so their fathers did to the prophets."

3. *Diatessaron* 8.36: "rejoice and be glad, for your reward is great in heaven: for so persecuted they the prophets before you."[32]

4. Tertullian, *Apology* 46: "the Christian, even when he is condemned, gives thanks."[33]

Good Results from Bad Treatment

What is God's purpose in commanding such self-denying—even unnatural—responses? The ancient authors indicate four categories of objectives for the reactions described above:

The first was to become like God. The early sources state:

1. Matthew 5:45: "so that you may be sons of your Father who is in heaven; for he makes his sun to rise on the evil and on the good, and sends rain on the just and unjust."

2. Luke 6:35: "you will be sons of the Most High; for he is kind to the ungrateful and selfish."

3. *Diatessaron* 9.18: "ye may be the children of the Highest: for he is lenient toward the wicked and the ungrateful."[34]

4. In his exegesis of 1 Corinthians 6:1–6, Clement makes the same point as Matthew 5:45, and adds that complete forgiveness of enemies, and lack of resentment and other negative feelings toward them, builds up long-suffering and conformity to the nature of the Almighty: "'For God makes His sun to shine on the just and the unjust,' and sent the Lord Himself to the just and the unjust."[35] Because God loves all humanity, it is through loving all people (including those who hate and cause trouble for a Christian) that the Christian becomes more like God, i.e., the sort of person God wants him/her to be.[36]

Second, was to train Christians in love for *all* people:

32. *Diatessaron*, ANF 10:56.
33. Tertullian, *Apology* 46 (ANF 3:51).
34. *Diatessaron*, ANF 10:58.
35. Clement of Alexandria, *Stromata* 7.14 (ANF 2:548).
36. Clement of Alexandria, *Stromata* 7.14 (ANF 2:548).

1. Justin Martyr wrote that praying for enemies, blessing those who curse us, etc. was only part of what Christ taught concerning "our love to all."[37]

2. Tertullian, *Apology* 37: "If we are enjoined, then, to love our enemies, as I have remarked above, whom have we to hate?"[38]

3. According to Clement of Aleandria's *Stromata* 7.12, the early Christian ideal was to be "equal and like" toward all people, be they neighbors, domestic servants, "or lawful enemy, or whosoever." As such, Christians are therefore to relieve and help everyone in need, including people who persecute and hate them.[39]

4. My own general gleaning from ancient Christian literature is that loving one's enemies is good practice and training for loving one's family, neighbors, and fellow Christians.

Third, that we might exercise our Christian freedom. A Christian's free love of people that injure him/her is an important application of the liberty that is in Christ, for s/he is independent of actions of other people. According to Irenaeus, Jesus extended the law of Moses in such things as giving offerings generously in addition to tithes, prohibiting anger and retaliation for injuries in addition to murder, forbidding lust in addition to adultery, and loving one's enemies in addition to neighbors and brothers. Jesus did this, wrote Irenaeus, so that a Christian can act in freedom, dignity, and willingness toward everyone, including those who hate and do him/her harm. In this way the Christian conforms his or her mind and behavior to God, "'who maketh his sun to rise upon the evil and the good, and sendeth rain upon the just and the unjust.'"[40]

The fourth and final purpose of the proper Christian response described in this chapter toward hatred, opposition, slander, and persecution is that it may well lead to the reform and even conversion of our enemies, and a consequent end to their hostility, whereas retaliation escalates hostility:

---

37. *1 Apology* 15 (ANF 1:167).
38. Tertullian, *Apology* 37 (ANF 3:45).
39. Clement of Alexandria, *Stromata* 7.14 (ANF 2:542).
40. Irenaeus, *Against Heresies* 4.13.3 (ANF 1:477–78).

1. Remember Aristides's comment above that Christians pray for their detractors and persecutors "that these may repent of their error."[41]
2. As Justin Martyr said to a Jewish opponent, "we pray for you and for all other men who hate us; in order that you, having repented along with us, may not blaspheme Him . . . Christ Jesus; but, believing on Him, may be saved."[42]
3. The teaching for Christians, according to Irenaeus, is that "when themselves wickedly dealt with, to be long-suffering, and to show kindness toward those [that injured them], and to pray for them, that by means of repentance they might be saved."[43]
4. The last word goes to Clement of Alexadnria:

   > For oblivion of injuries is followed by goodness, and the latter by dissolution of enmity. From this we are fitted for agreement, and this conducts to felicity. And should you suppose one habitually hostile, and discover him to be unreasonably mistaken either through lust or anger, turn him to goodness.[44]

Why Not Us?

Have you been harrassed by persecutors because of your faith? Probably not. If Christians are not opposed and spoken against in our daily lives in the twenty-first century, perhaps it is because we do not take a strong enough stand (or any stand) against injustice and evil in our world. Perhaps we are not open and vocal enough in opposing wrongdoing in our society or in advancing the kingdom of Christ among the people around us. If this is the case, we should pray and act such that we merit the negative reactions described above and thus receive the blessings God has promised there.

---

41. Aristides, *Apology* 17 (ANF 10:279).
42. Justin Martyr, *Dialogue with Trypho* 35 (ANF 1:212).
43. Irenaeus, *Against Heresies* 2.32.1 (ANF 1:408).
44. Clement of Alexandria, *Stromata* 2.18 (ANF 2:367).

Chapter 15

Envy

The Malignant Poison of Envy

Envy is not a light matter, at least not for a Christian. Scripture and the earliest Christian consensus after it contain an abundance of disapprovals and condemnations of envy. Such teaching dates from so early a period, before the middle of the third century AD, that it can have originated only in the instructions of Jesus and the apostles, and applies to all Christians because it predates the division into modern-day denominations.

By "envy" we mean resentment that another person possesses a personal quality or material goods that the envious person does not have. It is different from "jealousy," which I define as an inordinate desire to keep full possession or control of one's own personal quality, relationship, or material possession. "Covet," which is condemned in many places in many authors, including the Ten Commandments, is mere yearning to possess something that belongs to another person but without the resentment or ill-will that is an essential element of envy.

The first postbiblical mention of envy is in *The First Epistle of Clement to the Corinthians*, a letter dating from the middle or late first century, when some apostles were still alive. It gives a number of Old Testament examples of the evil effects of envy. Readers of the present book might be familiar with some of the cases mentioned.

The first example is that of Cain and Abel. Both brothers offered sacrifices to God, but God only accepted Abel's. Cain became bitterly envious of the favor shown to his brother and grieved. According to *1 Clement*, God counselled Cain, saying: "Be at peace: thine offering returns to thyself, and thou shalt again possess it." Nevertheless, Cain's envy became so great that he killed Abel. "Ye see," says 1 Clement, "how envy and jealousy led to the murder of a brother."[1]

Another example is the brothers Jacob and Esau. Jacob envied Esau's birthright and greater inheritance as the firstborn so much that he tricked him out of them. When Esau discovered this, he was enraged. This necessitated Jacob fleeing the country and living for decades far away from home.

While still a teenager, the patriarch Joseph in the Old Testament received visions from God that he would one day rule over his brothers, and was insensitive enough to tell them about said visions. Moreover, their father openly loved Joseph more than them. "When his brothers saw that their father loved him more than all his brothers, they hated him, and could not speak peaceably to him" (Gen 37:4 RSV). Their envy grew so great that when they were far from home, they kidnapped him with the intent of later killing him. They eventually let him live, but sold him into slavery, which resulted in his being taken to Egypt and living there as a servant.

"Envy compelled Moses to flee from the face of Pharaoh king of Egypt,"[2] also resulting in decades away from the only home he had known. The letter gives other examples of envy resulting in evil consequences: Aaron and Miriam were banished from the camp of Israel in the desert; and Dathan and Abiram were swallowed up by the earth as a punishment for envying Moses' leadership and rebelling against it. Although such severe and far-reaching results seldom follow envy today, and as heirs of over a millennium of Christian teaching where we try to damp down our envy, 1 Clement's point still remains that people often do bad things out of envy, with undesirable consequences for both sides.

Speaking generally, the letter points out:

> Look carefully into the Scriptures, which are the true utterances of the Holy Spirit. Observe that nothing of an unjust or counterfeit character is written in them. There you will not find that the righteous were cast off by men who themselves were holy. The righteous were indeed persecuted, but only by the wicked. They were cast into prison, but only by the unholy; they were stoned, but only

---

1. *1 Clement* 4 (ANF 1:6).
2. *1 Clement* 4 (ANF 1:6).

by transgressors; they were slain, but only by the accursed, and such as had conceived an unrighteous envy against them.[3]

First Clement also gives examples from "our own generation,"[4] i.e., the first century AD. Let us quote the letter:

> Through envy and jealousy, the greatest and most righteous pillars of the Church have been persecuted and have come to a grievous death[5]. . . . Peter, through unrighteous envy, endured not one or two, but numerous labours; and . . . at length suffered martyrdom[6]. . . . Owing to envy, Paul . . . [was] . . . seven times thrown into captivity, compelled to flee, and stoned . . . and suffered martyrdom[7]. . . . Through envy . . . being persecuted . . . suffered terrible and unspeakable torments[8]. . . . Envy has alienated wives from their husbands[9]. . . . Envy and strife have overthrown great cities and rooted up mighty nations."[10]

The letter follows each of these Christian examples with the observation that the envied persons all received a fitting reward from God, which means that those that envied did not really accomplish their purpose but only gave their victims a higher standing with the divine. Nevertheless, envy always fostered bad results on earth. According to this letter, envy is the source of all manner of sinful motives and actions.

So pernicious is envy that 1 Clement sees fit to remind readers of the deuterocanonical Bible book the *Wisdom of Solomon* 2:24 to the effect that "through the devil's envy death entered the world" (RSV). In the same vein, Novatian, a cleric who later guided the church at Rome through a severe government persecution in the middle of the third century, wrote that it was "the malignant poison of envy" that caused Adam to lose immortality through eating from the forbidden tree.

Over a century after this first Clement lived, another Clement, called Clement of Alexandria, who was the dean of the world's foremost Christian school. He wrote that a person truly has free will only when they do not act

---

3. *1 Clement* 45 (ANF 1:17).
4. *1 Clement* 5 (ANF 1:6).
5. *1 Clement* 5 (ANF 1:6).
6. *1 Clement* 5 (ANF 1:6).
7. *1 Clement* 5 (ANF 1:6).
8. *1 Clement* 6 (ANF 1:6).
9. *1 Clement* 6 (ANF 1:6).
10. *1 Clement* 6 (ANF 1:6).

out of envy, and that a characteristic of love is that it is free from envy, as did the apostle Paul in 1 Corinthians 13:4 in some Bible translations.

First Corinthians 13:4 was also quoted by a student of Clement of Alexandria named Origen, who was later an outstanding church scholar in his own right, and whose writing and preaching influenced the church for centuries to come. His Bible commentaries and homilies frequently list envy as among the "works of the flesh" that Christians are to remove from their lives. To do so, he recommended placing the cross of Jesus before one's eyes (whether in imagination or looking at an actual crucifix is not specified) and faithfully retaining it in one's mind and fixing attention on his death. This mental exercise, Origen wrote, would forestall envy and other sins from getting an upper hand in a Christian's life.

Including the deuterocanonical books, there are thirteen clear disapprovals or condemnations of envy in the Old Testament. Taking together the New Testament and Christian teaching passed along by the church fathers and other Christian writings, there are sixty-four in Christian literature before AD 250, mostly in lists (e.g. Mark 7:21–22). These are in addition to the dozens against the related evils of jealousy and covetousness. The lists rank envy with such serious failings as debauchery, greed, wrath, and slander. In addition to these are the notes at Matthew 27:18 and Mark 15:10 to the effect that it was through envy that the Jewish chief priests brought Jesus to Pilate in order to be crucified. Seeing the magnitude of the pernicious results of this instance of envy, we should all the more hold Jesus' cross in our mind's eye when we catch ourselves tempted to envy, as Origen advised.

Scripture quotations are from the Revised Standard Version of the Bible (RSV), copyright 1946, 1952, 1971 by the Division of Christian Education of the National Council of the Churches of Christ in the USA. Used by permission.

Chapter 16

Fasting

Introduction

This chapter studies fasting in the Christian church prior to AD 250. This was an age when the practices of Jesus and the apostles were openly continued and shared. During this era, any deviation from these practices would have been detected in any group of Christians within the widespread and alert community of believers. It also describes what fasting is, the reasons for it, the times and circumstances in which Christians fasted, minority beliefs about fasting, alternatives to literal physical fasting, and the manner in which fasting is to be performed. From time to time, differences in fasting practices will be noted between the majority, mainstream, catholic, or "great" church, and denominations separated from it. The most noteworthy as regards abstinence were the Montanists, a rigorous, apocalyptic movement that originated around AD 172 and was embraced by Tertullian in the middle of his writing ministry.

Meaning of "Fasting"

Fasting is the voluntary abstaining for a predetermined time from foods and beverages. This may be from all foodstuffs and drink, or only from particular foods and particular beverages, such as meat and wine. Older readers might remember that for Roman Catholics meat was forbidden on Fridays, and that no food or drink except water was permitted after the midnight before receiving Holy Communion. Both fasts had parallels in the ancient church.

Ancient Christian fasts could entail total abstinence, as in the Paschal Vigil from Good Friday to three o'clock in the morning of Easter Sunday. This is attested to by the *Didascalia* 21, a manual of individual and corporate Christian practice compiled in the first three decades of the third century; by Tertullian's *On Prayer* 18, written around AD 200 (before he became a Montanist); and by Hippolytus's *Apostolic Tradition* 29. The *Apostolic Tradition* 32.1 also prescribed absolute fasting before communion, but does not indicate how long. Hippolytus was a bishop in central Italy who produced this book in AD 217 to describe existing church practice as it had descended from the apostles, in order to guide clergy in the proper practice, and to equip clergy and laity to detect and stop deviations from it.

More commonly, fasting meant merely confining one's diet to plain bread and water—the simplest, least luxurious, and cheapest of nourishment. Although the contexts in many ancient writings are unclear, this is the meaning of "fasting" in Tertullian's *On Fasting*, in *Didascalia* 21, from the day after Palm Sunday to Maundy Thursday, and in *The Shepherd of Hermas* Similitude 5.3.7. *The Shepherd of Hermas* is a compendium of teachings, purportedly from heavenly beings, recorded by a brother of a bishop of Rome in the early- or mid-second century. This was the diet for pregnant women and the ill in *The Apostolic Tradition* 29.2, during the otherwise nutrient-free two days before Easter Sunday.

According to Tertullian's *On Fasting* 1, Montanists also abstained during regular preset periods from meals with liquids, meat, gravy, and juicy or succulent fruit.

Orthodoxy of Fasting

Church leaders today who inculcate fasting have not departed from the faith nor heeded seducing spirits and doctrines of demons, nor are their consciences seared with a hot iron, because they command abstinence from foods God created (1 Tim 4:1–3). Nor do they "judge other Christians in matters of food and drink" (Col 2:16). They do not ban particular categories of food on a lifelong basis the way Jews and Muslims do with pork, but merely call for a delay of foods, or smaller portions, or reduced desires for them.[1]

Jesus set an example by fasting himself (Matt 4:2//Luke 4:2). He imposed restrictions, not on fasting itself, but on doing so ostentatiously (Matt

---

1. Tertullian, *On Fasting* 2, 14, 15, 17.

6:16–18). In fact, he stated that his disciples would later fast (Matt 9:15//Mark 2:19–20//Luke 5:35). As for a fast in which Christians eat only bread, remember that Christ bade us to pray "Give us this day our daily bread" (Matt 6:11//Luke 11:3), not ask for banquets of steak, wine, and delicacies.

When to Fast

For early majority/mainline Christians, there was no blanket, inflexible commandment to abstain from food or drink at fixed times. All fasting was voluntary, with designated periods of abstinence being a matter of custom and for the purpose of providing guidelines and balance for an entrenched practice. *Hermas* Similitude 5.1 and 3 regarded physical fasting to be more than God requires. However, it added he appreciates the sincerity behind it and willingness to trouble oneself out of religious devotion. Fasting brings joy to the Christian, and will be written down in heaven to his or her credit.

Recording longstanding church practice, Hippolytus's *Apostolic Tradition* 25 stated in AD 217 that laypeople and church elders (presbyters) are to fast frequently, but at their own individual option and time. On the other hand, the bishop was restricted to periods when the whole congregation fasted. To avoid offending a donor of foodstuffs, the bishop must eat some of it, and he was therefore free to fast only during its general public fasts; donors would presumably know the times of public fasts.

In the late 240s AD, Origen wrote that Christians "do not set great store on refraining from eating," and reminded readers "Not that which goeth into the mouth defileth a man; but that which cometh out of the mouth, this defileth a man" (Matt 15:11//Mark 7:18), "What God hath cleansed, that call not thou common" (Acts 10:15), and "meat commendeth us not to God: for neither, if we eat, are we the better; neither, if we eat not, are we the worse" (1 Cor 8:8).[2] The foremost Christian scholar, preacher, and Bible commentator of the first half of the third century, Origen was best positioned to know and relate widespread and local Christian practices because he traveled frequently throughout the eastern Mediterranean as an authority on Christianity at the request of local bishops/pastors.

Montanists were the extremists. They insisted upon a strict, systematic, and thoroughgoing set of regulations about when to eat, when to drink, when not to eat, and what to drink at permitted meals. They instituted frequent days and seasons for fasting. Their spokesman Tertullian condemned

---

2. Origen, *Against Celsus* 5.49 (ANF 4:565).

the attitude of the mainstream church in a passage that incidentally reveals the great church's practice:

> They think that fasting is to be indifferently observed under the New Covenant, of choice, not of command, according to the times and needs of each individual. They take a wide range according to individual judgment, [not] being subject to the law of a given precept.[3]

About AD 211, one churchman was so opposed to Montanist rigidity that one of the accusations he made was that the founder promoted the separation of spouses, systematically compelled donations, received bribes, loaned on usury, gambled, and "made laws for fasting."[4] This great church author apparently approved of fasting but not of legalistic, comprehensive, hard-and-fast regulations. Christians of the majority group generally viewed Montanist fasting teachings and practices as "very much akin to heathenish superstition."[5]

In a word, freedom was the hallmark for fasting among the majority group. They did not see it as a duty, such as attending church on Sunday—still less as a command, such as loving one's neighbor. Although everyone was encouraged to fast, nobody was compelled. The minority that sought to diminish the liberty that is in Christ was regarded by mainstream Christians as being so far from orthodox teaching that they refused fellowship with them, even when in prison awaiting martyrdom.[6]

Christians Encouraged to Fast

Fasting was strongly encouraged or mandated in the *Didache* 1.3 and 8.1, a first-century church manual, and a few decades later in *The Letter to the Philippians* 7.2 by Polycarp, who was probably "the angel of the church in Smyrna" addressed in Revelation 2:8. Before the decimating epidemic, persecution, and mass apostasy of AD 249–251, abstinence from foods and beverages for preset periods was quite frequently referred to as common among Christians. There are incidental references, sometimes with instructions, in Matthew 6:16–18; 1 Corinthians 7:5; *Apology* 15 by the Athenian

---

3. Tertullian, *On Fasting* 2 (ANF 4:103).
4. Apollonius, quoted in Eusebius *Church History* 5.18.2, 11.
5. Tertullian, *On Fasting* 2 (ANF 4:103).
6. *To Abercius Marcellus*, in Eusebius, *Church History* 5.16.22.

thinker Aristides (around AD 125); the *Sentences of Sextus* 267 (in the mid-second century); the *Letter to Flora* 5.13 by Ptolemy the Gnostic; the *Second Letter of Clement* 16.4 (both around the same time as *Sextus*); *Hermas* Similitude 5.1 and 3 (the same era or earlier); and Tertullian's *To His Wife* 2.4 and *On Prayer* 18 (both between AD 198 and 206). Ptolemy was a Valentinian gnostic in Italy. The *Sentences of Sextus* was a Western European collection of maxims for the Christian life that was very popular and was translated into many languages. At the end of our period of study, Origen approved *Sextus* 267's sentiment on fasting and attributed it to the apostles.[7] In *Commentary on Romans* 2.14.15, Origen included fasting among "the works of faith," together with mercy, studying God's law, enduring persecution, and martyrdom. In *Homilies on Leviticus* 7.1.3, he called for abstinence from food and alcohol before and during public worship by God's priests, with all Christians being priests.

The early third century saw extended treatment of the topic in Tertullian's treatise *On Fasting*, Hippolytus's *Apostolic Tradition* 25, 29, and 32.1, and the entire second section of Origen's tenth sermon on Leviticus. The last-mentioned contains the only reference to a forty-day Lent in this period. The *Didascalia* 21 notes that during Holy Week (the Monday to the Saturday before Easter) "all the faithful throughout the world fast." Except for the *Didache* and Polycarp, all the sources in the previous two paragraphs of this essay did not aim so much to promote fasting as to instill salutary guidelines to prevent extremes in a well-established tradition.

Reasons for Fasting

Early Christians saw numerous reasons and benefits for fasting. The most geographically widespread was also the most unselfish, because it helped the less fortunate. Aristides in Greece, Origen in Palestine, Hermas in Italy, and *The Sentences of Sextus* elsewhere in the Western Mediterranean encouraged deliberately going without food in order to share with the needy and hungry. Even Christians who possessed barely enough food for their own needs were counseled to fast and donate to the totally destitute the money they would have spent on food. The *Didascalia* 19 widened the circle of beneficiaries to encompass Christians who had been condemned and imprisoned for their faith, and urged believers to provide them with food and to secure better treatment in an era when prisoners had to provide

---

7. Origen, *Homilies on Joshua* 10.2.6.

their own food, bedding, and other jailhouse necessities now supplied by governments.

Other reasons or purposes Origen often cited were to mortify the flesh, subdue the body, humble it and the soul, and put to death the deeds of the flesh.[8] These are also put forward in Tertullian,[9] but Origen's lifestyle is a stronger witness in that he fasted often, never married, slept on the bare floor, permitted himself not even modest luxuries, and practiced other austerities to keep his desires and bodily inclinations under control.

Fasting was also an aid in exorcisms or casting out evil spirits, according to Matthew 17:21//Mark 9:29, Origen's *Homilies on Exodus* 2.3, and in *Two Letters on Virginity* 1.12 (a Syrian work dating from the first half of the third century).

Origen's other reasons for fasting were: to conquer temptation,[10] to prepare to worship God,[11] to fight for God,[12] and to train oneself in moderation in eating and other aspects of life.[13] Both *2 Clement* 16.4 and Origen's *Homilies on Joshua* 1.7 regard fasting as concomitant with repenting from sin. Dated at the middle of the second century, *2 Clement* is the oldest surviving Christian sermon outside the New Testament.

Tertullian's treatise *On Fasting* propounds the views of the rigorous Montanist denomination, with its demands for extreme abstinence and other austerities. Chapter 7 details many additional reasons for fasting: it bespeaks awe of God, reconciles an angry God to humans, enabled the Israelites to win battles, gives children to barren women, changes nature, averts perils, obliterates sins, and merits knowledge of the hidden mysteries of God. Chapters 5 through 9 recite the benefits and rewards of fasting to Old and New Testament saints, to argue that God delighted in a nation, priests, prophets, and ordinary individuals that fasted.

More individual reasons for fasting are to seek heavenly blessing on a church endeavor (Acts 13:2–3, 14:23), to thank God for a blessing or to obtain another from him (*Acts of Peter*, AD 180 to 200), as a form of intercession with heaven on behalf of the Jews (*Didascalia* 21), and to find the

---

8. Origen, *Against Celsus* 5.49, Origen, *Homilies on Joshua* 15.3; Origen, *Homilies on Leviticus* 10.2.3; Origen, *Homilies on Jeremiah* 20.7.5.

9. Tertullian, *On Fasting* 2, 9.

10. Origen, *Homilies on Exodus* 2.3.

11. Origen, *Homilies on Leviticus* 7.1.3.

12. Origen, *Homilies on Numbers* 25.4.1.

13. Origen, *Homilies on Leviticus* 10.2.6.

Kingdom of God (*Gospel of Thomas* 27). The last-mentioned, dating from the second half of the second century, contradicts itself in that it elsewhere condemns fasting.

Times for Fasting

Because of the wide latitude allowed and the needs of individual Christians, any time of year was open to fasting.[14] Within this liberty, it was customary to keep fasts weekly. There was also an annual fast, in the week before Easter Sunday.

Fasting every week of the year, on Wednesdays and Fridays, is attested in many sources: in the first-century church manual *Didache* 8.1; during the opening decades of the third century by *Didascalia* 21 and Tertullian's *On Fasting* 2 and 14 in describing mainstream practice; and around AD 240 by Origen's *Homilies on Leviticus* 10.2.6. In criticizing the tolerance and relative infrequency of fasting in the great church, the Montanist Tertullian sarcastically quipped that it regarded Wednesday and Friday as "the only legitimate days for Christian fasts."[15]

As early as AD 198, Tertullian in his pre-Montanist period wrote that Good Friday always saw a general fast in the mainstream church. According to *Didascalia* 21, all the world fasted in the week before Easter Sunday. From the Monday before Easter to Maundy Thursday, *Didascalia* 21 permitted only the regular fasting fare of bread and water. It forbade even this meager nourishment on Good Friday and Holy Saturday and demanded abstinence from all food and drink until 3 a.m. on Easter Day. In the same era as the Syrian *Didascalia*, Hippolytus's *Apostolic Tradition* 29.2–3 in Italy allowed pregnant women and the ill who could not go two days without food to consume bread and water on Saturday. The *Apostolic Tradition* provided that if sea travelers had lost track of the day, they were to fast after Pentecost upon learning the truth.

The week preceding Easter was the nearest known equivalent to the six-week Lent of later times. Although Origen's *Homilies on Leviticus* 10.2.6 refers in passing to "forty days dedicated to fasting," while outlining opportunities to fast and the freedom of the individual to abstain at almost any time, neither he nor anyone else in our period of study elaborated on these forty.

14. Tertullian, *On Fasting* 2; Origen, *Homilies on Leviticus* 10.2.3, 10.2.6.
15. Tertullian, *On Fasting* 2.

In addition to regularly recurring fasts, it was customary for bishops to call on their people to fast for a special cause, such as the state of the universal church.[16]

When Not to Fast

More common were prohibitions against fasting during particular days and seasons. Christians before AD 250 did not fast on the Lord's Day (Sunday), according to the *Didascalia* 21 and the non-Christian *Babylonian Talmud*, both dating from this era. Around AD 211, Tertullian cited refraining from fasting on Sunday as a tradition so old and so well accepted that it equaled Scripture in authority.[17] He likewise noted a prohibition on fasting between Easter and Pentecost,[18] which explains fasting after Pentecost in *The Apostolic Tradition* 29.3 by confused sea travelers.

Because its authors believed hypocrites fasted on Mondays and Thursday, *Didache* 8.1 forbade fasting then, with Wednesday and Friday being the proper days for sincere Christian practice. No other ancient writer repeated this prohibition.

Fasting was also forbidden on the Sabbath (Saturday), as recorded in *Didascalia* 21, the *Talmud* Taanith 27b and Tertullian's *On Fasting* 15. The last-mentioned pertained to Montanist and catholic alike, although Tertullian did note that some mainline Christians violated this prohibition.[19]

Part of the millennia-long controversy over what elements of Judaism Christianity should retain, Christian authors before the middle of the third century stressed avoiding Jewish fasting habits. Around AD 190, the *Acts of Peter* pronounced them abolished for Christians. About the same era or a little later, the *Letter to Diognetus* 4.1 stated they were forbidden for the new people of God. Even though he taught that Christians could fast at all times and at any time throughout the year, Origen preached twice around AD 240 against incorporating Mosaic precepts and Jewish traditions into fasts. Anti-Judaizing throughout, the *Didascalia* advocated extra measures to avoid importing any elements of the older religion into the new. For instance, Christians are to fast when Jews feast at Passover (ch. 21).

---

16. Tertullian, *On Fasting* 13.
17. Tertullian, *De Corona* 3; cf. Tertullian, *On Fasting* 14.
18. Tertullian, *De Corona* 3.
19. Tertullian, *On Fasting* 14.

The only exception to fasting during Jewish feasts and feasting during Jewish fasts was that Christians not fast on the Saturday Sabbath, which was also forbidden to Jews. Even so, Christians did fast on one Sabbath a year, the day before Easter—which usually occurs near the time of Passover.[20]

Although "enrolled widows" (the forerunners of nuns) were expected to spend much of their time in fasting and praying for the church,[21] they were forbidden to do so without the permission of a bishop or deacon. This was to prevent the widows from going from house to house and performing their duty only where there was a likelihood of being rewarded. Being already supported by the local church, their only motive could have been greed rather than necessity.

Origen warned his congregation not to fast for the wrong reason, such as excessive regard for physical fasting as an observance in itself.[22] Ptolemy the Gnostic wrote that it does not help the soul if done to imitate other people, out of habit, or out of regard for special days or seasons.[23]

Some second-century gnostics rejected fasting entirely. The recently discovered *Gospel of Judas* 40 categorizes fasting as among the corruptions and improper religious observances then being introduced into the mainstream church, along with abortion and homosexuality. The *Gospel of Thomas* seemingly contradicts itself. Logion 14 totally condemns fasting, prayer, and almsgiving, while Logion 27 warns that unless we "fast from the world" we will not "find the Kingdom." However, Logion 27 might indicate not literal physical fasting but spiritual fasting, which found support among many mainline authors.

Spiritual Fasting

Although acknowledging the benefits and service of literal abstinence from foods and beverages, some great church authors laid more stress on spiritual fasting, i.e., abstaining from evil deeds and replacing them with good ones. To Origen this meant, on the one hand, abstaining from every sin, malice, passion, luxury, heresy, and blasphemous philosophy, and, on the other hand, giving oneself to contemplating God, to humbling one's soul,

---

20. Connolly, *Didascalia apostolorum* 21.
21. Hippolytus, *Apostolic Tradition* 25.1; Connolly, *Didascalia apostolorum* 15.
22. Origen, *Homilies on Leviticus* 10.2.6.
23. Ptolemy, *Letter to Flora* 5.13.

and to moderation of an appetite that leads to gluttony.[24] *The Shepherd of Hermas* saw no benefit or value in physical fasting or any contribution to righteous living in it, unless the Christian also cultivates a pure heart, trust in God, and obedience to God's mandates, and fortifies him/herself against evil desires, evil words, the vanities of the world, and other sins.[25] If the highest and fullest obligation of the Sabbath was to rest and refrain from sin, then the highest and fullest form of fasting is to rest and refrain from it, although even today some denominations believe both literal and spiritual aspects are binding.

While acknowledging "some benefit to the soul," Ptolemy opined that the physical practice was less important than abstinence from evil, and than positive acts of praise, thanksgiving, and glorifying God, and than charity toward neighbors. He regarded fasting and other ordinances of the Mosaic Law to be "images and symbols" which Jesus later fulfilled and transformed into these spiritual observances. For instance, literal abstinence from food was one of the "types and shadows" that trained the Israelites to accept spiritual fasting.[26]

This allegorical method of Scripture interpretation and of reconciling the New Testament with the Old Testament was also characteristic of Origen, who was its most famous and most prolific exponent, although he did not significantly employ it when discussing fasting in his *Homilies on Leviticus*.

The allegorical method's most thoroughgoing application as regards fasting is found in the *Letter of Barnabas* 3, written in an Egyptian milieu sometime between AD 70 and 132, i.e., before the other commentators on spiritual fasting. Its author so completely spiritualized Mosaic laws and ordinances as "images and symbols" that he eliminated any room for their literal application. Instead, he quoted Isaiah 58 as the only possible Christian interpretation and practice:

> To us He saith, "Behold, this is the fast that I have chosen, saith the Lord, not that a man should humble his soul, but that he should loose every band of iniquity, untie the fastenings of harsh agreements, restore to liberty them that are bruised, tear in pieces every unjust engagement, feed the hungry with thy bread, clothe the naked when thou seest him, bring the homeless into thy house, not

---

24. Origen, *Homilies on Leviticus* 1.2.4–5.
25. Herm. Sim. 5.1, 5.3.
26. Ptolemy, *Letter to Flora* 5.9–14.

despise the humble if thou behold him, and not [turn away] from the members of thine own family.²⁷

Any other exegesis, he said, constituted rash acceptance of outdated Jewish laws.

Conduct to Accompany Fasting

Starting with Jesus, personal deportment and outward conduct were as important as physical fasting itself. He preached:

> when ye fast, be not, as the hypocrites, of a sad countenance: for they disfigure their faces, that they may appear unto men to fast. Verily I say unto you, they have their reward. But thou, when thou fastest, anoint thine head, and wash thy face; that thou appear not unto men to fast, but unto thy Father which is in secret: and thy Father, which seeth in secret, shall reward thee openly. (Matt 6:16–18)

This was phrased another way at *Diatessaron* 9.31–41, a consolidation of Matthew and other gospels that reflects what was regarded as the essence of Jesus' teaching by its editor in the mid-second century, and by the Syrian church until the fifth century:

> When ye fast, do not frown, as the hypocrites; for they make their faces austere, that they may be seen of men that they are fasting. Verily I say unto you, they have received their reward. But when thou fastest, wash thy face and anoint thy head; that thou make not an appearance to men of fasting, but to thy Father which is in secret: and thy Father which seeth in secret shall reward thee.

The Didache 8.1, which may have predated the Gospel of Matthew, forbade fasting with hypocrites. Around AD 200, Tertullian, in his pre-Montanist period, emphasized concealing as much as possible from other people, including other Christians, that one is fasting.[28] Origen discountenanced fasting for the purpose of how one appears to other people.[29] In mid-second century Italy, Ptolemy wrote against fasting just to imitate other people or out of excessive regard for particular days.[30]

---

27. *Letter of Barnabas* 3.3 (ANF 1:138).
28. Tertullian, *On Prayer* 18
29. Origen, *Commentary on Romans* 8.1.3.
30. Ptolemy, *Letter to Flora* 5.13.

Origen interpreted Matthew 6:16–18 allegorically: washing one's face was to better contemplate the glory of the Lord "with open face" (2 Cor 3:18), while the spiritual anointing oil is the oil of mercy, joy, and exultation.[31]

Tertullian interpreted the Matthew passage as saying that fasts are to be "without sadness" and commented that, being for a salutary purpose, fasts should not be occasions for sadness.[32]

Why No Fasting on Weekends

Mr. John Ernst, a reader in First Peninsula, Lunenburg County, Nova Scotia, has asked why Christians were not to fast on the Saturday Sabbath or the Sunday Lord's Day. As mentioned earlier, not even Montanists fasted on weekends.[33]

The early literature does answer his question, although the most succinct part of the answer comes from a writing later than the cutoff date elsewhere in this article, i.e., AD 249–251. The answer below deals first with the issue of fasting on the Saturday Sabbath, then with Sunday, and then with later sources that encompass both.

Sabbath: In *Against Marcion* 4.12, Tertullian found the reason for the prohibition against Sabbath fasting in Scripture itself. When God, in Exodus 16:22–29, commanded the Israelites in the wilderness to gather manna for only one day at a time, he told them to collect two days' supply on Fridays. This indicates, wrote Tertullian, that God did not want them to go without food on the Sabbath. Another example was Luke 6:1–5, where Jesus excused his disciples for plucking handfuls of standing grain and eating them on a Sabbath, to the consternation of the Pharisees. By excusing this act, said Tertullian, the Lord of the Sabbath regarded relief of hunger to be more important than the Sabbath rules, and thus he would hardly approve of seventh-day Sabbaths as regular fast days. In both cases, Tertullian opined, that the Creator "maintains the honor of the Sabbath as a day which is to be free from gloom rather than free from work."[34]

Sunday: Referring to Christians as "we," one of the earliest of Christian documents said: "we keep the eighth day with joyfulness, the day on

---

31. Origen, *Homilies on Leviticus* 10.2.4.
32. Tertullian, *On Fasting* 8.
33. Tertullian, *On Fasting* 14.
34. Tertullian, *Against Marcion* 4.12 (ANF 3:363).

which Jesus rose again from the dead."[35] Fasting is incompatible with such joyfulness.

A century or so later, chapter 21 of the *Didascalia* commented three times that Sunday is to be a day of joyfulness or good cheer. The same chapter states that Jesus forbade fasting on Sunday because it is the day of his resurrection, and prohibits afflicting one's soul on the Lord's Day.

Dating from AD 375 or 380 (i.e., after Christianity became an official religion of the Roman Empire), the *Apostolic Constitutions* are a synthesis of earlier church manuals, such as the *Didache*, the *Didascalia*, and Hippolytus's *Apostolic Tradition*. Although it came after this chapter's period of study, it does contain more concise answers to Mr. Ernst's question about why there was to be no fasting on weekends.

According to 5.15, fasting is forbidden on the Sabbath because it is "the rest from the creation." The Sabbath commemorates the creation. Like the *Didascalia*, exception is made for the Saturday before Easter because it was the day on which Christ the Creator was in his grave.

An exhortation in 7.23 is "keep the Sabbath, and the Lord's Day festival; because the former is the memorial of creation, and the latter of the resurrection. But there is only one Sabbath to be observed by you in the whole year, which is that of our Lord's burial, on which men ought to keep fast."

Conclusion

Thus it appears that the earliest Christians fasted for many purposes. However, fasting was not an end in itself, nor were experiencing physical weakness, rumbling stomachs, or diminished ability to concentrate. The common concerns were to damp down preoccupation with the fleshly, and to attain more intimate union with God. The only exception was financial: to enable Christians with barely enough food to raise money to buy some for people who had none at all. Yet even this reason was in obedience to the command that we are to love our neighbor, especially the destitute.

---

35. *Letter of Barnabas* 15.9 (ANF 1:147).

Chapter 17

Food

Genetically Modified Food

Scientists are producing meat by in-vitro cell growth, with the prospect that it will replace raising livestock. If it becomes commercially affordable, there will be no greenhouse gases or killing of animals. As with every change, some people question whether Christians may use this new development.

The Christian consensus before the mass apostasy of AD 249–251 was that no food is religiously forbidden or unclean. Jesus himself declared all foods clean (see Mark 7:18–19; Matthew 15:11–18). In Acts 10:10–16, the Lord told Peter not to call "unclean" any animal God has made clean (fit to eat).

The church scholar Origen commented on the concept of regarding as unclean and religiously forbidden even foods which Jewish law permitted. He said this is foundationless in the objective reality of God's will and arises from failure to correctly perceive the real sources of defilement. Origen was the dean of Christianity's foremost educational institution of the early third century. Christianity, Origen wrote, recognizes no food as unclean, although simplicity of mind and faultiness in one's powers of reflection mislead some hyper-scrupulous Christians to believe otherwise. He forbade judging the uncleanness of animals. However, he allowed for sensitive consciences that have reservations about foods sacrificed to idols, in which case the strong in the faith should not disturb weaker Christians by eating any in their presence.

Ancient Christians opposed deliberate abstinence from particular foods if the abstainer thereby considered himself closer to God. Romans 14:3 reads: "Let not the one who eats despise the one who abstains, and let not the one who abstains pass judgment on the one who eats," while 1 Timothy 4:1–3 warns of evil spirits and liars who require abstinence from foods that God created.

Clement of Alexandria, Origen's predecessor as dean, wrote similarly in the 190s AD. He observed that the Bible allows eating animal flesh, such as ravens bringing Elijah bread and meat (1 Kgs 17:6) and Samuel giving Saul a leg of meat to eat (1 Sam 9:24),[1] and also referenced Romans 14:2–3. Clement dismissed as "blockheads and atheists" people who ungratefully abstain from reasonable food. Many early authors considered that abstaining from particular foods shows ingratitude to God who provided them.[2] Clement summarized, "We are not, then, to abstain wholly from various kinds of food, but only not to be taken up about them. We partake of what is set before us, as becomes a Christian, out of respect to him who has invited us."[3]

The only mainline Christian reservations about food in early times were blood, meat that had been sacrificed to idols, and strangled animals (Acts 15:29).

As for blood, the Christian Minucius Felix, sometime between AD 166 and 249, said, "We do not use the blood even of eatable animals in our food."[4] In-vitro meat uses no blood, but relies on synthesis of vegetable matter.

Around AD 125, the Christian apologist Aristides of Athens wrote of his co-religionists, "Of the food which is consecrated to idols they do not eat."[5] The pagan Roman governor of Bithynia reported around AD 112 that Christians refused to buy sacrificial meat at public meat markets.[6] Origen reasoned that to eat meat from sacrifices to demons is to join the table of demons.[7]

---

1. Clement of Alexandria, *Stromata* 3.6 (52).
2. Clement of Alexandria, *Stromata* 3.7 (60).
3. Clement of Alexandria, *Paedagogus* 2.1 (ANF 2:239).
4. Minucius Felix, *Octavius* 30 (ANF 4:192).
5. Aristides, *Apology* 15 (ANF 10:276).
6. Pliny the Younger, *Letter 10.96*, 31.
7. Origen, *Against Celsus* 8:30; Origen, *Commentary on Matthew* 10.12.

Strangled animals are forbidden by Scripture because the blood is still in them; and blood, especially the odor arising from it, is reputedly the food of demons, thus causing the eater to dine with them.

A Christian is to refrain from particular foods if they constitute a stumbling block to someone who is weaker in Christian knowledge and discernment. This principle dates from the apostle Paul. "It is good not to eat meat or drink wine or do anything that causes your brother to stumble" (Rom 14:21), and "we are no worse off if we do not eat, and no better off if we do. But take care that this right of yours does not somehow become a stumbling block to the weak" (1 Cor 8:8–9). This sentiment is repeated in Origen, and in a Syrian manual of Christian instruction of his era, saying a Christian should not abstain from particular foods if it will cause uneasiness for other Christians.

Around AD 177, there was a Christian who had "lived an exceedingly austere life, confining his diet to bread and water." While in prison awaiting martyrdom, a pillar of the church persuaded him that he "was not pursuing the right course in refusing to use the creatures of God, and living an example which might be a stumbling-block to others." He thereupon "partook freely of all kinds of food."[8]

Whether we eat meat from stem cells or from traditional means, Christians ought to eat and drink to the glory of God and his community (1 Cor 10:31). According to Origen, "A Christian should eat if another Christian is edified by it; and a Christian should not eat if God's work grows by abstaining."[9]

---

8. Vienne and Lyons Churches, *Letter of the Churches*, ANF 8:784.

9. Origen, *Commentary on Romans* 10.3.5.

Chapter 18

Gambling

THE New Testament contains brief references to gambling but is silent as to its morality. Few other Christian sources in the first three centuries considered the ethics of engaging in games of chance for gain, but they all indicate that Christianity discouraged it.

Pilate's soldiers cast lots to divide Christ's clothing just after he was nailed to the cross (Matt 27:25; Mark 15:24; Luke 23:34; and John 19:23–24), but the Scriptures do not comment on whether such a game of chance was wrong in itself. The background in all four Gospels is the mockery and indignities heaped on Christ; the dice game appears to have been recorded as just one of the many examples of indifference to his agony.

The next reference to deciding an issue by fortune is Acts 1:23–26, where the apostles cast lots to choose between two candidates for the office vacated by Judas Iscariot. The prayer before they were cast indicates that the apostles used this method in order to learn whom God preferred. There is no other reference to this method of church decision-making elsewhere in the New Testament, not even in situations where we might otherwise expect to find it, for example: the election of the seven deacons in Acts 6, the selection of missionaries in Acts 13, the resolution of the circumcision controversy in Acts 15, and the selection of congregational officers elsewhere in Acts. Employed only once in the New Testament, the method was soon replaced by elections and other methods of collective participation by church members. Also note that no money or other material gain was at stake in Acts 1:23–26.

As regards the Bible being silent on the issue of the morality of gambling, we turn to the earliest generations of Christians after the apostles.

Their writings are valuable to us for at least three reasons. First, in any endeavor, knowledge of the thought and events of an era is most accurately obtained from contemporaries of it or—as second best—from material dating from neighboring times and neighboring geographical regions, i.e., with people who were well acquainted with the language, culture, thought processes and actions of the personages whose words and deeds are being studied. More reliable information can be obtained about the events in the New Testament and the thought of its writers by consulting ancient people who spoke the same language and shared the same culture, and were familiar with—or shared—their way of looking at and perceiving the world. Second, the church fathers and other ancient Christian writers show the response to life, and solutions to problems formulated by believers who were closer than we to the ultimate source of Christian ethics, before there was much opportunity for the original Jesus message to be corrupted. Third, much early Christian literature recorded contemporary beliefs and practices during a period in which most present-day Christians agree the Holy Spirit was still actively guiding the church.

The earliest known Christian comment on the ethical dynamic in gambling dates from the final decade of the second century. Clement of Alexandria was the president of the foremost Christian educational institution of this period. In his *Paedagogus* 3.11 he wrote: "The game of dice is to be prohibited, and the pursuit of gain, especially through dice, which many keenly follow. Such things the prodigality of luxury invents for the idle." The context is not clear whether Clement opposed gambling as an evil in itself or only as a waste of time.

After a distinguished career as a lawyer, Tertullian was converted to Christianity and became a clergyman at Carthage in what is now Tunisia in northern Africa. In denouncing many of the popular amusements of his day, his *De Spectaculis* (written between AD 197 and 202) included gambling as forbidden to Christians. In chapters 15 and 16, he argued that certain entertainments are prohibited because they excite rage, internal agitation, excessive craving, and other emotions contrary to Christian calmness, gentleness, and peacefulness. When focusing on the ancient Roman circus (fatal contests among animals and gladiators), Tertullian began chapter 16 with:

> Since then, all passionate excitement is forbidden us, we are debarred from every kind of spectacle, and especially from the circus, where such excitement presides as in its proper element.

See the people coming to it already under strong emotion, already tumultuous, already passion-blind, already agitated about their bets.[1]

Tertullian's main opposition to gambling was rooted in the effects it exerts on the emotions, not because it was an evil in itself. However, he also considered it as intrinsically wrong. For him, betting made the matter even worse.

A stronger indication that most Christians regarded games of chance as ethically wrong is found in *Against Montanus*, a tract written about AD 211 by Apollonius, a clergyman in Western Turkey, near Ephesus. In combating the Montanist heresy, Apollonius appealed to what were apparently well-accepted Christian norms; if they had not been commonly shared by Christians, Apollonius would not have used them in his attempt to enlist his readers' support against Montanism. Among his accusations were that its leaders received improper gifts and played with tables and dice. His tract assumes the prohibition as well established among Christians.

The next references to gaming are in Origen's *Homilies on Joshua*, preached during the persecution of AD 249 to 251. No discussion of early Christianity is complete without reference to him. Origen was the successor of Clement as dean of the seminary in Egypt. Later, Origen established "the first Christian university"[2] in Palestine around AD 230. Origen was the father of systematic theology, one of the most prominent preachers in the first half of the third century, the most influential Christian teacher and Bible scholar in both his own day and for centuries afterwards, and greatly helped make Christianity appealing to educated and philosophical pagans. His *Homilies on Joshua* 23 and 25 constitute a detailed study and full commentary on many passages of Scripture that mention the casting of lots (Lev 16; Josh 9, 13, 17–19, and 21; Prov 18:18; Jonah 1:7; Acts 1: 23–26; Eph 1:11–12, and Col 1:12—the last two only in the Greek). Despite this great work of learning, Origen did not pronounce on the ethical status of the practice. However, an examination of his other writings and sermons reveal that he frequently discussed Scripture passages touching on other moral issues but refrained from addressing the ethical implications of the conduct described.

Cyprian of Carthage left no doubt. He was the pastor of the city where Tertullian had ministered two generations earlier. Cyprian, in writing to

1. Tertullian, *De Spectaculis* (ANF 3:86).
2. McGuckin, *Westminster Handbook to Origen*, 1.

the provincial governor in *Ad Demetrianum* (AD 252), condemned evil and wickedness in general, but singled out pride, greed, cruelty, intemperance, envy, lust, inordinate anger, and "prodigality with gambling."[3] By linking it to these others, Cyprian indicated that both he and the addressee of the letter ranked gambling among the more serious vices.

All the preceding comments on games of chance are very brief, and occupy only a few words or a few lines. By far the longest work against gambling in the first three Christian centuries was *De Aleatoribus* ("*Of Dice-Players*"). The date of this sermon is between AD 180 and 280, and its most probable origin is Rome or Carthage. The name of the preacher of *De Aleatoribus* is unknown, but its wording and themes indicate that he was a prominent clergyman, probably a bishop. He stated outright that gambling is not permitted to Christians, and denounced it as a snare of the devil and a sink-hole of death. He considered it to be in the same class as adultery, greed, fraud, drunkenness, murder, jealousy, cursing, and false witness. The preacher's main concerns were not only that gambling was a waste of time and money that could be otherwise better applied, but also that it was sinful in itself, was addictive, and had close links with superstition. Early Christian writers generally equated superstition with idolatry.

De Aleatoribus warns more than once that hell is the sure destination of gamblers, and that dice-playing is incompatible with full membership in the church (sections 4, 8, 9, and 10). The sermon stresses the wrongfulness of the results and accompaniments of games of chance for gain, but also states that they are evil in and of themselves.

In addition to these pronouncements by individual Christians is Canon 79 of the Council of Elvira in Spain (around AD 306), which decreed that if a Christian engages in dice-games for money, he or she is to be excluded from the Christian community; if he or she repents and mends their ways and stops gambling, he or she may be admitted to Holy Communion after one year. The one-year suspension was among the mildest penalties prescribed by the Council, which indicates that it regarded gambling as a comparatively minor misdeed, although nevertheless a sin.

In summary, the New Testament refrains from pronouncing on the ethics of gambling but other Christian authors of the first three centuries who reflected on its mortality were unanimous that games of chance for gain were inconsistent with a Christian lifestyle. The only difference among them was its seriousness as a moral offense.

---

3. Cyprian, *Ad Demetrianum* 10 (my translation), 357.

Chapter 19

Gluttony

Do You Eat Too Much?

"Whether ye eat, or drink, or whatsoever ye do, do all to the glory of God."
—1 Corinthians 10:31

People in the Western world habitually consume too much food. Eating becomes immoral when it is done to such an excess that a person sacrifices other good things to pursue it, such as a healthy body weight, reputation for moderation, and Christian prudence and charity. Overeating becomes obsessive when we ignore warning signs from nature and other people, making food not only our god but also our overriding concern in human interaction.

The arguments against overuse of alcohol and tobacco also to apply to a person's favorite foods, for they are addictive and take an undue toll on both pocketbook and physical wellbeing. Lack of control and of inclination to moderate one's eating habits sometimes indicates a self-importance to the exclusion of God and one's neighbor.

It is no wonder church fathers before AD 249–251 opposed overeating. The most outspoken were Clement of Alexandria, dean of Christendom's foremost institute of learning in the 190s AD, and Origen, his successor as dean, and the most influential Bible scholar, preacher, and teacher of the first half of the third century his own right. Both Clement and Origen considered overeating to be harmful to body, mind, and soul. To them, excessive eating or gluttony was any consumption simply for the pleasure of it and beyond what is sufficient for life and health. Their general observations are still valid in the twenty-first century.

Physically, overeating was seen as the source of stomach disorders, was harmful to general health, and weighed down the body due to inactivity. Overeating, said Clement to a group of new converts, contradicts the Christian virtues of quietness in word and deed, and controlling one's passions. Clement and Origen also warned that once self-control in eating slackens, and consumption is pursued for pure pleasure, self-control in other aspects of life (such as over passions) also weakens. Both church fathers counselled against becoming slaves to food, especially luxury foods, for God appointed foods to be slaves to humans. Failure to rein in one's appetite, wrote Origen, reduces a person to being wholly caught up about not so much the necessity of eating, but excess in itself. "Dabbling in luxuries," Clement wrote, "glides into mischievous pleasures,"[1] such as those of the flesh. Clement believed that "the diet which exceeds sufficiency injures a man, deteriorates his spirit, and renders his body prone to disease."[2] Such diseases today include heart disease, sleep apnea, and diabetes.

Surrender of oneself to the pleasures of food slows down intellectual capacity, thought Cyprian, bishop of Carthage (Tunisia) toward the end of Origen's ministry. Origen himself believed it limits the brain, while Clement saw it as imposing a limit on a person's reasoning capacity, as "too much food drags the rational part of man down to the condition of stupidity."[3]

But by far the greatest evils of overeating, wrote Clement and Origen, are to the soul. Food was, as Origen pointed out, Satan's first temptation of Christ in the wilderness after his baptism (Matt 4:3; Luke 4:3). Both authors frequently used the Bible phrase "their belly is their god" (Phil 3.19) and urged that the only proper purposes of eating be "health and sustenance" and "sufficiency."[4] Origen preached that a person makes a god of anything s/he serves. If we exert our best efforts toward gratifying our taste buds, ever looking for opportunities to eat and eat more, we are servants of food and make it our god (just as some people serve and deify money), and we cease to be suitable servants of the real God. To weigh down the body with

---

1. Clement of Alexandria, *Paedagogus* 2.1 (ANF 2:237).
2. Clement of Alexandria, *Paedagogus* 2.1 (ANF 2:238).
3. Clement of Alexandria, *Paedagogus* 2.9 (ANF 2:258).
4. Clement of Alexandria, *Paedagogus* 2.1 (ANF 2:238, 242).

excess food, noted Origen, also weighs down and slows the soul it contains. Abundant feasting, wrote Cyprian, often enervates a person to the extent that it decreases his/her capacity to be watchful in prayer.

Ever quotable, Clement produced a neat summary of our subject: "Pleasure has often produced in men harm and pain; and full feeding begets in the soul uneasiness, and forgetfulness, and foolishness."[5]

Also, as regards other people, great scandal and alienation from the Christian faith can be caused by perfectly acceptable food if a Christian eats too much of it in the wrong circumstances. What can the starving children of central Africa think of persons of European extraction who indulge themselves in chocolates, expensive seafood, or pricier cuts of beef, but do not offer them a single crumb? This situation is a sin, according to a compilation of revelations in the early second century by a Christian some scholars believe was a brother of a bishop-pastor of the City of Rome, and which found a place in some early editions of the New Testament:

> Some through the abundance of their food produce weakness in their flesh, and thus corrupt their flesh; while the flesh of others who have no food is corrupted, because they have not sufficient nourishment. And on this account their bodies waste away. This intemperance in eating is thus injurious to you who have abundance and do not distribute among those who are needy.[6]

---

5. Clement of Alexandria, *Paedagogus* 2.1 (ANF 2:242).
6. Herm. Vis. 3.9 (ANF 2:16).

Chapter 20

Gossip!

"Thou shalt not go up and down as a talebearer among thy people."
—Leviticus 19:16 KJV

Do you find gossip interesting? Relaxing? Informative? Do you know that it can be a sin or lead to sin?

According to the dictionary, gossip is casual conversation containing unproven statements about other people, usually about their private lives. Gossip can be either complimentary or derogatory, but usually is negative, and delights in harmful allegations. In older English translations of Scripture, the word "whisper" means "gossip," which in modern speech survives in the expressions "whispering campaign" and "be whispered about," meaning "be the subject of gossip." Perhaps the word "whispering" comes from the circumstance that gossipers often speak in low voices because they do not want passersby to detect that they are violating Christian rules regarding the tongue.

Everyone agrees that—in Christian conversations—untrue, derogatory, and slanderous statements are out of place. However, Scripture and early church teachings also condemn any chitchat about what is none of the speaker's or the hearer's business concerning a third person's life. Perhaps even such innocent gossip borders on sin in that such neutral conversations easily slip into malice and untrue remarks against the subject's character.

Scripture discountenances such gossip. The wisdom literature of the Old Testament and deuterocanonical books states that a gossip separates close friends (Prov 16:28), defiles his/her own soul, and is eventually hated by his/her neighbors (Sir 21:28). Sirach 28:12–18 offer an extended treatment of gossip, e.g., "curse the whisperer and deceiver, for he has destroyed many who were at peace," and "many have fallen by the edge of the sword, but not so many as have fallen because of the tongue."

According to Saint Paul, gossip is on a par with envy, jealousy, selfishness, and conceit (Rom 1:29–31; 2 Cor 12:20; 1 Tim 5:13), probably because the purpose of relating derogatory statements is often to prove that the speaker is a better human being than the person being gossiped about. The same apostle also links gossip with slander, selfishness, pride, covetousness, malice, heartlessness, deceit, idleness, hatred of God, strife, and being a plain busybody.

A book from the first or second century AD sometimes used by early Christians contains two lists just like Saint Paul's, but links gossip not only with slander, envy, jealousy, and strife, but also with such more serious misdeeds as adultery, robbery, fornication, drunkenness, and idolatry.[1]

Dating from the middle or late first century, when some apostles were still alive, the *First Letter of Clement* exhorted readers to practice concord, humility, self-control, and to stay well away from "all whispering and evil-speaking" (*1 Clem.* 30.3). It too contains a list that places gossiping (whispering) and evil-speaking in the same class as covetousness, hatred of God, deceit, pride, and strife (*1 Clem.* 35.5). Clearly the earliest disciples of Jesus, those in the first and early second century, opposed any form of gossip.

Dating from early-third-century Syria, and once considered to have also been written by the same Clement, are two letters concerning nuns and friars. It disapproves of Christians—especially widows dependent on the church—who, instead of working, wander around the neighborhood looking for rumors and "carry them from house to house with much exaggeration."[2] It especially condemns people who

> meet together for vain and trifling conversation and merriment, and that they may speak evil of one another; and they hunt up tales against one another, and are idle: persons with whom we do not allow you even to eat bread.[3]

---

1. *Greek Apocalypse of Baruch* 8.5 and 13.4.
2. *Two Letters to Virgins* 1.11 (ANF 8:58).
3. *Two Letters to Virgins* 1.10 (ANF 8:58).

The last clause touches on another aspect of the earliest teachings: it forbids even listening to gossip and approving of gossipers. Sirach 19:6 considers those people who hate gossip to be blessed. Proverbs 20:19 counsels readers not to associate with gossips. Saint Paul ended one list of evil deeds with a statement that not only people who engage in gossip are sinners, but also people who approve of them (Rom 1:32), as does *1 Clement* 35:6.

In the first half of the third century, the church scholar Origen from Egypt preached that if a conversation turns to matters that are shameful, empty, improper, or evil, a Christian should close his/her ears and act as if deaf and dumb. Christians, he said, should listen only when the speaker promotes morals, encourages virtues, restrains vices, and otherwise builds the hearers' spiritual life. The only exception Origen would allow is listening long enough to be able to respond to statements that might mislead more simple Christians.[4]

About the time and locality as Origen, a manual for Christian life instructed widows not to be talkative, but to turn away whenever the talk became unseemly, and to act as if they had not heard it. Widows who are gossips, it said, "stir up quarrels."[5] Both this book and Origen's *Homilies on Joshua* 1.7 fault them and other women for gossiping in church instead of paying attention to the liturgy.

Scripture and early tradition lay a further restraint on Christians who hear negative remarks about someone in a private conversation: we must not believe, approve, or accept such derogatory comments as true. This may be only common sense, for if the remarks could be proved true, they would have come to us through the media and not as private gossip. Nevertheless, the Bible and early church reinforce this prohibition.

In some translations, Exodus 23:1–2 prohibits accepting as true any negative report against a person's character that comes through unsubstantiated rumors. The *Epistle of the Apostles* 49, in the middle of the second century, used Exodus 23:1–2 as a reinforcement for its instruction that Christians are to give no credence to statements that blacken the character of another Christian brother or sister, and are not to delight in listening to them. Origen commented that what this Scripture forbids is not *hearing* uncomplimentary statements—for this often cannot be avoided when we

---

4. Origen, *Homilies on Exodus* 3.2.
5. Connolly, *Didascalia apostolorum* 15.

live in a community—but internally *accepting* or *believing* such statements. When we hear negative gossip we are to be deaf to it.[6]

A student of the apostle John wrote that Exodus 23:1–2 applies especially to clergy. Ministers, said Bishop Polycarp of Smyrna in the early second century, are to be merciful and compassionate and neither severe in judgment nor quick to credit an uncomplimentary rumor against anyone.[7] It was probably clergy that Origen had in mind as Christians that are permitted to listen to gossip long enough to formulate a reply that would forestall more simple Christians from being misled.[8]

Lastly are the words of Christ himself in Matthew 12:36–37:

> I tell you, on the day of judgment men will render account for every careless word they utter; for by your words you will be justified, and by your words you will be condemned.

Except where otherwise indicated, all Scripture quotations in this article are from the Revised Standard Version of the Bible © copyright 1946, 1952, and 1971 by the Division of Christian Education of the National Council of Churches of Christ in the USA. Used by permission.

---

6. Origen, *Homilies on Exodus* 3.2.
7. Polycarp, *Letter to the Philippians* 6.1.
8. Origen, *Homilies on Exodus* 3.2.

Chapter 21

Greed

Introduction

ALTHOUGH we are surrounded by it and it encroaches more and more each day into our society and economy, we hear precious few pronouncements against the evil of avarice. It is so much touted as good for the individual and the world economy that Christians tend to mute their opposition to it. This article breaks the silence and—rather than concur with those who extol avarice as good for everyone in the world—the following chapter shows that the Bible and its first readers and the earliest disciples of Jesus considered it a sin, not a virtue. Dating from a time before the division into modern-day denominations, their statements are applicable to members of all Christian denominations.

Avarice, or greed, is the intense and inordinate desire for money and temporal goods. Although usually a venial sin, it becomes a mortal one when a person in his or her greed neglects the virtue of charity. The earliest Christians, who were much closer than we are to the writing of the New Testament and to the teachings of Jesus and his apostles which were not written down until generations later, were at one in condemning it as sinful rather than a trait beneficial for individuals and society as a whole.

The Essence of Greed

The essence of avarice is usually considered to be or is summarized as the love of money. According to the apostle Paul, "the love of money is the root of all evils" (1 Tim 6:10). Polycarp of Smyrna, a bishop and martyr of the first half of the second century who had known the apostle John and other early disciples, repeated this statement in a letter to a Christian congregation. The Christian *Sibylline Oracles*, a work bearing the name of a pagan prophetess into which early believers inserted Christian ideals and values, also said that such love is the source of all evil.

Even the desire to accumulate a lot of money is sinful. According to Saint Paul, "those who desire to be rich fall into temptation, into a snare, into many senseless and hurtful desires that plunge men into ruin and destruction" (1 Tim 6:9). The *Sibylline Oracles* called it a double-edged sword that destroys the spirit.

The New Testament

The earliest Christian documents, the books of the New Testament, contain instruction about avarice. First Corinthians 5:9–11 condemns associating with greedy people, especially greedy Christians. It includes the greedy in the same category as idol worshippers, the sexually immoral, and robbers. Second Corinthians 6:10 states flatly that the greedy will not inherit the kingdom of heaven. Hebrews 13:5 exhorts, "Keep your life free from love of money and be content with what you have." Second Peter condemns those who from the motive of avarice exploit Christians with false words (2:3) and have "hearts trained in greed" (2:14).

Origen on Greed

The early church writer who said the most against greed was Origen, a preacher, teacher, lecturer, and author who was active in Egypt and Palestine in the first half of the third century. The father of systematic theology, he was the first to produce a connected, organized and methodological presentation of Christianity so that intelligent and cultured pagans would accept it as a rational religion. Writing more than any single Christian before the sixteenth century, he influenced Christian thinkers for centuries to come.

Origen's *Commentary on Romans* and homilies on various books of the Bible include over forty-seven disapproving references to avarice. He called greed "most offensive"[1] and considered it as bad as false testimony and violence. He said that it is a vice that should be restrained and fled from. He preached that Christians should master and exterminate this vice from their land. He warned his hearers not to be harassed by thoughts of it. He even said that avarice violates the Christian virtue of generosity because the greedy shut their hearts from brothers and sisters in need. He opined that avarice is the source of many disputes and quarrels, and that it impairs the mental faculties, and even went so far as to say that greed is worse than idolatry, and that Jesus does not love those who even think of avarice.

Other Writers against Greed

Some other early Christian writers also disapproved of avarice. Among them, Clement of Alexandria, Origen's predecessor as dean of the world's foremost Christian educational institution, opined that it was a symptom of uncontrolled appetite, while a second-century collection of sayings for the Christian life considered that it demonstrated an excessive love of body. Writing in Tunisia during the earlier part of Origen's career, the church father Tertullian condemned the person who esteems money more than charity to the poor. Nearly a dozen other writings from the first two centuries of Christianity regarded greed as inconsistent with a Christian lifestyle.

A Pitiable Vice

Avarice was seen as an evil not only for its effects on other people but also because it harmed the greedy themselves. In his *Commentary on Matthew*, Origen called avarice a "sickness of the soul" for which people should come to Jesus for healing. He deplored as unhealthy the state of "lovers of money wholly intent on money and on preserving and gathering it" whose avarice impaired them like sleep "drowsy in their reflections" and existing in "an atmosphere of vain and dream-like fancies concerning realities, not admitting the things which are actually true, but deceived by what appears in their vain imaginations."[2]

Origen's student Saint Gregory the Wonder Worker called for pity on the person "who is left entirely alone, having neither brother nor son, but

---

1. Origen, *Homilies on Exodus* 6.3, 288.
2. Origen, Com*mentary on Matthew* 10.24 (ANF 9:430).

prospered with large possessions, lives on in the spirit of insatiable avarice, and refuses to give himself in any way whatever to goodness." Gregory further wrote that such a person is "full of terror to himself."[3]

The teacher of them both, Saint Paul the apostle, wrote in 1 Timothy 6:10 that because of the love of money "some have wandered away from the faith and pierced their hearts with many pangs."

Greed among Clergy and Members of the Order of Widows

Clergy especially are to be on guard that they not be greedy or lovers of money. According to 1 Timothy 3:3, a bishop is to be "no lover of money." The Letter to Titus 1:7 prohibits a bishop from being greedy for gain. Origen echoed this command in his *Commentary on Romans*. Perhaps because they handled all monies in the very early church, deacons were also singled out not to be lovers of money.[4]

Greedy widows posed a problem in the ancient church. A church manual of the early third century found it necessary to tell them to refrain from being actively concerned with obtaining money for themselves. According to Origen, the blessing from dedicating their sex lives to God was cancelled out by their greed. Polycarp too condemned those who loved money.

Near Occasions of Avarice

The early writers exhorted Christians to avoid even near-enticements to avarice. Origen, in his *Commentary on Romans,* counsels us not to attend theaters or other amusements that would inflame our souls to greed. Along with the apostle Paul (1 Cor 5:9–11), he tells us not to be friends or partners with the greedy or even eat with them. This is particularly the case if the greedy person is a Christian (1 Cor 5:11). Second Timothy 3:2–5 also instructs Christians to avoid "lovers of money."

---

3. Gregory Thaumaturgus, *Metaphrase of the Book of Ecclesiastes* 4 (ANF 6:12).

4. 1 Tim 3:8; Polycarp, *Letter to the Philippians* 5:2; Origen, *Commentary on Romans* 8.10.4.

Conclusion

Thus we have ample witness from the early, undivided, and apostolic church that greed is a very bad or even pitiable vice, especially when it has a negative impact on the greedy persons themselves or on those whom their avarice prevents them from helping. Today, on the one hand, we have the free-market economists and advocates of the view that the single-minded pursuit of money and profits by every individual and corporation (or at least by those that are already wealthy) will result in a more prosperous society and world, with more goods and services for everyone. On the other, we have the apostles, the Bible, the church fathers, and other saints who unanimously condemned such ideas and courses of action as sin. Which do you choose?

Chapter 22

Hate Commandment

LUKE 14:26 reports Jesus Christ as saying: "If any man come to me, and hate not his father, and mother, and wife, and children, and brethren, and sisters, yea, and his own life also, he cannot be my disciple."

How can I hate my mother and father, who gave me life, raised me, and made sacrifices for me? How can I hate my wife after I married her because I love her? How can I hate my children when I have a duty to love and care for them?

A solution to this seeming endorsement of hatred, which is contrary to many other verses of Scripture, is found in the *Second Sermon on the Song of Songs* preached by the Christian scholar Origen in the early 240s AD. Origen was the most outstanding Bible scholar, teacher, and preacher of the first half of the third century, and influenced the church for centuries afterwards.

Origen preached that God really does want Christians to love their fathers, mothers, wives, children, and other relatives, but wants us to love Jesus even more. Origen preached that it is a matter of setting our priorities in order. A Christian's first priority must always be Christ. We are indeed obliged to love our close relatives, but we must not be consumed by love for them, but put our affections in correct order. We must not love father, mother, etc. first, and Christ afterwards. Christians must not be consumed by love of their children at the expense of love of Jesus.

Origen quoted Matthew 10:7, the parallel passage to Luke 14:26, to show that, rather than advocating general hatred and ingratitude, Christ wanted merely an ordering of priorities: "He that loveth father or mother more than me is not worthy of me: and he that loveth son or daughter more than me is not worthy of me." Here it is "love less," not "hate."

Origen then exhorted his listeners to examine their consciences and compare their relationships and priorities in order to determine whether they had more love for their earthly relatives than for the Lord himself.

In cases of conflict, and only in cases of conflict, Jesus and Origen taught that we must hate our families if the only alternative is not loving Christ.

Chapter 23

The Homeless

CHRISTIANS have a serious obligation to respect and help the homeless and other poor. This is not just one possible interpretation of the Bible among many, but was an essential teaching of Christianity in its first two and a half centuries before it was divided into present-day denominations, a time when most Christians today believe the Holy Spirit was still guiding the church.

Christians are not to forget or disregard the homeless. Alluding to Isaiah 58:7, Bishop Irenaeus of Lyons in France in the 180s AD mandated "Deal thy bread to the hungry willingly, and lead into thy house the roofless stranger."[1] Theophilus, bishop of Antioch in Syria in the third quarter of the second century, concurred in almost identical words.

In its formative years, Christianity instilled affirmative duties to help the economically marginalized instead of waiting for them to ask. Clement of Alexandria, who flourished in Egypt as the dean of Christianity's foremost educational institution in the 190s AD, and his successor Origen commanded Christians to actively seek out those who ought to be benefited by their gifts and compassion. The elder church father also taught that when wondering whether or not to give to a beggar, if we have doubts about whether they are deserving we should give anyway, on the chance that they might be in real need. Tertullian, a church father who flourished around AD 200 in what is now Tunisia, regarded it as a law of God to give even to the poor man who does not ask.

Early Christian literature is full of statements about how *not* to treat the poor. The New Testament itself rhetorically asks "if anyone has this

---

1. Irenaeus, *Against Heresies* 4.17.2 (ANF 1:483); Theophilus, *To Autolycus* 3.12.

world's goods and sees his brothers in need, but closes his heart against them, how does God's love abide in him?" (1 John 3:17) At least four other early Christian writings or writers condemn turning away a person in want: (1) a first- or second-century Syrian or Palestinian church manual, (2) the related *Letter of Barnabas* of about the same era, (3) Tertullian, and (4) Origen sometime between AD 238 and 244.

Nobody ought to oppress the poor, at least according to *The Shepherd of Hermas*, a Christian book compiled in Rome in the early- or mid-second century. This sentiment found agreement in Irenaeus and an early third-century manual for clergy and laity.

Origen also said that we should not despise or abase the poor, or shame their faces. It was (and is) forbidden to view economic marginality as God's punishment, say, for laziness. According to Clement, "those who have paid the penalty of protracted penury should not suffer a life-long punishment."[2]

---

2. Clement of Alexandria, *Stromata* 2.18 (ANF 2:366).

Chapter 24

Homosexuality

Not Singled Out

COMPARED to twenty-first-century believers, early Christians were surprisingly unconcerned about homosexuality. While some Christian writers in the first two and a half centuries appear to condemn all forms of homoerotic behavior, most commented on only specific aspects of it, such as intercourse with minors. No author of this period singled it out as an especially repulsive sin, but mentioned it only incidentally when discussing other matters.

Disapproval of homosexual activity—or certain aspects of it—appeared early in the church. Examples in the New Testament are 1 Corinthians 6:9 and 1 Timothy 1:10. Contrary to some misinterpretations, Romans 1:27 does not say it is a sin, but a punishment for prior misdeeds.

Some church fathers in the second century continued this seemingly negative bent: Aristides of Athens[1] in AD 125, the well-traveled Justin Martyr in Rome in mid-century,[2] Athenagoras (also of Athens),[3] Bishop Melito of Sardis in Turkey[4] in the 170s, Bishop Irenaeus in France[5] in the 180s, and Clement of Alexandria (dean of the world's foremost Christian educational

---

1. *Apology* 8, 9, 13, and 17.
2. 1 *Apology* 27; 2 *Apology* 12.
3. *Legatio* 34 (ANF 2:129–48, at page 147.).
4. *On Pascha* 53.
5. *Against Heresies* 4.27.4 and 5.11.1.

institution)[6] in the 190s. Another second-century bishop who made passing references against it was Polycarp,[7] a disciple of the apostle John and, later, teacher of Irenaeus. Polycarp was probably "the angel of the church in Smyrna" addressed in Revelation 2:8. Another book of revelations, those of the apostle Peter, was of like mind in the first half of the century.[8] The recently discovered *Gospel of Judas* (also second-century) condemns it,[9] inferring that it was a corruption newly introduced into Christianity by mainstream believers, i.e., not gnostics.

Transitioning into the early third century was Tertullian,[10] a converted ex-lawyer who became a clergyman in Tunisia, and the founder of Latin Christian literature. Always a rigorist, he was more prepared to condemn debatable practices as sin than were other writers before the middle of the century.

The present study concludes at AD 249–251, a time of severe persecution, mass apostasy, and upheaval in the church. It approximately coincides with the death of Origen, who had succeeded Clement as dean, and later became the leading Bible scholar, teacher, and preacher of his own day and for centuries afterward.

These were all voluminous authors who touched on homoeroticism only a few times amid a mass of material on other activities.

The most commonly mentioned aspect of same-sex gratification was intercourse with young boys. Pedophilia was considered sinful by some church fathers who wrote nothing against relations between adult males. Among them were a bishop of Antioch (Syria) in the mid-second century,[11] and a friend and financial backer of Origen.[12] Four comprehensive collections of Christian ethics and life were produced before AD 230, none of which forbids adult homosexuality.[13] One prohibits oral sex, but only by a woman on a man.[14]

---

6. Clement of Alexandria, *Paedagogus* 2.1, 2.10.
7. Polycarp, *Letter to the Philippians* 5.3.
8. *Revelation of Peter*, 32.
9. *Gospel of Judas*, 38, 40.
10. *Apology* 46; *Against Marcion* 1.29.4; *De Corona* 6; *On Modesty* 16.
11. Theophilus, *To Autolycus* 2.1.
12. Ambrose the Deacon, *Hypomnemata*.
13. *Letter of Barnabas, Didache, Didascalia apostolorum, Sentences of Sextus*.
14. *Letter of Barnabas* 10.8.

Depending how broadly or narrowly their wording is interpreted, some ancient believers may have censured only particular types of homosexual acts while allowing others. Polycarp, the *Revelation of Peter*, Irenaeus, and Origen prohibited "men abusing themselves with men" and "men defiling each other."[15] The question arises whether homosexual acts in themselves are abusive and defiling or whether God forbids only those homoerotic positions that abuse or defile due to other factors. After all, heterosexual relations may or may not be abusive or defiling, even between spouses. By being specific, did these early Christians suggest that some kinds of same-sex relations could be loving and enriching, and therefore permitted to Christians?

Some of the abovementioned authors quoted Leviticus 18:22 to the effect that males are forbidden "to lie with a man as with a woman." Although some homoerotic acts are imitations of heterosexual ones, others are anatomically possible only between males. A conservative interpretation of Leviticus and these church fathers would forbid only the simulations of regular sex but permit uniquely male-male positions. Those magazines at the drugstore indicate that gays use a wide variety of techniques, and do not lack imagination.

In addition to how restrictive an interpretation is to be given to "men lying with men as with a woman," there is the issue of whether this prohibition is binding in our day. It would not apply if its sinful nature was rooted in social/cultural factors rather than eternal anatomical differences. In the world of the Bible and the early church, women occupied a position subordinate to males, with a status little different from slaves or animals. Thus, treating a man sexually as if he were a woman may have been forbidden only because it subjected him to an inferior status, thus abusing and defiling him psychologically and socially in that culture. If so, the ban was not aimed at same-gender sensual gratification as an evil in itself, and thus might not apply in an age of equality between the sexes.

Anal penetration with a penis (sodomy properly so described) was condemned in the middle of the second century by Justin Martyr[16] and the *Acts of John* 36. They did not mention other homoerotic positions, and forbade such penetration in heterosexual relations also. It is strange that so

---

15. Polycarp, *Letter to the Philippians* 5.3 (ANF 1:33); *Revelation of Peter* 32, 510; Irenaeus, *Against Heresies* 4.27.4 (ANF 1:500); Origen, *Commentary on Matthew* 14.10 (ANF 10:500).

16. *2 Apology* 12.5.

few early Christian writers condemned it, for it is harmful in itself because too frequent indulgence weakens the rectal muscles and creates problems in defecation. The rarity with which it was discountenanced may indicate that some New Testament and other early Christian authors meant only sodomy when condemning all homosexual activity.

The foregoing study raises a number of questions. Are all homosexual relationships abusive and defiling in themselves or are they permissible when these elements are absent? Are all varieties of homoerotic acts a sin or only those positions in which a participant is demeaned or degraded by the standards of his own culture, or are imitations of heterosexual positions? At what age does a boy become a man, thus rendering intercourse no longer pederasty?

The foregoing presentation partly distorts the focus and preoccupations of early Christians in two respects. First, homoeroticism was touched upon by less than seven percent of the 500-plus extant Christian writings of the period. Ninety-three percent did not mention homosexuality. Still less did any single it out for special condemnation, but regarded it as one sin among many. As in Origen's opposition to "the lovers of money, and the lovers of ambition, and the lovers of boys,"[17] the ancient Christian writers always mentioned it in company with other offenses, never alone. All the citations against homosexuality in this chapter appeared only in lists or general discussions; one passing mention amid a host of other material. No author in the first three centuries devoted a chapter, let alone a book, to the phenomenon. Most references consist of only a few words. Unlike some in the twenty-first century, early Christians did not treat it as the greatest sin or as especially important.

Secondly, early Christian writers condemned gluttony, greed, and untruthfulness at significantly greater length and with much more frequency than homosexuality. Individual authors and the consensus of Christians before AD 251 regarded these offenses as more deserving of condemnation than what a minority does in their bedrooms. This may help account for the absence of adult homoeroticism in ancient Christian moral codes. Selfishness, gossip, and lying appear to have been much more common and to have warranted more frequent condemnation in Christian antiquity than homosexuality.

---

17. Origen, *Commentary on Matthew* 10.24 (ANF 10:430).

Chapter 25

Honor Your Parents

WHAT does the commandment to "Honor thy father and thy mother" include? It recurs frequently in early Christian teaching. Jesus repeated it in Matthew 15:4 and 19:19, Mark 10:19, and Luke 18:20, while Paul the apostle cited it in Ephesians 6:2.

It was restated by two Christian philosophers in Greece—Aristides in AD 125 and Athenagoras around AD 177—and also by Bishop Theophilus of Antioch and by Bishop Irenaeus in France, both about the same time as Athenagoras. The present chapter extracts the extent and parameters of such honor from its wider context of biblical and early postbiblical Christian literature to see how to apply it today.

Ancient Christians enjoyed an advantage over us because they lived when unwritten teachings and Bible interpretations of Jesus and his apostles were still fresh in church memory, and before there had been time for Christian observances and understanding to be significantly altered. Irenaeus is a good case in point. His early Christian training came from men who had personally associated with the apostle John.

Origen was another important witness to early Christian understanding. Raised in a Christian home, he became the most outstanding Bible scholar, preacher, and teacher of the first half of the third century. He traveled extensively throughout the Near East, and was therefore better able to observe and record church practice in different countries. His *On First Principles* and his commentaries on Matthew, Romans, and Ephesians stated the commandment to honor one's parents ought to be observed in his day. Shortly before AD 250, which coincides with the end of Origen's ministry, an anonymous compilation of Christian precepts repeats the fifth commandment as still operative (*Three Books of Testimonies*).

The Command to Hate and Love

Jesus taught that his followers are to hate their parents (Luke 14:26) and prophesied that the gospel will create conflict between family members (Matt 10:34–37). These two passages were quoted by later Christian writers, but seldom by ones that counseled honoring one's parents. Nor did most of those that restated the fifth commandment refer to Matthew 10:36–37 or Luke 14:26.

In the late second and early third century, Tertullian regarded both the hate and the honor commands as binding. Tertullian had been a prominent lawyer in a system of secular law that prized the cohesion of the family and the authority of fathers over it, much more than the Mosaic law or our own. After being converted, he was ordained and became a Christian author. Somewhat strangely, he stated that we are also to "love" our parents—one of only two references to loving them in Christian writings before the mass apostasy of AD 249–251.

Attempts to Reconcile the Precepts

We must both hate and honor our father and mother

Origen's predecessor was Clement, the principal Christian writer of the 190s AD. He pointed out that a literal interpretation of Luke 14:26 would conflict with Christ's directives to love one's enemies. Clement explained that a Christian is to oppose and resist, even hate, anyone who tempts them to do anything detrimental to their soul's salvation, or who constitutes "a hindrance to faith and an impediment to the higher life,"[1] inside or outside the family. The key factor is whether they lead us to or away from Christ.

What honor entails: general

We can determine what sorts of behavior fulfill the duty of honoring if we examine specific actions and attitudes the New Testament and near-biblical

---

1. Clement of Alexandria, *Quis Dives Salvetur* 22 (ANF 2:597).

writers advocated in relation to parents. Then, to tease out the full scope and meaning of the fifth commandment, the present essay will consider categories of other people we are to honor, and apply the implications to relations with one's parents.

Both New Testament and early postbiblical Christian literature contain specific precepts as to how Christians are to treat their parents, which presumably indicate what is entailed in honoring them. Starting with the most obvious, we are not to murder them; this is attested by 1 Timothy 1:19, the Christian philosopher Aristides of Athens AD 125, Bishop Melito of Sardis in the third quarter of the second century, Tertullian, the anonymous *Oratio ad Graecos* in the first half of the third century, and the mid-second century *Acts of John*.

Melito also preached against assaulting one's father.

Jesus forbade cursing one's parents and speaking evil of them (Matt 15:4, Mark 7:10). Matthew 15:5 and Mark 7:11–12 and Origen condemned trust fund arrangements whereby an adult child could evade the obligation to support their parents in old age.[2]

Ridiculing one's father and dishonoring one's mother are condemned by the Christian *Sibylline Oracles*, a collection of prophecies into which Christian material was inserted. The Sibyl also denounced abandoning parents in old age, disrespectfully talking back to them, and hostility to them because of money matters.

What honor entails: obedience

Obedience to parents was inculcated by Ephesians 6:1, Colossians 3:20, Tertullian, and Origen's *Commentary on Ephesians* 6:1–3 and *Homilies on Luke*. Disobedience by either Christians or non-Christians was condemned in Romans 1:30, 2 Timothy 3:2; the *Sibylline Oracles*, and Origen's *Homilies on Judges*. However, they contained limits and restrictions on such obedience. For instance, Origen pointed out that Ephesians 6:1 reads "obey your parents in the Lord" rather than "obey your parents in the flesh," and indicated that children are to obey only when father and mother command something that accords with God's will; they are not to obey their "parents in the flesh" who command something contrary to it.

---

2. However, a child need not save up money specifically for a parent's support: 2 Cor 12:14.

However, some people outside the family have an equal or greater claim on a Christian's obedience than parents. Speaking of bishops (pastors) and presbyters (church elders), Bishop Ignatius of Antioch around AD 107 exhorted: "obey the bishop and the presbytery with an undivided mind," and commended a particular deacon "inasmuch as he is subject to the bishop as to the grace of God, and to the presbytery as to the law of Jesus Christ."[3]

In the mid-second century, the oldest surviving Christian sermon outside the New Testament predicted a hellish afterlife for people that "knew not and believed not and obeyed not the elders who show us plainly of our salvation."[4]

In the 180s AD, Irenaeus stated that "it is incumbent to obey the presbyters who are in the Church."[5] Origen preached that believers must exhibit courtesy to clergy. Just as Jesus Christ submitted to Joseph and the Virgin Mary, so Christians are to submit, not only to fathers, but also to their bishop and presbyters/church elders.

Complicating the matter further is the attribution to Jesus in the mid-second century that all Christians are to obey each other (*Epistle of the Apostles*). The apostle Peter would have us obey every human ordinance, not only Christian ones (1 Pet 2:13).

Honor others

Christians are to honor people other than their father and mother. There are many positions and offices in society and church that the ancient sources said should be honored. By observing who these categories were, we can ascertain how and to what extent parents are to be honored in our time and our lives.

First of all, Christians are to honor church officers (Heb 13:7; 1 Thess 5:12–13.) A first-century manual of church and personal Christian practice mandated: "him that speaketh to thee the word of God remember night and day; and thou shalt honor him as the Lord."[6]

A few decades later, Ignatius of Antioch wrote:

---

3. Ignatius of Antioch, *Letter to the Magnesians* 2 (ANF 1:59).
4. *2 Clement* 17.5 (ANF 10:255–56).
5. Irenaeus, *Against Heresies* 4.26.2 (ANF 1:497).
6. *Didache* 4.1 (ANF 7:378).

> It is well to reverence both God and the bishop. He who honors the bishop has been honored by God; he who does anything without the knowledge of the bishop, does [in reality] serve the devil.[7]

First Timothy 5:17 says "Let the elders that rule well be counted worthy of double honor, especially they who labor in the word and doctrine." Double honor to church elders/presbyters, and apparently only single honor to parents. What actions manifest "double honor?" Tertullian, around AD 210, deplored that for the majority of Christians it meant giving a presbyter twice as much food at a church supper than to a layperson. This is corroborated by a Syrian church manual compiled at roughly the time when Tertullian made his comments. According to this church manual, deacons were to be given twice the helping of "widows" (forerunners of nuns), and presbyters four times as much, because "they ought to be honored as the apostles."[8] Parents were accorded no such privileged status at church suppers.

The phrase "double honor" calls for further examination among the persons Christians were obliged to honor. Should parents be honored more than other people? The ancient Christian evidence is mixed. Tertullian stated that Christian morality demands that we "honor and love next to God Himself"[9] mother, fathers, and nearest kinfolk. The *Sibylline Oracles* agrees: "First, honor God, then your parents."[10] On the other hand, the *Sentences of Sextus* has "After God, honor the sage."[11] A collection of practical maxims and instructions for the Christian life, *Sextus* proved very popular among Christians after the mid-second century. Comparing it to Tertullian and the Sibyl reveals that there was no agreement as to the degree and priority of honor due to parents, only that they be honored in some fashion.

However, if presbyters and other clergy stand for God in relation to an individual Christian, there is no conflict. This would render the Sibyl as directing: "First, honor your clergy, then your parents," and Tertullian as "honor and love parents next to clergy."

Christianity before the mass apostasy and epidemic of AD 249–251 required that honor be shown toward all elders, not just holders of the office of church elder. In the middle or late first century, when some apostles

---

7. Ignatius of Antioch, *Letter to the Smyrnaeans* 9.1 (ANF 1:90).
8. *Didascalia* 9, 90.
9. Collins, *Sybilline Oracles* 2.60, 346.
10. *Sentences of Sextus,* Sentence 244, 45.
11. *Sentences of Sextus,* Sentence 244, 45.

were still alive, the church at Rome exhorted at Corinth: "Let us reverence the Lord Jesus Christ, whose blood was given for us; let us esteem those who have the rule over us; let us honor the aged among us."[12] Describing the Christian community about a century later, Athenagoras noted that "to the more advanced in life we give the honor due to fathers and mothers."[13]

There are yet other categories of people Christians are to honor. First Timothy 5:3 instructs that well-behaved widows be honored, as does *Three Books of Testimonies*. Origen called on Christian brothers to honor everyone that performs good works in the churches, including women. *Sextus* opined that anybody that does not honor seekers of knowledge and wisdom shows ingratitude to God.

Husbands have a duty to "honor" their wives (1 Pet 3:7). According to 1 Peter 2:13–14 and 17, and Origen, Christians are to honor and submit to kings and other secular rulers. For example, we address secular judges as "Your Honor."

Indeed, all Christians have a duty to honor each other (Rom 12:10). Quoting Psalm 15:4, Origen preached that honor will be shown to all who fear God.

First Peter 2:17 commands "Honor all people" in a context that indicates that it is to be shown to non-Christians as well. The Christian Tatian in the mid-second century pleaded that "Man is to be honored as a fellow-man."[14] Paul would have a Christian honor his or her own body of flesh (1 Thess 4:4).

Conclusion

There thus appears to be great diversity as to who is to be honored and to what extent. We must keep this scope and variety in mind when selecting the most appropriate dictionary meanings of "honor" for the fifth commandment. These are "respect," "esteem," and "be courteous toward." A person can exhibit these to one person without diminishing those to another, and more honor can be displayed to one person than another. Twice as much respect, esteem, and courtesy ("double honor") can be demonstrated toward one person or category of persons, and a lesser degree toward others.

---

12. *1 Clement* 21.6 (ANF 1:11).
13. Athenagoras, Legatio 32 (ANF 2:146).
14. Tatian, *Address to the Greeks* 4 (ANF 2:66).

The thrust and meaning of the many exhortations to honor your father and mothers indicate, and require no more than, being civil to your parents and refraining from needlessly harming them. No more honor, respect, esteem, or courtesy need be shown to them than other people.

Chapter 26

Hospitality

HOSPITALITY is an ageless virtue in the church, although lately we do not hear sermons or read much about it in church magazines. The earliest Christians, on the other hand, said much about it long before separation into present-day denominations. Their counsel as to being hospitable therefore applies to all Christians alike.

According to my dictionary, hospitality is the friendly and generous reception and accommodation of guests and visitors. Saint Paul in Romans 12:13 encouraged his readers to be "given to hospitality" as well as to contribute to the needs of other Christians. First Peter 4:9 exhorts us to practice it ungrudgingly, as well as to be engaged in other forms of charity. One New Testament author and some other ancient Christian writers highly commended hospitality to strangers, of which more can be seen below.

In the middle of the second century AD, a brother of a pastor-bishop of Rome put forth commandments for the Christian life in a book called *The Pastor of Hermas*. It says that in hospitality is a fruitful field for goodness. Half a century later, Clement of Alexandria in Egypt was dean of the world's foremost Christian educational institution. He encouraged Christians to be "given to hospitality,"[1] like St. Paul, in a long list of what he considered desirable conduct for Christians, such as helping the poor and weak. In another book Clement wrote "akin to love is hospitality."[2]

Clement's successor as dean was Origen, the most outstanding Christian professor, writer, and preacher of the first three centuries. So great was his knowledge of the Christian faith that he was called upon as a theological

---

1. Clement of Alexandria, *Paedagogus* 3.12 (ANF 2:294).
2. Clement of Alexandria, *Stromata* 2.9 (ANF 2:357).

consultant by pastor-bishops throughout the eastern Mediterranean. In his *Commentary on Romans*, he regarded receiving guests as a Christian virtue, along with rescuing the innocent and helping the poor, especially the hungry and naked. He said that great grace is to be found in hospitality, both with God and with people. In one sermon he valued hospitality in the same list as justice, mercy, patience, gentleness, and helping the poor.

Strangers were singled out as special objects of hospitality. The Letter to the Hebrews 13:2 says, "Be not forgetful to entertain strangers: for thereby some have entertained angels unawares." Biblical examples are found in Genesis 18 and 19. Clement called hospitality "a congenial art devoted to the treatment of strangers," and also "Hospitality, therefore, is occupied with what is useful for strangers."[3]

In some localities, hospitality to fellow Christian strangers was a standing institution. A first- or second-century church manual from Syria or Egypt called *The Didache* prescribed detailed regulations for the reception and accommodation of traveling Christians, especially clergy. About the same time as Origen, the church father Tertullian in Tunisia placed hospitality to Christian travelers in the same class of Christian activity as relief of the poor and attending church. A little later, papyrus letters of recommendation for travelers indicate there was a network of hospitality among early churches.

Although especially for strangers, hospitality was not confined to travelers by the earliest Christians. Clement widened the scope of the term "strangers" as a category, writing: "guests are strangers; and friends are guests; and brethren [i.e., Christians] are friends."[4] In an even more universal statement, he wrote "And those are strangers, to whom the things of the world are strange."[5]

The Bible considers being hospitable as a desirable quality especially by bishops, which in the early writings were the equivalent of today's parish pastors. First Timothy 3:2 includes it in the same passage with such qualifications as being above reproach, an apt communicator, and not a lover of money. Titus 1:7 has hospitality in a list with such traits as being self-controlled, upright, and a lover of goodness. In a paraphrase of 1 Timothy, Origen, in his *Commentary on Romans,* considered a hospitable nature as

---

3. Clement of Alexandria, *Stromata* 2.9 (ANF 2:357).
4. Clement of Alexandria, *Stromata* 2.9 (ANF 2:357).
5. Clement of Alexandria, *Stromata* 2.9 (ANF 2:357).

necessary for a pastor-bishop as also being above reproach, vigilant, and respectable.

The early authors' frequent listing of hospitality along with relief of the poor was probably not accidental. Christian hospitality, as well as Christian life in general, has always been concerned for guests and strangers no matter what their financial circumstances. The ancient authors promoted the virtues of generosity and helping all people, including strangers, regarding them as brothers and sisters in Christ and as being entitled to the same reception and accommodation as Jesus. In his *Homilies on Luke,* Origen exhorted his hearers to invite into their homes Christian friends, even the poor ones, and also people who have trouble expressing themselves, the developmentally disabled, and other persons who are intellectually impaired. Jesus himself commanded: "when thou makest a feast, call the poor, the maimed, the lame, the blind" (Luke 14:13).

The New Testament and other early Christian writings and sermons were directed to all readers and to all people present in congregations. Their admonitions are put to all of us to provide generously for people we barely know or do not know, simply for the name of Christ and without regard to their means, status, or circumstances. Jesus himself provides a special blessing for the hospitable. In Matthew 10:11–12 and Luke 10:5 he instructed Christian travelers to salute and wish peace on the homes of hosts who showed them hospitality. These hosts might well have been hospitable to angels unawares. So might you.

Chapter 27

Humor in the Christian Life

Did the apostle Paul forbid Christians to tell jokes? Does God want us to never laugh? A convincing argument could be made from the earliest documents of our faith that Christians are to always be grim and gloomy. These documents, the New Testament and Christian writings that followed soon after it, date from a time when the unwritten teachings and Bible interpretations of Jesus and his apostles were still fresh in Christian memories, a time when most Christians in our own day believe the Holy Spirit was still actively guiding the church.

The King James Version of Ephesians 5:4 prohibits "foolish talking" and "jesting," which in the Revised Standard Version are "silly talk" and "levity," and in the NIV are "foolish talk" and "coarse joking." Many translations of Luke 6:25 have Jesus pronouncing eventual woe and doom "unto you that laugh now." A collection of sayings for the Christian life compiled in the next century goes into detail: (1) believers are to be serious rather than frivolous, (2) lightheartedness is to be "rare and timely," (3) Christians are to confine their levity to smiling and are never to laugh, and (4) a believer is to make a lifelong struggle at being serious.[1] A church manual compiled in the early third century AD actually contains the proverbial condemnation against laughing in church, with the instruction that deacons are to stop worshippers from doing so.[2]

But what is the larger context of these restraints on creating and reacting to humor? A precept must be interpreted within the book in which it appears, and then within the setting of other Christian writers of the same

---

1. *Sentences of Sextus* Sayings 278–282, 49.
2. Connolly, *Didascalia apostolorum* 12.

time period. We must examine the spiritual literature as a whole, seeking the points on which its authors agree. Where they appear to differ, we must go deeper in an attempt to harmonize them and resolve whether they are merely looking at the same subject from different viewpoints. Only in this way can we find the whole meaning. Like a human being, a moral precept is known from its associates.

Like many moral considerations, foolish talking and jesting in Ephesians 5:4 are part of a list. The verse also contains the word translated as "filthiness" in many English translations, while the NIV renders it as "obscenity." A Christian exposition of instructions for life, dating from the first half of the third century AD, lumps foolish talking with "buffoonery" (described below) and "boisterous laughter," fornication, and wantonness in a list setting forth manifestations of "the mind of the flesh."[3] Later, the collection speaks against laughter in a context that includes shameful sexual passion and "looseness" as opposites of chasteness and purity.[4]

The fullest discussion on humor in ancient Christianity is found in chapter 2.5 of the book *The Pedagogue* by Clement of Alexandria. Clement was well educated and well versed in both Greek philosophy and Christian teaching. He wrote *The Pedagogue* while dean of Christendom's foremost institution of higher learning between AD 192 and 202. This chapter is followed by one strongly against "filthy speaking," including "corrupt communications," shameful deeds, unnecessary nudity, and immodesty, licentiousness, and conversations dwelling on subjects such as adultery and pedophilia—commonly the subject of risqué humor even today.

Chapter 2.5 itself curtails many aspects of joking and laughter. It opposes savage and insulting merriment, laughing too long, too often, and on all occasions, laughter that goes beyond appropriate bounds, licentious humor, and filthy speaking, because they constitute a "travesty the gift of speech, which is the most precious of all human endowments."[5] Dirty jokes in particular cause both speaker and listener to think of sinful acts, which may lead them more readily to committing such acts themselves. According to Clement, laughing at such jokes only furthers people's inclinations to shameful deeds.

Clement in 2.7 would allow a certain amount of constructive humor that builds up a person's good feelings about him/herself, and edifies

---

3. *Two Letters on Virginity* 1.8.
4. *Two Letters on Virginity* 2.11.
5. Clement of Alexandria, *Paedagogus* 2.5 (ANF 2:250).

listeners or the speaker. In 2.5 he was against making a human being the butt of jokes, even if that person is oneself. A Christian is not to be a buffoon, or "play the clown." We are not to make ourselves laughingstocks, or stir up laughter by foolish antics. As representatives of Jesus and his kingdom, we should be grave and dignified instead of making ourselves and them to be regarded as laughing matters.

Clement's approach is illustrated in two paragraphs of 2.5:

> Pleasantry is allowable, not waggery. Besides, even laughter must be kept in check; for when given vent to in the right manner it indicates orderliness, but when it issues differently it shows a want of restraint.
>
> For, in a word, whatever things are natural to men we must not eradicate from them, but rather impose on them limits and suitable times. For man is not to laugh on all occasions because he is a laughing animal, any more than the horse neighs on all occasions because he is a neighing animal. But as rational beings, we are to regulate ourselves suitably, harmoniously relaxing the austerity and over-tension of our serious pursuits, not inharmoniously breaking them up altogether.[6]

He especially opposed wags and waggery, which in the language of this translation means someone who makes jokes one after another, on all occasions, and on all subjects, including sex and religion.

A little later, Clement wrote:

> We are not to laugh perpetually, for that is going beyond bounds; nor in the presence of elderly persons, or others worthy of respect, unless they indulge in pleasantry for our amusement. Nor are we to laugh before all and sundry, nor in every place, nor to every one, nor about everything.[7]

Clement's successor as dean and, in his own right, the most influential Bible scholar and teacher of the first half of the third century and for centuries afterwards, added valuable insights as to what kind of humor displeases God. In his first sermon on Psalm 38 he discountenanced laughing after sin, and other happiness over one's misdeeds. He explained that "Woe unto you that laugh now! for ye shall mourn and weep" in Luke 6:25 is directed to persons that do so.[8]

---

6. Clement of Alexandria, *Paedagogus* 2.5 (ANF 2:250).
7. Clement of Alexandria, *Paedagogus* 2.5 (ANF 2:250).
8. Origen, *Homilies on Psalm* 37.1.5.

Clement's successor wrote a commentary on the Song of Solomon, the Bible's only explicit love poem, in which many readers find sexual innuendos. When interpreting "sweet is thy voice" in 2:14, he reminded readers of Jesus' warning in Matthew 12:36–37: "every idle word that men shall speak, they shall give account thereof in the day of judgment. For by thy words thou shalt be justified, and by thy words thou shalt be condemned," and Paul's injunction in Colossians 4:6 to "Let your speech be always with grace, seasoned with salt, that ye may know how ye ought to answer every man."[9] Years earlier, Clement himself had applied Matthew 12:36–37 against foul language, in chapter 2.6 of *The Pedagogue*, following the chapter on laughter.

So joke, laugh, and speak as would an ambassador of your country, remembering that you are a representative of a higher sovereign. In order for our message about the kingdom of heaven to be taken with the importance and seriousness it deserves, we must not intersperse nonessential jokes into it, for this may lead listeners to dismiss the whole presentation as a joking matter or an idle tale intended for amusement rather than for earnest consideration. Humorous points may arise, as Clement indicated, but our seizing on them must be rare and timely, and calculated only to uplift other people. Still less are Christians to be buffoons and invite laughter at themselves, for this inclines listeners to think less highly of representatives of the heavenly king, and consequently of God himself.

Incidentally, the same passage of the church manual that forbids laughing in church also discountenances whispering, sleeping, and making signs with the hands there;[10] in short, irreverent conduct and failing to pay attention to the worship service then in progress. The restraint on laughter and these other diversions fits well within the teaching of all ancient Christian authors that we accord due attention and respect to all serious matters pertaining to our souls and bodies—and the souls and bodies of others—and not treat as trifles either sex or religion, unless we can thereby edify another person.

---

9. Origen, *Commentary on the Song of Songs* 3.13.
10. Connolly, *Didascalia apostolorum* 12.

Chapter 28

The Husband's Role and His Duties

IN early Christian teaching, a husband's role was best described as head of the wife, just as Christ is the head of the church. This appears in Ephesians 5:23, as well as in Origen's *Commentary on Ephesians* concerning 5:22–23. Origen was considered the greatest Bible scholar, teacher, and preacher of the first half of the third century. Dean of "the first Christian university,"[1] he was well situated to know and record the consensus of Christian beliefs and practices from region to region, because he traveled frequently throughout the eastern Mediterranean at the invitation of local clergy as a theological consultant. He composed his *Commentary on Ephesians* sometime between AD 232 and 244.

The husband's headship is also indicated in the *Didascalia apostolorum* 3, a Syrian manual of church and individual Christian practice compiled in the first three decades of the third century.

Origen also designated a higher but nevertheless loving status for the husband. Husbands, Origen wrote, are to relate to their wives in the way that Jesus relates to the church, while wives are to relate to their husbands as the church does to Jesus. In the same vein, Origen instructed husbands to think and do the things of Christ while wives are to think and do those of the church.[2]

---

1. McGuckin, *Westminster Handbook to Origen*, 1.
2. Origen, *Commentary on Ephesians* 5:22–23, 233.

A wife is under the further duties of helping her husband in all things, and to "fear" him,[3] which is the word that older ancient Christian translations use where we say "respect," the latter being employed for the same feeling in Heine's translation of Origen's *Commentary on Ephesians* 5.33.

There are many passages in early Christian literature that instruct wives to submit to their husbands (Eph 5:22, 24; Col 3:18; Clement of Alexandria, *Paedagogus* 3.12; *Didascalia apostolorum* 3; Origen, *Commentary on Ephesians* 5.24; 1 Pet 3:1; Titus 2:5). Unlike the patriarchalist abuse of the Bible in comparatively recent times, this is not submission like a slave but springs from the acknowledgment that the wife is a "weaker vessel" (1 Pet 3:7), whose conformity to her husband materially aids him in his role as the "stronger vessel" that protects and provides for her. In his *Homilies on Joshua* 3.1, Origen explained it as an analogy from why men but not women fought as soldiers in the ancient Israelite army: a weak vessel is not sent into conflicts lest it become broken and useless.

Today's Olympics and other sporting events recognize that women are weaker when they provide separate competitions for them. This is not men lording it over women but recognition of differences in ability and specialization conferred by nature. The difference in function and status that results from being weaker does not mandate abject subordination; rather, 1 Peter 3:7 commands Christian husbands to honor wives as the "weaker vessel." It is the duty of the husband to brave conflicts in order to protect his wife.

Besides being equipped by nature to fight in literal battles, husbands until the twentieth century possessed a greater knowledge of "the world"—workplaces, business, and evil men therein—acquired by working and associating with many people outside the home, at a time when females were confined to home and family. For this reason, says Origen's *Commentary on Matthew*, specifically 14:24, a Christian husband has a right and duty to prevent his wife from doing what is not fitting, and from associating with such men he knows from general experience to have dishonorable intentions. Clement mentioned the additional duty of keeping his wife from acting in a way that contravenes virtue and salvation.[4]

To maintain the balance of wifely submission and husbandly leadership, the church father Tertullian, around AD 200, forbade husbands to be

---

3. Connolly, *Didascalia apostolorum* 3.
4. Clement of Alexandria, *Stromata* 4.19.

ruled by their wives,⁵ and for a woman to select a man to marry on the basis that she could dominate him.⁶ Tertullian was the founder of Latin Christian literature from his base in Tunisia. Before being converted and ordained, he had been a lawyer in a system of secular law that gave great power to husbands and fathers, and allowed women a status little higher than slaves.

Paul's instructions in 1 Corinthians 14:34–35, that women must not voice questions aloud in church but must ask them at home from their husbands, are not evidence of female subjection or disenfranchisement. Origen's *Homilies on Joshua* 3.1 explains that one person cannot help another unless the intended helper can teach something to the other person. Husbands thus have a duty to help, teach, and inform their wives and themselves on spiritual matters.

Origen received his formal theological education at the world's foremost institute of Christian learning at Alexandria in Egypt. The dean at the time was Clement, the most outstanding Christian thinker of the day. In the 190s AD, Clement wrote much about relationships between spouses, particularly the sexual aspects. While the celibate Origen wrote in generalities that husbands are to regulate the matters of marriage,⁷ the married Clement gave details. The husband, wrote Clement, is under an obligation to control and regulate himself and his desires so that he loves and delights in his wife as a person more than as a source of pleasure in intercourse.⁸

According to Clement, a husband's trustworthiness, reliability, good behavior, self-control, honesty, and love of others—all of which should characterize a Christian in his relations with outsiders—were also to be exhibited to his wife. Indeed, said Clement, marriage should be the training ground for developing and practicing love of neighbor.⁹

Clement also taught that the husband has a duty to ask the wife's consent to sex, a novel idea at the time. In an age when wives and other slaves were considered mere playthings and tools for a free man's pleasure, Clement opened new ground by allowing a woman to veto her husband's advances.¹⁰

---

5. Tertullian, *On Patience* 16.
6. *To His Wife* 2.8.
7. Origen, *Commentary on Ephesians* 5:22–23.
8. Clement of Alexandria, *Stromata* 3.7 (58).
9. Clement of Alexandria, *Paedagogus* 2.10.
10. Clement of Alexandria, *Stromata* 3.7 (58).

THE HUSBAND'S ROLE AND HIS DUTIES

Christianity, before the middle of the third century AD, introduced yet another novel (and, for its time, outrageous) duty for husbands. Husbands were obliged to actually love their wives. In fact, there are many more injunctions in the early Christian literature that a husband love his wife than that she should love him. Husbands are instructed eight times to love their wives (1 Cor 7:33, Eph 5:25, 28, and 33, Col 3:19, Clement's *Paedagogus* 3.12 and *Stromata* 3.7 [58], and *Letter from Ignatius to Polycarp* 5.1). Ignatius was a bishop of Antioch who had worked alongside apostles and was martyred around AD 107. Love by wife for husband, without mentioning that he love her, is found only in Titus 2:4, Polycarp's *Letter to the Philippians* 4.2, and Origen's *Commentary on Romans* 10:20. Writing in the first half of the second century, Polycarp was a bishop who in his youth had associated with the apostle John and other first-generation Christians. He was probably "the messenger of the church in Smyrna" in Revelation 2:8.

What was this new love? Ephesians 5:25, Clement (*Paedagogus* 3.12) and Ignatius (*Letter to Polycarp* 5.1) said that the husband is to love the wife "as Christ loved the church and gave himself for it," while Ephesians 5:28 commands husbands to love their wives "as their own bodies," adding that "he that loves his wife loves himself."

Of course, men can "love" many things: their dogs, their automobile, their football team, and—among Roman men in the early Christian centuries—a sex partner of either gender. But these are means to an end, put aside when he becomes more interested in something else. Love for wife was to be permanent and constant. A husband must spend time with the wife and for the wife's benefit by teaching her, considering her sexual needs,[11] controlling his sexual passion, protecting her from evil-intentioned persons, living considerately with her and honoring her,[12] and leading the way toward God.[13] Such love excludes bitterness and harshness.[14] To perform these responsibilities he needs to be head of the wife.

There was a wide contrast between Christian teaching and Roman law of the time, when a wife was just another of a male's possessions, and a father had the right to put a family member to death, while Christian literature before AD 250 was remarkably lacking in the concept of a husband owning his wife. The Christian husband's role and the sort of "submission"

---

11. 1 Cor 7:3–5 and Clement of Alexandria, *Stromata* 3.15.
12. 1 Pet 3:7.
13. Origen, *Homilies on Genesis* 4.4.
14. Col 3:19.

his wife was to render him were more like the relationship between a loving, benevolent teacher and an eager pupil, not between a master and his serf as it became many centuries later in Christian society.

The duties and relationship between spouses were to produce the happy Christian marriage described in Tertullian's *To His Wife* 2.8:

> Together they pray, together prostrate themselves, together perform their fasts; mutually teaching, mutually exhorting, mutually sustaining. Equally are they both found in the Church of God; equally at the banquet of God; equally in straits, in persecutions, in refreshments. Neither hides ought from the other; neither shuns the other; neither is troublesome to the other. The sick is visited, the indigent relieved, with freedom. Alms are given without danger of ensuing torment; sacrifices attended without scruple; daily diligence discharged without impediment. There is no stealthy signing, no trembling greeting, no mute benediction. Between the two echo psalms and hymns; and they mutually challenge each other which shall better chant to their Lord. Such things when Christ sees and hears, He joys. To these He sends His own peace.[15]

---

15. ANF 4:48.

Chapter 29

Imitate

Many New Testament authors and early church fathers exhorted their readers to emulate the good deeds and traits of both Old Testament personages and also other Christians, especially clergy. Their writings are valuable to us because they preserved the background and mindset of Christianity in its formative period and the unwritten Bible interpretations and teachings of Jesus.

According to a description of the Christian Sunday liturgy written in the middle of the second century, "the memoirs of the apostles or the writings of the prophets are read, as long as time permits; then, when the reader has ceased, the president verbally instructs, and exhorts to the imitation of these good things."[1]

The category of example most often cited by early Christian authors was the prophets. In the New Testament, James 5:10 urges Christians to emulate the Old Testament prophets as examples of patience and bearing with afflictions. *The First Letter of Clement* mentions Ezekiel, Elijah, and Elisha as examples worth emulating, as do two letters on church discipline once ascribed to the same author. *First Clement* was composed in the middle or late first century, while some apostles were still alive, but the two letters date from almost two centuries later. One of them said to copy these prophets's sinless lives.

First Clement put forth Moses as a model of humility and submission toward God that Christians should imitate, as well as Abraham, Job, King David, and the prophet Ezekiel.

---

1. Justin Martyr, *1 Apology* 67 (ANF 1:186).

Recall the three young Hebrews in the book of Daniel who braved the fiery furnace rather than worship an idol. For their faith and steadfastness to God they were held up as worthy of emulation by *1 Clement* and by Hippolytus, a bishop in central Italy writing in AD 203. Hippolytus encouraged copying the good ways and good habits of Daniel himself and also the chastity of the patriarch Joseph, who resisted the attempts of his master's wife to seduce him.

Origen was the most outstanding theologian, Bible scholar, and preacher of the first half of the third century. He encouraged his listeners to read all the Old Testament books to observe who became righteous and to thus follow their example, and to see who were reproached in order to avoid their shortcomings.

Besides Old Testament figures, early Christians were exhorted to emulate contemporary Christians. The apostle Paul encouraged his congregations to imitate him and his ways, in the way he imitated Christ (1 Cor 4:16; 11:1; Phil 3:17; 4:9). One of the third-century letters once ascribed to Clement encouraged taking Paul as an example of faith and practice, and also Paul's companions Barnabas and Timothy, for it considered all three to have loved and practiced exemplary chastity and to have been flawless imitators of Christ.

Nor are Bible personages the only suitable examples for Christians to copy. We can take cues for behavior from any worthy believer. *First Clement* encouraged copying all the persecuted, not just prophets. More generally, a later letter ascribed to Clement exhorts: "Let us contemplate and imitate the faithful who have conducted themselves well in the Lord,"[2] especially those who skillfully dispense the word of truth, are concerned for other people's salvation, and do not mislead the innocent or regard their leadership status only as a means of making money. Hebrews 6:12 admonishes Bible readers to follow the example of all "who through faith and patience inherit God's promises."

Clergy were specially singled out as examples to be followed. Remember Paul, Barnabas, and Timothy? The former two were clergy in that they were apostles, while Timothy was a parish pastor and bishop/overseer. Origen preached that we should imitate the deeds of our clergy, while Hebrews 13:7 instructs readers to remember our leaders that spoke God's word to us and to observe the results of their way of life and imitate their faith. In near-apostolic times, around AD 107, Bishop Ignatius of Antioch prayed

---

2. *Two Letters on Virginity* 1.13 (ANF 8:60).

that church members be like their bishop-pastor, "a man of inexpressible love,"[3] and that they all try to be like him.

Being frequently put forward as examples, clergy have a duty to be good examples, worthy of imitating. First Timothy 4:12 mandates the pastor or bishop to be an example to other Christians in word, conduct, love, spirit, faith, and sexual restraint. Written by one cleric and addressed to others, 1 Peter 5:3 admonishes them to be "examples to the flock."

In exercising church discipline in the case of consecrated widows and deacons involved in questionable conduct in the 250s AD, Bishop Cyprian of Carthage opined:

> overseers and deacons should be careful for this, that they may afford an example and instruction to others concerning their conversation and character. For how can they direct the integrity and continence of others, if the corruptions and teachings of sin begin to proceed from themselves?[4]

One aim in imitating prophets, clergy, and other saints is so that each individual Christian may become a good example to others. We should ourselves be worthy of being emulated. There was another church father named Clement, in the city of Alexandria in Egypt, who wrote about Christian topics in the 190s AD. He extended to all believers, lay and clergy, the duty of being an example in word, conduct, love, faith, and sexual continence. He also recommended that Christians:

> become an example to those who wish to exercise temperance, not encouraging each other to eat greedily of what is set before us, and not to consort inconsiderately with women. And especially is it incumbent on those entrusted with such a dispensation to exhibit to disciples a pure example.[5]

In particular, he said the Christian layperson or cleric ought to be an example in moderation in drinking wine, in order to teach people how to avoid becoming drunk.

Clement's student Origen said each Christian ought to be a guide and motivator, and present a model of conduct to other people. He also opined that we are to be very conscious about the example we set. The soul ought to have such self-knowledge as to know when it is making progress and

---

3. Ignatius of Antioch, *Letter to the Ephesians* 1 (ANF 1:49).
4. Cyprian, *Epistle* 61.3 (ANF 5:358).
5. Clement of Alexandria, *Stromata* 4.15 (ANF 2:427).

growing in all the virtues, and whether such progress improves only the soul itself or benefits other people by its actions.

Clement of Alexandria even went so far as to consider a reflection attributed to the apostle Matthias: "if the neighbor of an elect man sin, the elect man has sinned. For had he conducted himself as the Word prescribes, his neighbor also would have been filled with such reverence for the life he led as not to sin."[6] Although this saying shifts the responsibility much further than most ancient and modern-day believers would place it, we should be mindful of the possible consequences our example may set.

As regards finding and being an example of the Christian life, all early and present-day believers can agree with the *Sentences of Sextus,* 166: "The faithful person is a guide to every good deed." This was a collection dating from the first half of the second century, which was so popular among believers that it was translated into many languages.

---

6. *Traditions of Matthias*, quoted in Clement of Alexandria, *Stromata* 7.13 ANF (2:547).

Chapter 30

Immigrants and Racism

Any chapter on attitudes to racism in the Christian church's foundational period would be necessarily short. There simply was none. The matter was sometimes different for foreigners and strangers in general.

Racism was absent in the earliest church and in the non-Christian society surrounding it. Christians and other subjects of the Roman Empire simply did not make distinctions based on race. In fact, mentions of a person's skin color are so rare as to be insignificant. For instance, the Christian Bardesanes in early-third-century Eastern Syria mentioned people coming in different colors as an example of what everyone agreed was inconsequential.

The only discriminations were based on cultural factors. Jews divided the world into themselves and gentiles, while for Greeks the distinction was between themselves and "barbarians," i.e., people who did not share Greek language or culture. The Romans divided people between citizens and noncitizens, and then among various economic classes of citizens. The main Roman xenophobia was of hostile peoples outside the empire. In each case, however, individuals could cross the divides by joining the preferred group through financial or military achievement or by changing their religion. Any antipathy was cultural, not ethnic, and was directed most against "oriental cults" or "superstitions," of which Christianity was one. In fact, there is only one ethnic slur by a Christian in the whole of the New Testament, and even that is a quotation from a member of the maligned group (Titus 1:12–13).

On the other hand, Scripture and other ancient Christian writings say much about how to regard individuals new to a community, whether they come for employment, business opportunities, or conditions in their homelands. The term "immigrant" nowhere appears in the early literature, because strict separation into nation-states, with restrictions on travel, employment, and trade, did not yet exist. The ancients did not generally think much about the reasons why newcomers had come, unless they were military invaders.

The use of the term "stranger" in the early Christian period was thus wide enough to include all persons new to a locale. Christian writers before AD 200 encouraged welcoming and generous treatment of immigrants and other strangers.

The earliest instruction about strangers is Christ's preaching that they be welcomed and protected, and whoever does so to the least of strangers does it to Jesus himself (Matt 25:34-45). One apostle wrote that Christians are loyal to God when they render any service to newcomers (3 John 5).

A description of Christianity for heathens written around AD 125 in Athens reported that it was the Christian custom to take strangers into one's home and rejoice over them as if brothers and sisters. A similar book by a Christian teacher who was martyred for the faith in Italy around AD 165 records that local Christian congregations used their funds to provide for orphans, widows, the sick, the needy, and strangers. It also details that among the effects of conversion to Christianity was that "we who hated and destroyed one another, and on account of their different manners would not live with men of a different tribe, now, since the coming of Christ, live familiarly with them."[1]

In showing how elevated Christian ethics were, a bishop in France in the 180s AD encouraged giving lodging in one's own home to "the roofless stranger" and to "give rest to those that are shaken,"[2] which would cover a newcomer experiencing culture shock from moving to a new country. About the same era, the bishop of Antioch in western Syria wrote similarly. Both clerics quoted Zechariah 7:10 in support.

Clement of Alexandria in Egypt was dean of the world's foremost Christian educational institution from AD 192 to 202. He praised hospitality, which he described thusly: "Akin to love is hospitality, being a congenial art devoted to the treatment of strangers."[3] His illustration of its width and why Christians should welcome and assist newcomers was "Hospitality,

---

1. Justin Martyr, *1 Apology* 14 (ANF 1:167).
2. Irenaeus, *Against Heresies* 4.17.3 (ANF 1:483).
3. Clement of Alexandria, *Stromata* 2.9 (ANF 2:357).

therefore, is occupied in what is useful for strangers; and guests are strangers; and friends are guests; and brethren are friends."[4] Even more universal is his statement "those are strangers, to whom the things of the world are strange."[5] Christian morality, wrote Clement, obliges us

> to love strangers not only as friends and relatives, but as ourselves, both in body and soul .... Accordingly, it is expressly said, "Thou shalt not abhor an Egyptian, for thou wast a sojourner in Egypt;" designating by the term Egyptian either one of that race, or any one in the world.[6]

These authors lived so early and were so geographically widespread that their sentiments could have originated only with Jesus himself. Because they predate the division into present-day Christian denominations, and before racism and immigration were subjects of controversy well before Christianity was a state religion, their comments are relevant to Christians of every shade and hue in the world today.

---

4. Clement of Alexandria, *Stromata* 2.9 (ANF 2:357).
5. Clement of Alexandria, *Stromata* 2.9 (ANF 2:357).
6. Clement of Alexandria, *Stromata* 2.18 (ANF 2:367).

Chapter 31

Jealousy

ALTHOUGH jealousy is noted in both Testaments, eight church fathers, and three New Testament apocrypha before the mass apostasy of AD 249–251, none of them discussed it at length or described it. Most mentions appear only in lists with other vices, without individual treatment.

Properly so called, jealousy is the resentful, even suspicious protectiveness and vigilance for one's own rights, advantages, or possessions against someone who would deprive him or her of them or make them be or appear to be less valuable. As such, it is not necessarily a vice because the person is merely taking care of his or her own legitimate interests.

The Bible refers to God's jealousy about two dozen times, usually when he was upset that Israelites, who had formed a covenant with him to be his people before wrongfully replacing him with false gods. In both Exodus and Deuteronomy, the Ten Commandments state that the Lord their God is a jealous god. The Bible includes human examples also, such as (1) a husband jealous of his wife in Numbers 5:11–31, (2) King Saul, who was jealous and suspicious that David might deprive him of the throne or at least of the Israelites' affections, (3) the brother of the prodigal son in Luke 15:11–32, who was jealous because the restoration of the prodigal to a favored position with alacrity and rejoicing diminished his own contribution of working on the farm and being a good son, and (4) Paul's "godly jealousy" in 2 Corinthians 11:2 for Corinthian believers as against false teachers who would lead them away from their proper loyalty to Christ. These examples indicate that jealousy is not always wrong or sinful, which makes me wonder why it is included in so many lists of vices. Perhaps it is only *excess* of jealousy that the ancient believers condemned, just as they discountenanced gluttony and foods that had been offered to idols, but not eating per se.

Outside lists of sins, jealousy is given special treatment in the doublet "jealousy and strife" or "envy and strife." The expression does not occur in the Old Testament. The combination appears as a single phrase in 1 Corinthians 3:3 and James 3:14, and 3:16, which suggests that the two are linked more closely to each other than either is to other vices, as the list in Romans 13:13 indicates.

The (Jewish) Old Testament is soft or neutral on jealousy, often attributing it to God, while in the early Christian literature it usually meets with blanket and oft-repeated prohibition, and is linked to strife in a special way. The difference is probably due to the different manners in which the Jewish and Christian communities were organized and the mechanics of becoming and advancing as a member. Under the old covenant, people were born into the community. The early Christians were mostly converts. Since the time of Ezra, if not before, a person was either in or out of the covenant people, with no semi-status at the margins of the community. On the other hand, early Christian literature is replete with references to people at the fringes mixing the gospel with Judaism, heresy, false teaching, or lukewarmness. The Jew was rewarded and improved his or her status within the community by good works and temple sacrifices. Christianity was based on faith, and accepted prostitutes, publicans, and other sinners on no other basis than faith. Late converts were accorded the same rights and advantages as long-time members. It was only human for people who had been Christians for decades to regard the ready acceptance and equality of a Johnny-come-lately as diminishing the value of their own positions, which had involved years of clean living and good works. In keeping with Christianity's penchant for factionalism and disunity, it is to be expected that strife enter an open community not based on accomplishments or ethnic descent. Although originally neutral in itself, jealousy had become divisive and a chronic nuisance among Christians and thus condemned as a vice.

Chapter 32

Judging Christians, Then and Now

SOME Christians refuse to serve on a jury because Jesus said "Do not judge" in Matthew 7:1 and Luke 6:37, a command restated in James 4:11–12, by Paul in Romans 14:13 and 1 Corinthians 4:5, and twice by the third-century church scholar Origen in his *Commentary on Romans*. However, a survey of the New Testament and other Christian writings before AD 250 shows that the earliest Christians did not share this interpretation but participated in courts and trials. To them and to us "Do not judge" has a very restricted and limited message. People who first received the gospel, who could ask New Testament authors for clarification of Christ's written and unwritten teachings, and fortunate Christians a few generations afterwards, regarded these words of Jesus to be like a parable or figure of speech in which he frequently expressed wider and less literal truths. Nevertheless, "Do not judge" does have an important meaning for Christians today.

Early Christians were Judges and Jurors

The earliest heirs of the apostles recorded that Christians in their day often served as judges (which would include jurors). This would have been an unbelievably abrupt and almost impossible departure from the faith of only a few years earlier if the apostles and their companions had interpreted "Do not judge" literally and applied it in a blanket manner. Usually these records are exhortations to "judge justly and righteously" (five ancient Christian authors, including ones in the late first or early second century),[1] "judge well and rightly" (Origen) and, in particular, "judge widows and orphans justly" (three authors,[2] including one in the second half of the first century). For example, in describing Christians and their traits around AD 125, the Christian philosopher Aristides noted "whenever they are judges, they judge uprightly."[3]

Church Courts Began in New Testament Times

Not only was judging in secular courts part of the early Christian experience, but the church itself had its own system of courts and trials. Matthew 18:15–17, 1 Corinthians 6:1–5, and 2 Corinthians 13:1–2 in the first century assume them to be well established for disputes between Christians and against backsliders. By the first half of the third century, church courts were considered routine by Origen, and had a code of procedure similar to modern secular courts in the church manual called the *Didascalia*. Judging is the whole purpose of such courts.

The influence of such courts is still with us. When the Emperor Constantine legalized Christianity and made it an official religion of the Roman Empire in the fourth century, he incorporated church courts as part of the government justice system, applying Christian teachings and principles to Roman law. They continued through the Reformation and were secularized and absorbed into the English judicial system, and exported to the United States and countries of the British Commonwealth. Their approach (but not their theology) survive today for such matters as divorce and family relations.

Private Judgment Forbidden Outside a Court

Matthew 7:1, Luke 6:37, Romans 14:13, 1 Corinthians 4:5, James 4:11–12, and Origen's *Commentary on Romans* 9:40 and 9.41.2 are not to be completely disregarded today. What they forbid is a Christian taking judging into his or her own hands, judging privately the actions of another without

---

1. *Didache* 4.3; *Letter of Barnabas* 19.11, 20.2; Christian Sibylline Oracles 2.64; Origen, *Homilies on Leviticus* 9.4.3; Origen, *Homilies on Psalm 36* 5.2; Theophilus, *To Autolycus* 3.12.

2. *First Epistle of Clement* 8.4; *Letter of Barnabas* 20.2; Theophilus, *To Autolycus* 3.12.

3. Aristides, *Apology* 15 (ANF 10:276).

the safeguards built into courts for a full and fair hearing, such as the right of the person being judged to know in full the accusations against him/her, to ask questions of the complainant, to have an opportunity to defend him/herself, to have the right to call witnesses to support his/her side of the story, to have the right to cross-examine the complainant's witnesses, to have the opportunity to explain his/her actions, and to have the right to be fully heard and judged by a neutral arbitrator, be it a church or secular court, by a judge alone, or by a judge assisted by jurors. Private judgment outside a duly constituted court, the kind of judgment Christ forbade, is like an individual taking the law into her/his own hands, which is prohibited to private citizens although allowed for, or even a duty of, a government judicial system. After all, most believers accept that a duly constituted court has authority to lock up offenders and keep them in distant jails, but for a private person to do so is universally regarded as abduction and kidnapping. Nobody doubts that a court can fine and seize property, but for an individual citizen to do so is theft.

Conclusion

What Christ meant by "Do not judge" was judging in private situations, without authority and safeguards; this command does not apply to jurors in Anglo-American courts. The New Testament and other Christian literature before AD 250 and centuries or millennia of judicial history indicate that "Do not judge" was not understood so widely or comprehensively by the well informed as to exclude jury duty.

Chapter 33

Keep Your Word Before AD 200

THE early people of God considered keeping one's word, or fulfilling one's promise, to be a serious obligation. This was particularly true of promises to God. Frequently one's word or promise was confirmed with an oath, and often was incorrectly considered to override other obligations.

The duty to perform as promised dates at least as far back as the law of Moses. Witness Numbers 30:2, "If a man vow a vow unto the LORD, or swear an oath to bind his soul with a bond; he shall not break his word, he shall do according to all that proceedeth out of his mouth," and Deuteronomy 23:23, "That which is gone out of thy lips thou shalt keep and perform; even a freewill offering, according as thou hast vowed unto the LORD thy God, which thou hast promised with thy mouth."

In Joshua 9, the Israelite leaders made a peace treaty with the Gibeonites even though it violated God's command to exterminate all previous inhabitants of the promised land. The leaders kept their word that had been confirmed by their oath even though there were five good reasons for breaking it. First, the Gibeonites had deceived them that they had come from a far country rather than from among the Canaanites, whom God had commanded them to exterminate. Second, they would not have given their word had they known the truth. Third, the Israelite leaders had not sought counsel from God before giving their word. Fourth, the bulk of the Israelites were dissatisfied with this act of their leaders and wanted them to repudiate it. And fifth, the agreement had been made in violation of God's general command that they not make treaties with the existing populations of Canaan, but instead were to destroy them.

When Nehemiah as governor confronted profiteers who preyed upon the common people and he demanded they restore their ill-gotten gains, the exploiters promised to do so. To cement their promise, Nehemiah had the priests administer oaths to them and laid on the oppressors a graphic curse in case they defaulted. Nehemiah 5:13 records that "the people did according to this promise."

This Israelite attitude is also evidenced in the New Testament. When King Herod was pleased with a dancing girl at his birthday celebrations, "he promised with an oath to give her whatsoever she would ask" (Matt 14:7). When she requested that John the Baptist be executed, Herod regretted his promise but granted the request to save face among the other celebrants at the party and because he had made an oath.

Early Christians also inculcated a duty to keep one's word. A church manual that may have been written before the Gospel of Matthew, or in the early second century at the latest, gives as one command among many: "Thy speech shall not be false, nor empty, but fulfilled by deed."[1]

The first description of a Christian worship service by an outsider indicates the importance of the sworn word. To eradicate Christianity, illegal at the time, from a Roman province in northwest Turkey, its governor investigated Christian faith and practices and reported to the emperor around AD 112 that Christians gathered before dawn and "they bound themselves with an oath, not for any crime, but not to commit theft or robbery or adultery, not to break their word, and not to deny a deposit when demanded."[2]

Besides the Hebrew Scriptures and prophets, some early Christians also heeded writings attributed to a pagan prophetess as a gentile teacher of Christian truths.[3] A prophecy dating to about AD 175 condemned "lovers of faithlessness," "breakers of faith," and "tyrants in fickleness," and other "violent sinners."[4]

"The good man must not prove false or fail to ratify what he has promised, although others violate their engagements."[5] So wrote the dean of Christendom's foremost educational institution in the 190s AD, who was well versed in both pagan Greco-Roman and Christian ethics.

---

1. *Didache* 2.5.
2. Pliny the Younger, *Letter 10.96*, 29.
3. Origen, *Against Celsus* 8.30; Origen, *Commentary on Matthew* 10.12.
4. *Sib. Or.* 8.185–87.
5. Clement of Alexandria, *Stromata* 7.15.

What about promises to sin or which otherwise violate God's will? This was precisely the situation with Joshua and Herod. True, the rules about promises contained in Numbers and Deuteronomy pertained to undertakings to God, and God cannot command contrary to his own will. The Israelite leaders are faulted because "they did not inquire of the LORD" (Josh 9.14). Nevertheless all the above pronouncements admitted no exceptions.

Perhaps the key is that the promises for other-than-godly purposes were confirmed with oaths. Christian literature in its first two centuries is full of prohibitions against swearing oaths, although there are a few exceptions where it is recognized that in some situations the general rule may not apply. Jesus spoke against oath-taking in Matthew 5:33–37 and his brother prohibited them in James 5:12. So also did Justin and Polycarp, both of whom were martyred for the faith in the middle of the second century. Justin wrote of refraining from oaths as a characteristic of Christians already well known to his pagan readers. Polycarp was probably "the angel of the church in Smyrna" in Revelation 2:8. He helped teach a man who later moved to a bishopric in France. This bishop repeated Christ's prohibition in the 180s AD.[6] The dean referred to above also discountenanced oath-taking. This was not a denominational distinctive of their communion, for even a gnostic writer in the mid-second century understood Jesus the same way (2 *Jeou* 43).

The sum of all this is that, while a good man keeps his word, the wise man avoids giving it, especially not under oath. We should follow the advice in the *Sentences of Sextus*, a book of adages for guidance in the Christian life dating from the first half of the second century that became extraordinarily popular: "Do great things rather than promise great things."[7]

---

6. Irenaeus, *Against Heresies,* 2.32.1, 4.13.1.

7. *Sentences of Sextus*, Sentence 198, 38 (my translation).

Chapter 34

The Medicine of Immortality

UNLIKE denominations with unstructured and informal forms of worship, the liturgical churches (Eastern Orthodox, Armenian, Episcopalian, Lutheran, and Roman Catholic) hold the Eucharist in great reverence and maintain firm regulations as to how communion elements are to be treated and to whom they may be distributed. These regulations are not modern inventions, nor did they originate with superstitious monks in the Dark Ages. The present essay looks at Christian regard for the Eucharist before AD 250 to show how the earliest believers shared the same practices as liturgical denominations today. The ancient writings are the common heritage of all Christians because they date from before the division into present-day denominations, and could have originated only in apostolic times.

In the earliest Christian centuries, extremely respectful treatment was shown toward the bread and wine (or body and blood of Christ). The reason appears in Justin Martyr, a Christian writer in the mid-second century who was later martyred for the faith: "not as common bread and common drink do we receive these . . . we have been taught that the food which is blessed by the prayer of His word, and from which our blood and flesh by transmutation are nourished, is the flesh and blood of that Jesus who was made flesh."[1]

Half a century earlier, another martyr, Bishop Ignatius of Antioch, described the Eucharist as "the medicine of immortality, and the antidote to prevent us from dying but which causes that we should live forever in Jesus

---

1. Justin Martyr, *1 Apology* 66 (ANF 1:185).

Christ."² This was not the better-known Ignatius Loyola, but his namesake fifteen centuries earlier.

In AD 217, Bishop Hippolytus in central Italy set out existing church practice as to how clergy were to continue to conduct worship services. He also intended it as a guide for the laity in detecting and taking action when clergy departed from the worship heritage passed down from the apostles. He wrote that the consecrated elements are not to be allowed to fall to the floor or be lost or treated carelessly; this is corroborated in the same era in Tunisia by the church father Tertullian. Nor were church mice and other animals to be permitted to consume them. The bread and wine were to be consecrated only according to a prescribed ceremony, which must be in an orderly manner, without talking or arguing, and such that Christians preserve their good reputation, and their worship practices not be ridiculed by non-Christians. Shortly afterwards, the church father Origen wrote that people are not to receive them "in haphazard fashion."³ These, of course, are echoes of Saint Paul the apostle, that church services must be conducted "decently and in order" (1 Cor 14:40).

This same Origen illustrated better than anyone else the great reverence with which Christians in the 240s AD held the sacramental elements. Unlike Ignatius or Hippolytus, he was not urging his hearers to show respect, but was using one existing church practice as the grounds or analogy for other spiritual exercises. Origen was taking the example of the treatment of the Eucharist as a standard practice on which to build his argument to encourage them to adopt an additional soul-building activity. His argument indicates that both he and his congregations took high respect for the sacramental elements for granted and as well established:

> You who are accustomed to take part in divine mysteries know, when you receive the body of the Lord, how you protect it with all caution and veneration lest any small part fall from it, lest anything of the consecrated gift be lost. For you believe, and correctly, that you are answerable if anything falls from there by neglect.⁴

Because he traveled much throughout the eastern Mediterranean at the request of local bishops, and once to Rome, his statements probably describe universal practice.

---

2. Ignatius of Antioch, *Letter to the Ephesians* 20 (ANF 1:57).
3. Origen, *Commentary on Matthew* 10.25 (ANF 10:431).
4. Origen, *Homilies on Exodus*, 380–81.

Partly because outsiders might not know how to demonstrate proper respect, it was forbidden to give Holy Communion to them. From the earliest times, it was considered sinful to consume the sacrament in an unworthy manner. According to the apostle Paul, "whosoever shall eat this bread, and drink this cup of the Lord, unworthily, shall be guilty of the body and blood of the Lord," and "he that eateth and drinketh unworthily, eateth and drinketh damnation to himself, not discerning the Lord's body" (1 Cor 11:27, 29). This was repeated almost two centuries later by Origen when he warned that Christians who partake unworthily will receive the Lord's judgment, again as a proposition accepted as a given by all his hearers.

The *Didache* was a church manual and guide to the Christian life written in the late first century, when some apostles were still living. It limited participation in the Eucharist to people who had been baptized, citing Jesus' command that we must not give what is holy to dogs. Half a century or more later, Justin Martyr similarly confined communion to people who believe Christian doctrine, have been baptized, and live as Christ had taught. Another sixty years later, Hippolytus's church manual would also admit to Holy Communion only people that had received Christian baptism. One of his charges against the leadership of a rival party within Christianity was that they indiscriminately gave communion to everybody.

To further safeguard against disrespect of the sacrament and prevent people from eating and drinking unworthily, there were restrictions even on the baptized. In the first century, Saint Paul required examination of conscience prior to receiving (1 Cor 11:28), while the *Didache*, not long afterward, mandated confession of sins. It also required resolution of disputes with other people before participating.

Liturgical denominations have always provided further protection by requiring communicants to come to the front of the church and to receive the sacrament only from the hand of a duly authorized minister commissioned for this purpose. In AD 212, Tertullian referred to this procedure as already ancient and universally accepted. The sacrament is not put into trays as among Calvinists and passed along the pews like a collection plate where anyone can serve themselves, even an unbaptized visitor who has never been in this church before.

Considering the veneration some churches accord the eucharistic elements—as witness the protections surrounding them—Christians of all denominations should show great respect for the sacrament and due consideration for the consciences of their hosts when attending a communion service in a church other than their own.

Further reading: John 6:48–58 and 1 Corinthians 11:20–36.

Chapter 35

Modesty in Dress and Appearance

THE principle that Christians should be modest—not unduly exposing their bodies or decorating themselves with finery—has a long history. It arose well before the twentieth century, and predates even the Protestant Reformation. Indeed, the principle goes back to the earliest years of the church, and is found in the works of prominent Christian writers from the first to third centuries. Those who commented on it taught that we are to wear unaffected dress and not embellish our bodies.

The principle starts in the New Testament itself, where 1 Timothy 2:9–10 commands "that women adorn themselves in modest apparel, with shamefacedness and sobriety; not with braided hair, or gold, or pearls, or costly array, but (which becometh women professing godliness) with good works."

A few generations later, in AD 125, a Christian named Aristides in Athens wrote a description of his coreligionists' practices and habits, noting that: "they go their way in all modesty and cheerfulness."[1]

The matter was explored in greater depth by Clement of Alexandria (Egypt), the dean or principal of ancient Christianity's foremost educational institution. Between AD 190 and 202 he wrote a number of books for the training and nurture of believers. One of them was *Paedagogus* (*The Instructor*) and another was *Stromata* (*Miscellanies*).

---

1. Aristides, *Apology* 15 (ANF 10:277).

The purpose of *Paedagogus* was to improve the soul and to advance it in the Christian life.² It stated that to attain virtue and properly practice Christianity, disciples are to avoid enhancing their physical attractiveness and refrain from wearing expensive or skimpy clothing.³ Clothing for both sexes must extend below the knee.⁴ Clement also taught that believing women are to keep their arms and heads covered.⁵ It forbade Christian men to voluntarily adopt the appearance and mannerisms of females, to wear earrings or finger rings, or to allow their hair to grow below the eyes. Wigs and other false hair were condemned as an affront to God.⁶

Describing the lifestyle of the sincere Christian in *Stromata*, Clement commended simple speech and a simple mode of life.⁷ This treatise condemns all luxury in dress, body, or manner, including expensive clothes and beauty ointments, which it calls "treacherous garments and treacherous unguents."⁸ It also describes how a believing wife is to conduct herself. She is not to adorn herself beyond what is becoming, for simplicity renders a wife free of suspicion while she earnestly devotes herself to prayer and supplications.⁹ She is not to leave her home too frequently but keep herself as far as possible from the view of all who are not related to her, and deem housekeeping of more consequence than useless frivolity.¹⁰

In an address to new converts, Clement encouraged modesty toward women.¹¹

Thus far, we have seen the attitude toward plain dress and bodily modesty in Egypt. Shortly before Clement wrote, a radical sect arose in Phrygia (now northern Turkey). To refute their false notions, a pastor named Apollonius wrote a treatise against them in AD 211. To prove that one of their leaders was not a prophet, Apollonius asked questions which reveal the contemporary Christian attitudes to cosmetics and dress:

Does a prophet dye his hair?

2. Clement of Alexandria, *Paedagogus* 1.1 (ANF 2:209).
3. Clement of Alexandria, *Paedagogus* 2.11.
4. Clement of Alexandria, *Paedagogus* 2.11.
5. Clement of Alexandria, *Paedagogus* 2.11.
6. Clement of Alexandria, *Paedagogus* 2.3, 3.11.
7. Clement of Alexandria, *Stromata* 1.10.
8. Clement of Alexandria, *Stromata* 1.10 (ANF 2:311).
9. Clement of Alexandria, *Stromata* 2.23.
10. Clement of Alexandria, *Stromata* 2.23.
11. Clement of Alexandria, *To Newly Baptized*.

> Does a prophet stain his eyelids?
> Does a prophet delight in adornment?[12]

Tertullian was a lawyer who became a clergyman in Carthage, in what is now northern Tunisia. He wrote on most aspects of the Christian life, including two books on the Christian rules for external appearance: *On the Apparel of Women* and *On the Pallium*. Written around AD 200, *On the Apparel of Women* began:

> If there dwelt upon earth a faith as great as is the reward of faith which is expected in the heavens, no one of you at all, best beloved sisters, from the time that she had first known the Lord,[13] and learned (the truth) concerning her own (that is, woman's) condition, would have desired too gladsome (not to say too ostentatious) a style of dress; so as not rather to go about in humble garb, and rather to affect meanness of appearance.[14]

The female tendency to beautify oneself, wrote Tertullian, can be traced to fallen angels mentioned in the Old Testament. As agents of Satan, they descended to earth and had relations with the female descendants of Adam. It was to sexually attract such demons that women started enhancing their outward beauty by artificial means.[15] To avoid falling into the same sin, said Tertullian, Christian women should be adorned only by "humility and chastity."[16] He condemned fancy clothing and elaborate dressing of the hair. *On the Apparel of Women* states that a woman's beauty, be it natural or artificial, will lead her into the sins of pride and vainglory unless she takes measures to avoid provoking carnal desire in men.[17] While disavowing any intention to encourage Christian women to become crude or wild in their appearance, or squalid or slovenly, Tertullian exhorted them to limit or hide much of their beauty.[18]

Tertullian's major concern was that Christian women not incite lust. Book 2 chapter 2 of *On the Apparel of Women* asks:

---

12. *Concerning Montanism* in Eusebius of Caesarea *Historia Ecclesiastica* 5:18.
13. Heb 8:11; Jer 31:34.
14. Tertullian, *De cultu feminarum* 1.1 (ANF 4:14).
15. Tertullian, *De cultu feminarum* 1.2.
16. Tertullian, *De cultu feminarum* 1.4 (ANF 4:16).
17. Tertullian, *De cultu feminarum* 2.3.
18. Tertullian, *De cultu feminarum* 2.5.

> Are we to paint ourselves out that our neighbours may perish? Where, then, is the command "Thou shalt love thy neighbour as thyself?" "Care not merely about your own (things) but about your neighbour's?"[19]

And shortly thereafter he answers the question with:

> Since, therefore, both our own interest and that of others is implicated in the studious pursuit of most perilous (outward) comeliness, it is time for you to know that not merely must the pageantry of fictitious and elaborate beauty be rejected by you; but that of even natural grace must be obliterated by concealment and negligence, as equally dangerous to the glances of the beholder's eyes.[20]

In the same chapter, he wrote:

> in the eye of perfect (that is, Christian) modesty, carnal desire of one's self on the part of others is not only not to be desired, but even execrated, by you: first, because the study of making personal grace (which we know to be naturally the inviter of lust) a means of pleasing does not spring from a sound conscience: why therefore excite toward yourself that evil passion? Why invite that to which you profess yourself a stranger? Secondly, because we ought not to open a way to temptations, which, by their instancy, sometimes achieve a wickedness which God expels from them who are His; (or,) at all events, put the spirit into a thorough tumult by presenting a stumbling-block to it. We ought indeed to walk so holily, and with so entire substantiality of faith, as to be confident and secure in regard of our own conscience, *desiring* that that gift may abide in us to the end, yet not *presuming* that it will. For he who presumes feels less apprehension; he who feels less apprehension takes less precaution; he who takes less precaution runs more risk.[21]

The purposes of all this were to mark off the handmaids of God from those of Satan, and to enable Christian women to set an example to the unsaved, to edify them, and to glorify God in their bodies and attire.[22]

---

19. Tertullian, *De cultu feminarum* 2.2 (ANF 4:19); the quotation is from 1 Cor 10:24; Phil 2:4.
20. Tertullian, *De cultu feminarum* 2.2 (ANF 4:19).
21. Tertullian, *De cultu feminarum* 2.2 (ANF 4:19); italics translator's.
22. Tertullian, *De cultu feminarum* 2.11.

Tertullian also addressed the assertion or excuse raised by some ladies to the effect that inner modesty is enough, and outer adornment is immaterial in God's eyes:

> Perhaps some woman will say: "To me it is not necessary to be approved by men; for I do not require the testimony of men:[23] God is the inspector of the heart."[24] *That* we all know; provided, however, we remember what the same God has said through the apostle: "Let your probity appear before men."[25] For what purpose, except that malice may have no access at all to you, or that you may be an example and testimony to the evil? Else, what is: "Let your works shine?"[26] Why, moreover, does the Lord call us the light of the world; why has He compared us to a city built upon a mountain;[27] if we do not shine in the midst of darkness, and stand eminent amid them who are sunk down? If you hide your lamp beneath a bushel,[28] you must necessarily be left quite in darkness, and be run against by many. The things which make us luminaries of the world are these—our good works. What is *good*, moreover, provided it be true and full, loves not darkness: it joys in being seen,[29] and exults over the very pointings which are made at it. To Christian modesty it is not enough to *be* so, but to *seem* so too.[30]

Although mostly about female believers, *On the Apparel of Women* does not forget Christian men. In agreement with Clement[31] and the *Didascalia*,[32] he stated that it is forbidden

> to cut the beard too sharply; to pluck it out here and there; to shave round about (the mouth); to arrange the hair, and disguise its hoariness by dyes; to remove all the incipient down all over the

---

23. John 5:34; 1 Cor 4:3.
24. 1 Sam 16:7; Jer 17:10; Luke 16:15.
25. Rom 12:17; 2 Cor 8:21; Phil 4:5.
26. Matt 5:16.
27. Matt 5:14.
28. Matt 5:15; Mark 4:21; Luke 8:16, 11:33.
29. John 3:21.
30. Tertullian, *De cultu feminarum* 2.13 (ANF 4:25). In ANF, the italicized "that" is within parentheses, but is not italicized. I removed unnecessary parentheses around some other words where they broke the continuity of the text. The other two italicized words are the translator's, not mine.
31. Clement of Alexandria, *Paedagogus* 3.3.
32. Connolly, *Didascalia apostolorum* 2.

MODESTY IN DRESS AND APPEARANCE

body; to fix each particular hair in its place with some womanly pigment; to smooth all the rest of the body by the aid of some rough powder or other: then, further, to take every opportunity for consulting the mirror; to gaze anxiously into it—while yet, when once the knowledge of God has put an end to all wish to please by means of voluptuous attraction, all these things are rejected as frivolous, as hostile to modesty.[33]

This would apply to the twenty-first century fad of men removing their chest and torso hair by waxing and similar procedures.

Around AD 210, Tertullian wrote *On the Pallium*, in which he exhorted Christian males against dressing the hair, cultivating the skin, consulting the mirror, gaudily dressing the neck, and effeminating the ear by piercing it.[34]

As Christian teachers, both Clement and Tertullian specifically condemned the wearing of gold and other jewelry (including that made of glass instead of precious stones),[35] rouge,[36] the ancient equivalent of mascara,[37] and bleaching or dyeing the hair[38] or clothing.[39] *Paedagogus*, *Stromata*, and *On the Apparel of Women* all forbade enhancing personal attractiveness by the use of ointments (the beauty creams of Christian antiquity).[40] The *Paedagogus* conceded God permitted unguents for medicinal purposes, but prohibited perfume.[41]

In the same era as Tertullian, a manual of Christian personal and community life, titled the *Didascalia*, was compiled in Syria. It decries some of the same practices in dress and bodily embellishment. Its main concern is that, by these means, women make themselves attractive to men other than their husbands, and men attractive to women other than their wives.

---

33. Tertullian, *De cultu feminarum* 2.8 (ANF 4:22).

34. Tertullian, *On the Pallium* 4.

35. Tertullian, *De cultu feminarum* 1.2, 1.6; Clement of Alexandria, *Paedagogus* 2, 13, 3.11; Connolly, *Didascalia apostolorum* 2.

36. Tertullian, *De cultu feminarum* 2.5; Clement of Alexandria, *Paedagogus* 3.2.

37. Tertullian, *De cultu feminarum* 1.2, 1.5; Clement of Alexandria, *Paedagogus* 3.2.

38. Tertullian, *De cultu feminarum* 2.6, 2.8; Clement of Alexandria, *Paedagogus* 2.8, 3.2–3.

39. Tertullian, *De cultu feminarum* 1.8; Clement of Alexandria, *Paedagogus* 2.11, 3.2.

40. Tertullian, *De cultu feminarum* 2.5; Clement of Alexandria, *Paedagogus* 2.8; Clement of Alexandria, *Stromata* 2.8.

41. Clement of Alexandria, *Stromata* 2.8.

The general Christian attitude was also disclosed by Clement's successor as principal or dean, Origen. Origen became the leading Bible scholar, teacher, and preacher of the first half of the third century, and influenced the church for centuries afterwards. His writings are especially valuable to us because he traveled much throughout the eastern Mediterranean as an expert on the faith at the request of local churches. In this way, he could observe and relate local views on modesty and immodesty, and what was the Christian consensus on them.

People and things are often better known or explained by observing what is associated with them. Three of Origen's Bible commentaries and sermons associate immodesty in the same class as fornication, uncontrolled rage, greed, and jealousy, which indicates the serious view Christians had of it.[42] His *Commentary on Romans* categorized it with deceit,[43] while his *Commentary on Titus* placed it in the same list as idolatry, witchcraft, and drunkenness.[44] Modesty itself, he preached, is akin to chastity and piety.[45]

A generation after Tertullian's death, Cyprian became pastor or bishop of his city. Cyprian was the leading churchman in northern Africa from Libya to the Atlantic and his influence spread to Europe and Asia Minor. In AD 252, he wrote *On Works and Alms*, in which he stated that wealthy Christian ladies are to anoint their eyes with good works and character instead of eye shadow.[46]

The foregoing were not the opinions only of self-appointed moralists who sought to impose a new practice on the church. Everyday laypeople incorporated the ethic into their lives, at least judging by the record of a martyrdom that took place in AD 202. Two Christian ladies were led into an arena to be mauled to death by a wild beast. Upon its first attack, one of them "fell on her loins; and when she saw her tunic torn from her side, she drew it over her as a veil for her middle, rather mindful of her modesty than her suffering."[47]

In short, the teaching that Christians exercise modesty by dressing as unpretentiously as possible and refraining from artificial enhancements

---

42. Origen, *Commentary on Romans* 5.9.9; Origen, *Commentary on Titus* in Pamphilus's *Apology for Origen* 31; Origen, *Homilies on Joshua* 8.6.
43. Origen, *Commentary on Romans* 5.9.9.
44. Origen, *Commentary on Titus*, Extract 31.
45. Origen, *Homilies on Joshua* 8.6.
46. Cyprian of Carthage, *De opere et eleemosynmis* 14.
47. *Passion of Perpetua and Felicitas* 6.3 (ANF 3:705).

of physical beauty dates back a long way in Christianity, right to the first century. Its ancient advocates were in good standing in the mainstream church, not members of small sects.

Although Clement's *Paedagogus* 2.12 and Tertullian's *On the Pallium* 5 forbade men to wear shoes, a prohibition no denomination today has adopted, this restraint does not appear in the other six authors,[48] nor even in Clement's *Stromata*. Even *The Paedagogus* 2.12 permits shoes to men in some circumstances. The same chapter regards footwear as always mandatory for female Christians. Tertullian banned only some types of shoes in *De Spectaculis* 23, not all footwear. The *Didascalia* proscribed only certain styles,[49] such as those that resembled those of prostitutes.[50] Here is another fashion that has reemerged in our own time. While shoes could be dispensed with in the Nile Delta, where Clement lived and wrote, it was impractical further north, where the others composed their books.

---

48. Paul the Apostle, Aristides, Apollonius, Cyprian, the author of *The Didascalia*, and the author of *The Passion of Perpetua and Felicitas*.

49. Connolly, *Didascalia apostolorum* 2–3.

50. Connolly, *Didascalia apostolorum* 3.

Chapter 36

Mutilate Yourself (Matt 18:8–9)

In Matthew 18:8–9, Christ commands:

> if thy hand or thy foot offend thee, cut them off, and cast them from thee: it is better for thee to enter into life halt or maimed, rather than having two hands or two feet to be cast into everlasting fire. And if thine eye offend thee, pluck it out, and cast it from thee: it is better for thee to enter into life with one eye, rather than having two eyes to be cast into hell fire.

How could anyone obey these injunctions literally, especially in the days before anesthetics and antiseptics, when they would result in death by either blood loss or infection?

Solutions to the stark harshness of a literal application were provided by Origen, an Egyptian who was the foremost Christian Bible scholar and teacher of the first half of the third century AD. People in the second century indicate that he was correct.

Origen cited Matthew 18:8–9 as a prime example of biblical injunctions that are impossible or unreasonable. He taught that the Holy Spirit placed such difficulties in the Scriptures in order to teach readers and interpreters not to confine themselves to the plain, literal wording, but to examine the passage more closely, to unveil the deeper meaning.[1]

Origen taught that the underlying message the Holy Spirit intended readers to draw from the text was that the parts of the body represent members of a Christian's family or circle of friends:

---

1. Origen, *On First Principles* 4.1.18.

it is possible to apply these words to our nearest kinsfolk, being considered to be our members of our bodies, because of the close relationship; whether by birth, or from habitual friendship. We must not spare them if they are injuring our soul. Let us cut off from ourselves as a hand or a foot or an eye, a father or mother who wishes us to do that which is contrary to piety, and a son or daughter who would have us revolt from the church of Christ and the love of Him. Even if the wife of our bosom, or a friend who is kindred in soul, become stumbling-blocks to us, let us not spare them, but let us cut them out from ourselves, and cast them outside of our soul, as not being truly our kindred but enemies of our salvation; for "whosoever hates not his father, and mother," etc. (Luke 14:26). We must hate them as enemies and assailants, that we may be able to win Christ, and be worthy of the Son of God. A lame person, so to speak, is saved when he has lost a foot—say a brother—and alone obtains the inheritance of the kingdom of God; and a maimed person is saved, when his parents are not saved, but they perish, while he is separated from them, and he alone obtains the blessings.[2]

Origen traveled throughout eastern Christendom at the request of local bishops as a theological expert. Although familiar with widespread Christian practice and with local variations, he never indicated that believers in some geographical areas or sects actually did amputate their hands, feet, or eyes.

A common lack of body parts among Christians in ancient times could not escape notice and comment by even the most casual observer as a common feature among Christians. We possess the accounts by the pagan Pliny the Younger around AD 112, and most of the attack on Christianity half a century later by the pagan philosopher Celsus. Pliny was Roman governor in Turkey, part of whose job was to detect and persecute Christians. His letter to the Emperor[3] described Christian faith and practices in some detail, but never mentioned self-mutilation. In his comprehensive denunciation of Christian behavior, Celsus would have jumped at the chance to ridicule voluntary destruction of body organs, or suicide by exsanguination or infection.

Justin Martyr wrote defenses of Christian beliefs and practices in the middle of the second century AD. Among other topics, he dealt with the pagan wish that Christians commit suicide rather than continue to bother

2. Origen, *Commentary on Matthew* 13:25 (ANF 10:489).
3. Pliny the Younger, *Letter* 10.96.

the world by their presence and preaching.[4] If believers of this period did indeed chop off their extremities, Justin would not have failed to mention that Christians did in fact court death, fulfilling the pagan hope.

Although we have tens of thousands of Christian denominations, ministries, sects, cults, divisions, and church parties in our own day, not one advocates self-mutilation in obedience to Matthew 18:8–9. Either all historic and contemporary Christianity has been heretical, or Jesus intended that not all his sayings be applied literally.

---

4. Justin Martyr, *2 Apology* 4.

Chapter 37

Nighttime Activities

NIGHT is a blessed time, a period that God wants us to spend in special activities. Both Scripture and the earliest postbiblical Christian writings encourage that our nighttime concerns be different from those of the working day. These two sources of faith and practice also show how ancient are the hours of prayer still practiced by nuns and other persons under religious vows.

Jesus himself remarked: "We must work the works of Him who sent me, while it is day; night comes, when no one can work" (John 9:4). This does not mean that Christians must be idle at night. Rather, God has provided in Scripture and the writings of its first heirs that we should relax from our daily toil and mundane concerns so that we will have time for activities that bring us closer to him and improve our spiritual lives.

Both the Bible and the early church fathers refer to a number of such kinds of activities. First of all, we should use the night for prayer. We should pray at all times, but especially during the hours of darkness. In Psalms, King David said that the Lord's song was with him at night, and his life was a prayer to God (41:8). Also in Scripture, the deuterocanonical book of Judith mentions that the people of her town called on God all night long when a disaster seemed certain. In 2 Maccabees 13:10, God's people were commanded to pray at night as well as the day to avert a danger threatening them and their religion. Later still, in a manual for Christians, Bishop Hippolytus in central Italy around AD 217 mentioned the custom of praying just before going to bed and of rising at midnight to pray, as some monks and nuns do to this day. In Tunisia about the same time, the church father Tertullian mentioned rising at night to pray as a standard Christian practice.

We should also use the night to praise God. David again in Scripture says "It is good to give thanks to the Lord, to sing praises to thy name, O Most High; to declare . . . thy faithfulness by night" (Ps 91:1-2). This reminds us of the prophet Isaiah's personal practice of yearning for and seeking God at night (Isaiah 26:9). Around the 190s AD, the church father Clement of Alexandria in Egypt, dean of the Christianity's foremost educational institution of the day, also recommended rising at night to praise God—as some monks and nuns still do. According to a tradition or legend related by Hippolytus, at midnight the angels and all nature stand still for a moment to praise God, which is one reason why we too should do so.

Praise also entails singing. King David, often called "the Sweet Singer of Israel" (2 Sam 23:1), had the Lord's song with him at night (Ps 41:8), and sang praises and declared God's faithfulness at this time (Ps 91:1-2).

Night is also a time for Bible study, an exercise we often have time to pursue only after the affairs of our busy days have come to an end. Clement advised waking at night to read and study. Origen, Clement's successor as dean and, in his own right, the most prominent father of the eastern church, urged that we meditate on the Bible at night as well as by day; since the daylight hours are not enough for taking in the full import of any passage, the night also is added. A few years later in Palestine, during the great persecution of Christians between AD 249 and 251, he commended those who nevertheless searched deeply into the Scriptures by persistent effort and uninterrupted nightly vigils, because Christians, Origen said, should not sleep while the devil is awake.

Even before Origen's time, Tertullian regarded nightly meetings of Christians as well-established practice. Around AD 202, he spoke of them as occurring so regularly that they posed problems in families where one spouse was not a Christian. In the same vein, he mentioned all-night Easter vigils.

In addition, night is a time to remember. Remembering is a natural exercise when life slows to its nighttime pace, especially at the time the authors of the Bible and early church fathers wrote, a time when there were no electric lights and remembering was one of the few things that could be done in the sparse glow of flickering candles and tiny oil lamps. In praising God's name and law, David, in the longest chapter of the Bible, sang that he earnestly remembered God's name during the night (Ps 118:55). Another early authority, which may have been written even before the Gospel of Matthew, also commented on nighttime remembering, in this instance as it relates to Christian clergy.

The greatest religious activity we have today had its beginning at night, which shows God's special concern for the period between sunset and sunrise. Those who study the Bible or at least pay attention during services of Holy Communion will recall that the Eucharist was instituted at night (Matt 26:20–29; Mark 14:17–25; 1 Cor 11:23–26). Today, this is the most repeated sacrament and the main nourisher of our souls. When Jesus instituted it, it was in a setting that harked back to the much earlier spiritual practice of commemorating God's grace and mighty deeds in freeing the Israelites from Egyptian slavery, an exodus that also took place at night.

But good things come to an end or are at least hedged with exceptions. Because our Lord is an understanding God and wants us to attend to all our needs, Christians are permitted to engage in tasks at night and on Sundays that are not spiritual in nature, even though we should devote nights, Sundays, and church festivals (as much as is feasible) to alternative, soul-building activities. Recall Luke 2:8, which records that the shepherds on the night of Christ's birth were watching their flocks in the dark. It would have been harmful to allow the sheep to roam unattended all night. Proverbs 31 describes the model housewife as one who rises before dawn to provide food for her family and give instructions to her household staff. This is repeated as being desirable for Christian women as well in a third-century Syrian church manual. Moreover, Proverbs 31:18 says "Her lamp does not go out at night."

The editor of this essay, when it was first published, asked me to include material about sleep, something everybody of every religion associates with nighttime. There is surprisingly little material about sleep in the early sources, and what little there is reveals a split between one ancient author and the rest. This difference illustrates the criteria of what is to be regarded as authority in religion.

Clement counselled Christians to sleep as little as possible, to be awake most of the night, to sleep in such a way as to be easily awakened, and to avoid sleeping, especially not in the daytime. Much less extreme, Proverbs 20:13 and 24:33–34 condemn love of sleep and warn that too much of it will lead to poverty. On the other hand, other verses of Scripture regard sleep as a gift from God (Ps 3:5; 4:8; 126:2; Eccl 5:11–12; Sir 31). Even Proverbs itself, at 3:21–24, recommends the study of wisdom and discretion so that a person's sleep will be sweet. One early Christian advocated self-control in sleep, not unreasonable abstinence from it. Except for Clement, excessive sleep is to be avoided while at the same time we must fulfill biological necessity.

The fact that Clement was alone in such extreme sentiments, and the fact that they are totally peculiar in light of other authors and of essential natural processes, illustrates an important aspect of the nature of early authors as a spiritual authority: we listen to the church fathers only when they agree and speak together in unison. We are to follow the consensus in Scripture and early Christian writers, and not count as authoritative the ideas of one who goes off on a weird tangent of his own.

Besides other activities in the hours of darkness, God wants us to get a good night's sleep, and the Scriptures indicate how we can do this. As above, Proverbs 3:21–24 promise sweet sleep to those who study wisdom and discretion. Ecclesiastes 5:11–12 and Sirach 31:19–20 warn against overeating as a hindrance to falling asleep. Elsewhere, Sirach says worry and anxiety about money cause insomnia (31:1–2), as does worry over a daughter (42:9). Instead, we should trust to the care and providence of God: when we go to bed at night we should remember that God will protect us (Ps 3:5 and 4:8) and give us peace and sleep (Ps 126:2). Before we climb into bed, we should pray, as Hippolytus recommended.

Because this chapter was originally written for a Roman Catholic magazine, the numbering of the Psalms is that of the Septuagint and Latin Vulgate Old Testaments.

Chapter 38

Patience

The good health of faith and the soundness of the Lord's discipline do not accrue easily to any person unless patience sits by his side. Patience is so set over the things of God that a person can obey no precept, fulfil no work well-pleasing to the Lord, if distant from it. The good of it, even they who live outside it honour with the name of highest virtue.

—Tertullian *On Patience* 1

How can a person train him/herself to be patient and thus wait for God's perfect timing? How can a Christian produce and increase the virtue of patience in their daily walk with the Lord? Written in the early 240s AD, Origen's *Commentary on Saint Paul's Epistle to the Romans* contains many ideas and pointers on how to foster and develop patience. The virtue of patience, Origen wrote, does not come all at once into a Christian's makeup nor is it acquired just because the Christian wills him/herself to be a patient person. Although the will is indeed necessary and must precede actual patience in a person, patience comes only after much effort, watchfulness, training, and practice. There may be lapses during this patience-building endeavor. It is like acquiring wisdom or chastity. Merely willing oneself to be chaste does not make a Christian totally chaste, i.e., free from temptations to lust. We must pick ourselves up after each lapse and must resume working at become chaste or patient.

Seeming calamities in one's life, continues the *Commentary on Romans*, help foster patience in one's Christian walk. Losses, illnesses, and bodily afflictions in righteous people enable them to build up the virtue, because misfortunes train them to resist their desires to be impatient or unchaste by harnessing their lust or impatience, keeping in check excesses of Christian liberty, and destroying other desires opposed to self-control.

In interpreting Romans 12:12 ("Be joyful in hope, patient in affliction") the commentary reveals a link between such joyfulness and hope. The Christian who is joyful in hope does not absorb him/herself in the present world, but remembers that "our present sufferings are not worth comparing with the glory that will be revealed in us" (Rom 8:18), and so is therefore patient in affliction because s/he knows they will be soon past them and subsequently rewarded. Indeed, "keep looking to the currently unseen world of heaven rather than the currently seen world here below"[1] is a frequent theme in Origen's writings. Patience, says the commentary, helps conform a soul to the future world.

More specific means of acquiring patience comes from other early Christian authors, such as by imitating Christians who are already patient. James 5:10 tells us to take the Old Testament prophets as "an example of patience." Polycarp, a pastor-bishop in Turkey who had associated with the apostle John, cited as examples both the apostles and the saints of his own time that are not mentioned in the Bible, thus indicating that we can be edified by the examples of Christians of our own day. Another exercise in developing patience is merely listening with attention while the Bible is being read during a church service, instead of engaging in private conversations in the pews, as Origen noted in a sermon preached at about the same time he wrote the *Commentary on Romans*.

Citing Romans 12:2, Origen prescribed renewing one's mind. He said this is accomplished through training and meditating on the word of God and proper interpretation of God's commandments. By reading the Scriptures every day, a Christian makes daily progress and acquires greater knowledge and understanding, and the soul is daily renewed. Because some individuals are mentally deficient, Origen wrote that not all minds are capable of being renewed to the point of understanding all knowledge. However, he wrote, all Christians can be renewed to faith, self-control, and patience.

---

1. Origen, *Against Celsus* 6.20; Origen, *Commentary on Matthew* 12.23; Origen, *Commentary on Romans* 2.13.21, 7.5.6; Origen, *De Principiis* 4.1.37; *Homilies on Genesis* 16.6; *Homilies on Leviticus* 7.6.2; *Homilies on Psalm 36* 2.8, 4.6.

Tertullian wrote that we should develop patience by remembering and living out the Beatitudes (Matt 5:3–12; Luke 6:20–23) in our lives outside church:

> For whom but the patient has the Lord called happy, in saying, "Blessed are the poor in spirit, for theirs is the kingdom of heaven"? No one, assuredly, is "poor in spirit," except the humble. Well, who is humble, unless he is patient? For no one can abase himself without patience, to bear the act of abasement. "Blessed," says He, "are those who weep and mourn." Who, without patience, is tolerant of such unhappinesses? And so, to such "comfort" and "laughter" are promised. "Blessed are the meek": under this term, surely, the impatient cannot possibly be classed. Again, when He calls peacemakers the "sons of God," we ask whether the impatient have any affinity with "peace." Even a fool may perceive that. When, however, He says, "Rejoice and be glad, because great is your reward in heaven," of course it is not to the impatience of exultation that He makes that promise; because no one will "be glad" in adversities unless he has first learned to disdain them, no one will disdain them unless he has learned to practice patience.[2]

Like Origen (first in Egypt, then in Palestine), Tertullian was a church father (in Tunisia). Tertullian wrote the above quotes around AD 200, a generation earlier than Origen, but their message is the same. Origen was particularly well placed to represent the Christian consensus on the subject of patience because he was he was dean of the world's foremost Christian educational institution and later of the first Christian university, and traveled widely throughout the eastern Mediterranean basin in response to requests by pastor-bishops as a theological consultant.

How can you tell whether you lack patience and are taking things into your own hands rather than waiting for and trusting God? According to Tertullian, you can know by examining what you wish to accomplish (your goal) and the means by which you plan to accomplish that goal. We are possessed by sinful impatience if the goal or the method violates Christian precepts or principles. For instance, we must not plan to take revenge to right an injustice done to us, but must be patient enough to wait for God to avenge it for us in his own due time.[3]

---

2. *On Patience* 11.

3. Lev 19:18; Deut 32:35; Rom 12:19; Tertullian, *On Patience* 8, 10, 15.

Chapter 39

Praying Without Ceasing

ACCORDING to the four Gospels, Jesus spent much time in prayer, frequently withdrawing from his apostles for this very purpose. His example should lead Christians to heed the Revised Standard Version of 1 Thessalonians 5:17, which exhorts readers to "pray constantly." In the King James Version it is "pray without ceasing." The Greek text has the same shade of meaning as the King James.

It is impossible to pray without ceasing and carry on the indispensable activities of daily life if we interpret "pray" to mean kneeling or standing motionless while talking to God and focusing only on him. The same problem occurred to Origen. He commented in his *Homilies on Samuel* that if this be the only meaning of "prayer," then anyone who tries to "pray without ceasing" will die of starvation or dehydration because eating and drinking would interrupt the prayer. First Thessalonians 5:17 would likewise forbid sleep. How can anyone pray without stopping? Did the apostle who urged constant prayer demand the impossible?

Origen formulated a solution in his *Treatise on Prayer* around AD 235, and in *Homilies on Samuel* five years later. The sermons inform us that a prayer is not interrupted by any action done in the service of God, nor by an act or word done or said in accordance with his will. As long as we perform our daily activities to the glory of God, we are praying constantly. As proof, Origen cited the prayer of Hannah in 1 Samuel 2:1–10. The Bible applies the term "prayer" to all that Hannah spoke, even though not all of it is speaking to God. Sometimes she refers to God as "he" or by one of his titles, and otherwise in the third person. She even says "Talk no more so exceeding proudly; let not arrogance come out of your mouth" (1 Sam 2:3

KJV)—something a human being would hardly say to the Almighty, particularly in a prayer. Yet during her discourse, said Origen, all her thoughts and words were for the glory of God, which indicates that the Bible must mean something other than solemnly speaking to the Lord while stock still. Prayer consists of all words and deeds spoken or performed in justice and in obedience to God's commandments—something Christians should never cease doing. As long as we speak and act in accordance with the divine will, said Origen, we are praying. When we do or think unjustly or sin, we cease praying.

Origen expressed the same thought with fewer words at *On Prayer* 12: if we count all good works and all obedience to God as part of prayer, a good person never stops praying. The only way we can pray without ceasing is to constantly practice our faith.

Chapter 40

Pride

MANY Scripture passages condemn pride. For instance, Proverbs 16:5 says "The Lord detests all the proud of heart," 16:18 says "Pride goes before destruction, a haughty spirit before a fall," and Romans 12:16 says "Do not be proud, but be willing to associate with people of low position. Do not be conceited." In 1 Corinthians 13:4, the apostle Paul tells us that love "is not proud." Wisdom, says Proverbs 8:13, hates "pride and arrogance." All these quotations are from the New International Version. Other translations use other words for pride, such as "haughty," "arrogant," "glory," "conceit," "self-glory," etc., or rephrase the verse and use the word "boast." There are also Job 40:11–12, Psalms 10:4, Proverbs 3:34, 8:13, 11:2, 15:25, 21:4, 29:23, Ecclesiastes 7:8, Jeremiah 13:15, Ezekiel 16:49, Mark 7:22, Romans 11:20, and 2 Timothy 3:2. Second Timothy 3:5 even instructs Christians to avoid and have nothing to do with proud people. Both James 4:6 and 1 Peter 5:5 tell us that "God opposes the proud."

There is a problem when we notice that the apostle Paul sometimes approved of pride and even was proud himself. The NIV quotes him as saying to the Corinthians "I take great pride in you" (2 Cor 7:4) and that he was giving them "an opportunity to take pride in us" (2 Cor 5:12), and to the Galatians (6:4) that "Each one should test his own actions. Then he can take pride in himself." The more literal Revised Standard Version translates the relevant words of Romans 15:17 as "I have reason to be proud of my work for God," 1 Corinthians 15:31 as "I protest, brethren, by my pride in you which I have in Christ Jesus," 2 Corinthians 1:14 as "you can be proud of us as we can be of you," and Philippians 2:16 as "so that in the day of Christ I may be proud that I did not run in vain or labor in vain."

How do we reconcile the clear teaching of many Scripture writers against the total opposite attitude elsewhere in the Bible?

The answer was provided by the church father Origen. A Scripture interpreter, preacher, and teacher from an early age, he wrote more about the Bible and Christian faith than anyone else before Martin Luther. Origen was better poised than any other church father before AD 250 to represent the consensus of early Christian teaching on pride, because he traveled frequently throughout the eastern Mediterranean basin as a theological consultant at the invitation of local pastor-bishops. Remember that the church of his day still possessed oral memories of Jesus and the apostles, which handed down his interpretations and explanations of the written Scriptures.

Origen resolved the seeming contradiction in the Bible when he preached against pride in a sermon in the 240s AD. His *Homilies on Jeremiah* 12.8.1–3 naturally condemned people who are proud that they have relatives who are in government or are otherwise important in a worldly sense, have power over other people, hold a high position, are wealthy, or possess a beautiful home or lands. However, he also chastised people who are proud for what seems a good reason to Christians: wisdom, chastity, and having borne chains for Christ. Origen said Christians should not be proud even of these. He mentioned that Paul had similar reasons to be proud: visions and revelations (2 Cor 12:1; Acts 16:9–10, 18:9), signs, wonders and miracles (Rom 15:17–19; 2 Cor 12:12), and ambition to preach the gospel in communities where Christ was previously unknown (Rom 15:20). According to 2 Corinthians 12:9, he was even proud about his weaknesses! Paul had reason to be proud also because he planted many churches in Turkey and Greece, and because of his sufferings on behalf of the gospel. Yet, said Origen, God strongly disapproved of such pride in Paul and took measures to counteract or balance it.

Origen reminded his congregation that God also gave Paul a thorn in the flesh, a demon from Satan to torment the apostle and thus dampen down any tendency toward pride. Paul three times asked the Lord to remove it but he refused, telling Paul that it was to remind him that he was and should be totally dependent on God's grace (2 Cor 12:7–9). That which comes by grace is no cause for pride, because God is the source and the means to any accomplishment. Paul was no exception, said Origen, to God's rule against pride.

In violation of many passages of Scripture, Paul may have drifted into pride, and even have encouraged others to be proud, but this does not mean God approved of it. All Christians have weaknesses, and Paul's was pride. We must follow the consensus of all the Bible writers rather than the lapse of one man. Paraphrasing 1 Corinthians 11:1, we should follow Paul's example only to the extent that he followed Christ's. The Bible is clear that we should curb our own pride before God, in his disciplining love, sends thorns in our own flesh to counteract it.

Chapter 41

Renewal

Starting Again

Romans 12:2: "Be not conformed to this world: but be ye transformed by the renewing of your mind, that ye may prove what is that good, and acceptable, and perfect, will of God."

Ephesians 4:23–24: "Be renewed in the spirit of your mind . . . put on the new man, which after God is created in righteousness and true holiness."

It is not enough to start the Christian life only once. Christians must repeatedly start again, being renewed by oneself or God.

The first start takes place in dying to sin and being buried with Christ in baptism, and raised to newness of life. Newness of life involves putting away the former sinful person and their sins, and putting on the new person, whom God has "renewed in knowledge after the image of him that created him" (Col 3:10). To do this, we must "put off all these: anger, wrath, malice, blasphemy, filthy communication out of your mouth. Lie not one to another, seeing that ye have put off the old man with his deeds" (Col 3:8–9).

A prominent church scholar of the first half of the third century continued on this theme. Origen wrote in his *Commentary on St. Paul's Letter to the Romans*, in 5.8.10–14 and 9.1.8–13, that renewing yourself once is not enough. The Christian must restart his efforts, being constantly renewed from day to day, to the extent that there is never a time when our newness does not increase. Christians ought always to be starting again on their spiritual journey. We are always to be renewing our minds, progressively transforming them to make them gradually more suitable for the heavenly world to come.

Origen wrote that we perform this by daily dying to sin, and reading the Scriptures and absorbing their wisdom, and meditating on them, delving ever deeper into their full, spiritual meaning. Such study is to become a habit, and new and fresh every day, so that our spiritual understanding increases. We must discard our old ways of pride, greed, lying, and slander, and adopt or readopt virtues such as patience, gentleness, faith, mercy, self-control, and truthfulness, so that virtues and good works fill our minds.

This scholar and teacher said Christians ought to be renewed enough to absorb the full measure of spiritual knowledge and wisdom so that they will not be deceived or led astray. The way to do this is to test (or prove) everything to determine what is the "good, and acceptable, and perfect, will of God" (Rom 12:2). We develop the ability to test by renewing—or starting afresh—our grasp of spiritual knowledge and enlightenment as to the will of God.

Chapter 42

Second Coming

Preparing for the Second Coming

How can we prepare for the second coming of Christ? At first sight, this appears difficult or impossible because nobody knows the day or hour he will come (Matt 24:32, 36–39, 25:13; Mark 13:32), and normal life will continue as usual until the last moment (Matt 24:38–39). However, early Christianity provided a plain answer: we are to continue to live good Christian lives as preparation every day, whether we believe the Lord will return this afternoon or in the distant future.

In discussing the second coming, 2 Peter 3 exhorts Christians to always "live holy and godly lives . . . and . . . make every effort to be found spotless, blameless and at peace" (vv. 12, 14). We must not scoff at the prospect or likelihood of Jesus' return (v. 3).

We must bravely endure any persecution and other attacks against Christianity, standing firm to the very end (Matt 10:22, 24:13; Mark 13:13; 2 Thess 2.15). Related to endurance and standing firm are the counsels to be watchful and on guard in Matthew 24:42, 25:13; Mark 13:23, 33 and 37; and Luke 21:36. A Christian source outside the received Scriptures is the *Didache*, which may have been written before Matthew's Gospel; it too exhorts to watch and be ready at all times.

We must be particularly vigilant against deceivers and false prophets (Matt 24:11; 2 Pet 3:17), who pretend to know more than everybody else about the second coming, with the implication that they enjoy some special relationship with or influence over it. They will perform seeming signs and miracles, and will hoodwink many believers into following them instead of Jesus (2 Thess 2:9–10; *Didache*). Some will even pretend to be the Messiah (Matt 24:5; Luke 21:8), or to know his exact geographical location (Matt 24:23–26; Mark 13:21–22).

In all this preparation, we are to remain calm and level-headed, not becoming upset or alarmed (Matt 24:6; Mark 13:7; Luke 21:9; 2 Thess 2:2).

The foregoing behavior applies both to a Christian as an individual and to whole congregations of believers, because it entails no more than following God's commandments—as we should be doing anyway. Other preparation for the last days can be fulfilled only by a group of Christians together, or must at least involve more than one person.

Matthew 7:1, Luke 6:37, Romans 14:13, and James 4:11–12 teach that individual Christians are not to judge other people. This applies in our ordinary lives, but the apostle Paul indicates that it especially applies as part of preparing for the Lord's return: "judge nothing before the time, until the Lord come, who both will bring to light the hidden things of darkness, and will make manifest the counsels of the heart" (1 Cor 4:5). When it becomes essential for congregational leaders to judge backsliders for the good of the Christian community, the church father Tertullian wrote in AD 197 that they are to take as their model the last judgment, by Christ and his saints, with the same seriousness and fairness.

In a description for pagan readers about the new Christian community, Tertullian narrated that believers habitually "assemble to read our sacred writings, if any peculiarity of the times makes either forewarning or reminiscence needful."[1] This would include what the Bible says about the last days. In its chapter on the end times, the *Didache* warns: "often shall ye come together, seeking the things which are befitting to your souls: for the whole time of your faith will not profit you, if ye be not made perfect in the last time."[2] At these gatherings, we are especially to encourage and comfort one another with Paul's description of what will happen in the last days (1 Thess 4:13–18).

There are four additional activities involving more than one Christian by which we are to prepare for the second coming. First, we must preach the gospel to all nations (Matt 24:14, 28:19; Mark 13:10, 16:15). The second was voiced by Origen, who exhorted his congregation to think and talk about Christ's second coming as much as about his birth and resurrection. Thus,

---

1. Tertullian, *Apology* 39 (ANF 3:46).
2. *Didache* 16.2 (ANF 7:382).

Christians who take time off work to hold joyous festivities for Christmas and Easter should by rights have a public holiday and special church services anticipating his second coming as well.

Thirdly, Origen formulated a symbolic and moral significance to the bells on the high priest's robe, which were always tinkling (Exod 28:31–35). This teaches, preached Origen, that we are never to be silent about the end times but should always discuss and speak about them. By remembering our last end in this manner, we will never sin.

Origen also composed the first text of Christian systematic theology, titled *On First Principles*. In the chapter on the end of the world, he cautioned readers to treat the subject with care and caution, as a matter of discussion and further exploration among Christians, rather than as cut-and-dried. Allowing no scope for intolerance or dogmatism, Origen would discountenance religious groups in his or our day that arrogantly claim they alone possess the only correct interpretation of Bible prophecies about the end times, and damn and exclude Christians that do not agree with them. There should be room for dialogue when talking about the second coming.

Because the best preparation for the last days is living an upright and pure Christian life—as we are obliged to do anyway—we must spend the time allotted us in brotherly love, cooperation in good works, toleration in nonessentials, sharing the gospel with unbelievers, and watching out for and warning one another when we encounter a false prophet or deceiver who would mislead us and them about the last days.

In short, we should follow Paul's advice at the conclusion of one of his passages on the second coming: "Brethren, stand fast, and hold the traditions which ye have been taught, whether by word, or our epistle" (2 Thess 2:15).

Chapter 43

Self-Correction

THE early undivided church advocated self-correction, i.e., examining one's own life for sins and failings, and then taking measures to correct them (Matt 3:2, 4:17; Luke 13:3, 5; Heb 12:1). This means more than just recalling individual sins; it includes knowing oneself and one's weaknesses, and searching for ways to avoid vices and prevent sinning again (1 Cor 9:27). It may even involve obtaining the continuing help of another Christian (Heb 13:17).

Self-correction and true repentance, Origen taught his students, benefits one's soul. As Christians, we do justice to our spiritual lives by turning inward and rendering frank evaluations of our own lives and behavior. We must endeavor to know ourselves, and be so at home with ourselves that we know our moral strengths and weaknesses, and what causes us as individuals to sin. Origen taught that this was a practical application of the principle "know yourself" (2 Cor 13:5; 1 Thess 4:4), which he considered to be the highest practical achievement of Greek philosophers, who were still widely quoted and followed in his day before Christianity became the majority religion. To succeed in the Christian life, Origen taught, we must hold up a mirror to ourselves and see our failings and weaknesses in it (Jas 1:23–24), and hopefully see a reflection of God as well (2 Cor 3:18).

Origen was an important preacher and teacher at prominent Christian educational institutions in the first half of the third century AD, where he imparted higher spiritual knowledge, such as that summarized in the paragraph above.

Origen wrote a text on the first principles of Christianity. In it he said that, in order to receive more blessings from God, we must first come to a knowledge of ourselves and learn what are our character flaws and defects, and what vices we most commonly fall into (Num 32:23). To do this completely, a Christian may even need to find a knowledgable member of the church, a spiritual advisor, who is especially qualified in the oversight and reconciliation of the soul with God, who can make up both for the Christian's deficiencies and failure to spot their own shortcomings (Ps 32:5; Matt 7:3–5; Heb 13:17).

Origen compared escaping vices, or taking care of the health of one's soul, to taking care of the health of the body. If we are not aware of a sickness or weakness, we do not know we are sick and will not seek a physician (Matt 9:12; Mark 2:17; Luke 5:31). Put another way, if we are not first aware of our sinfulness and spiritual defects and do not admit them to ourselves as individuals, we will not repent and thus will not continue to be forgiven. The Christian may even incorrectly believe s/he is always free from sin and in no need of any correction or repentance. This leads to spiritual pride and failure to acknowledge that only God is the source of righteousness and blessings (Luke 14:11). The Christian will thus not repent, and thereby fall into spiritual ruin. Without the discipline of self-correction, such a person loses the humility and simplicity God requires. Hence, I think, comes the need for a spiritual advisor knowledgable in the remedies provided by Jesus as the Great Physician.

Origen's books and sermons are full of exhortations to be watchful for one's soul, to guard against sin, to be alert to God's will, and to study the Scriptures in order to find one's duties and failings (Ps 1:2; Mark 13:37; 1 Cor 16:13; 1 Thess 5:6; 2 Tim 4:5). He encouraged constant self-correction and avoiding vices by unceasing vigilance over one's soul and behavior. Origen openly stated that this involves struggles with the devil, acquiring spiritually healthy habits, dogged perseverance in Christian life and virtues, and correcting sins as soon as they are detected. This was all to be centered on one's own soul, without attention to the failings of other people. Nor did Origen grant any room for comparing oneself to other Christians in order to rationalize that s/he was not as sinful as they (Luke 18:10–14).

In the 190s AD, Origen's own teacher also considered spiritual self-improvement to involve a gradual process. Although a person is steeped in sin, wrote Clement of Alexandria, it is possible to correct one's mistakes by increasing love and true repentance. Although it is possible for a repentant sinner who has led a dissolute life to overcome a long history of sin, the process requires continuing effort. In the same way that a body that has been afflicted with a protracted disease needs special attention (1 Tim 5:23), so a Christian cannot eliminate sinful tendencies all at once, instead requiring constant care and the help of God and the church (2 Cor 5:20; 1 Tim 3:2), prayer, and sincere repentance. For this purpose, Clement recommended submitting oneself to a more mature or more advanced Christian as a spiritual advisor, such as a godly pastor (Heb 13:7, 17). Under such an arrangement, we in effect freely open ourselves to criticisms and suggestions by the advisor (Ps 32:5). This is completely voluntary on the part of the person being criticized, an extension of self-correction. It is a world away from self-appointed busybodies looking high and low for conduct to criticize in others. Unlike them, spiritual advisors have knowledge of the subject, know what they talk about, and have the best interests of our souls at heart.

Instead of waiting to be criticized and being the involuntary subject of unbidden negative comments about one's behavior and character, we as Christians should first criticize ourselves and mend our ways, before our moral failings become a source of public comment. If we cannot discover our own failings, we as Christians should resort to a spiritual advisor.

Lastly, we must remember Christ's own words in Matthew 7:3–5 and Luke 6:41–42, that we should concentrate on eliminating our own faults and trespasses instead of looking to find fault in others.

Chapter 44

The Sick

You Too Can Make the Sick Better

LIKE Jesus, you can cure the sick or make them better. This truth is based not only on one possible interpretation of the Bible among many, but was shared by Christians that lived so early that they—or Christians not long earlier—knew the writers of the New Testament personally and could ask them for clarifications about or explanations of what they had written.

No doubt all readers of the present book are familiar with Christ's command in Matthew 10:7–8 and Luke 10:9 that missionaries and other traveling preachers are to cure the sick before telling them that the kingdom of God is near. Fewer readers will have heard of a writing from a minority of early Christians called the Gospel of Thomas. Although different from the majority of the four Gospels in many ways, it repeats the commandment and extends it to all who travel. Indeed, Mark 16:18 widens the power of healing to all who truly believe.

Christian healings continued after the first century. Irenaeus, a pastor in France, mentioned them as still current in the 180s AD.[1] So did Clement in Egypt, dean of the world's foremost Christian school in the next decade.[2] So also did the church father Tertullian in Tunisia early in the third century.[3]

Clement's successor as dean was Origen, who recorded in the late 240s that "traces" of the gifts of the Holy Spirit, including curing the sick,

---

1. Irenaeus, *Against Heresies* 2.32.4.
2. Clement of Alexandria, *Eclogae propheticae* 16.
3. *De Spectaculis* 29; see also *Against Marcion* 5.8.

remained in the church.[4] Although still occurring, they were apparently less common than in apostolic times.

Besides healings, Origen considered among the gifts of the Spirit to be "a marvellous meekness of spirit and a complete change of character."[5] He thought physical healing to be less important and less indicative of the working of the Holy Spirit than works of mercy and love. Even if you cannot perform a cure, you too can perform such works.

A chief way of helping the ill is to visit them. Remember Christ's teaching in Matthew 25:34–39 that it is deeds of love and mercy—such as feeding the hungry, visiting prisoners, and looking after the sick—that will be rewarded in heaven. This agrees with Matthew 7:21–23, where Christ says that performing miracles does not replace such works. What we do for the least sick person we do for Christ (Matt 25:40). Visiting might not cure the patient but it can make their symptoms less uncomfortable, making their lives better, although not perfect.

Visiting the sick was strongly encouraged in early Christianity. Clement quoted Matthew 25:34–40 to remind Christians of this duty in the 190s.[6] Tertullian spoke of it as one desirable fruit of a happy Christian marriage.[7] Another ancient Christian writing considered it a very serious duty.[8]

Shortly before AD 249, *Three Books of Testimonies* 109 classed visiting the sick to be among such important Christian activities as forgiving sins, helping the poor, loving enemies, and the golden rule itself—which indicates that Christians held visiting the sick in the highest regard. The author repeated Matthew 25:36 and quoted an earlier author: "Be not slack to visit the sick man; for from these things thou shalt be strengthened in love" (Sir 7:35).

It is particularly appropriate for ministers to visit the sick. James 5:14 instructs church officers to do so, adding that they should also pray for them and anoint them with oil. A church manual written around AD 217 encourages deacons to find out who is sick and inform the pastor so that he can pay a visit. Ill people, it says, are much comforted when they know the pastor (their high priest) is mindful of them.[9]

---

4. Origen, *Against Celsus* 1.46.
5. Origen, *Against Celsus* 1.67 (ANF 8:427).
6. Clement of Alexandria, *Quis Dives Salvetur* 30.
7. *To His Wife* 2.8.
8. *Apocalypse of Zephaniah* 7.4.
9. Hippolytus, *Apostolic Tradition* 30.

Your loving acts, such as visiting, can make the situation of the sick better. But can you actually cure them? Remember one thing: the Bible does not say that healing must *always* be caused by a miracle; you can contribute to their welfare by ordinary means. In describing Christian good deeds in the early third century, Bardesanes in Syria included healthy workers giving toward the support of the ill,[10] while one martyr for the faith around AD 165 noted that it was common for church funds to be used to relieve Christians in financial need due to illness.[11] Even the most ordinary person can donate to Christian medical missions and hospitals and thus (help) cure the sick.

Although the church fathers did not see visiting the sick and contributing to their material needs as miracles in themselves, they nevertheless regarded all cures as miraculous, and as evidence of divine power. For them, not all healings need be supernatural; divine love was the only factor necessary for the healing to be considered a miracle. This last thought is evidenced by the second-century instruction that cured Christians ought to give testimony about God's help in all healings, even those in which medications played a part.[12]

According to John 14:12, whoever believes in Jesus will do greater works than his. Although people gifted with the grace of divine healing have never been plentiful, certainly not all Christians, the Bible and earliest church fathers state that anyone at all can do great works equal in love and mercy to those of Christ. By visiting the sick, taking care of their bodies, and helping with their finances, we can all make the sick better and so fulfill the law of God.

---

10. *On Fate* (ANF 8:725).
11. Justin Martyr, *1 Apology* 67.6.
12. Tatian, *Address to the Greeks* 20.

Chapter 45
Silence

"It is better for a man to be silent and be a Christian, than to talk and not be one." So wrote Bishop Ignatius of Antioch around AD 107. He also indicated that it was a Christian characteristic soon after the New Testament that believers act as they speak, and are recognized by their silence in appropriate circumstances. Thus, Ignatius summed up the role of silence in the Christian life, which is evidenced in both Scripture and in actual church practice prior to the mass falling away from the faith in AD 249–251.

Christian ethics in its first 250 years decreed silence in some situations and forbade it in others. The first situation where it was commanded should be obvious but a lot of people forget it: silence is mandatory on topics that a person does not know about, counsels *The Sentences of Sextus*, a collection of instructions for the Christian life dating from the first half of the second century. *The Sentences* enjoyed widespread circulation and translation into many languages. It also recommended silence as being preferable to reckless words about God. A Christian in the next century even suggested the extreme of holding one's hand over one's mouth to avoid talking without understanding the subject matter.

In his multivolume guide to the Christian life, Clement of Alexandria, in the 190s AD, opined that, "It is better to be silent than to contradict, and thereby add sin to ignorance."[1] At that time, Clement was dean of Christendom's foremost educational institution. In an address to new Christians, he gave guidelines for speech and silence:

---

1. Clement of Alexandria, *Paedagogus* 2.7 (ANF 2:251).

> Be thoughtful in all your talk, and give back a useful answer, adapting the utterance to the hearer's need, just so loud that it may be distinctly audible, neither escaping the ears of the company by reason of feebleness nor going to excess with too much noise. Take care never to speak what you have not weighed and pondered beforehand; nor interject your own words on the spur of the moment and in the midst of another's; for you must listen and converse in turn, with set times for speech and for silence.[2]

The Sentences of Sextus advocated speaking when it would be wrong to remain silent. But what are the conditions and circumstances in which it would be wrong to be silent? This question is answered elsewhere in ancient Christian literature. A prominent lawyer before conversion and ordination, Tertullian warned around AD 200 that silence constitutes apostasy from the faith in circumstances where silence would be acquiescence in statements by other people that a person is not a Christian, e.g., an oath in the name of a pagan god or idol. To refute pagan allegations that believers perform atrocities and crimes at their assemblies, Tertullian denied that there was any wall of silence about what went on during Christian public worship. Silence is forbidden when the Christian religion is verbally attacked, but enjoined by Origen when the same happens to the private person and reputation of a Christian individual.

Clement's student Origen succeeded him as dean and wrote more on Christian topics than anyone before Martin Luther nearly thirteen centuries later. One of the reasons he wrote was so that his silence would not feed the assertions of heretics. He interpreted the noise of the bells on the high priest's robe in Exodus 28:33–35 as symbolizing that believers must not be silent about the last days and end of the world.

Jesus taught "resist not evil" (Matt 5:39), "bless them that curse you" (Matt 5:44), and "turn the other cheek" (Matt 5:39, 11) to a physical or verbal assailant. Origen distinguished between (1) attacks on an individual Christian personally, for which there must be no words in retaliation or repaying in kind, and (2) attacks on orthodox Christianity, which must be countered by an exception to the rule of Christian silence. In three places, his *Homilies on Psalm 38* command remaining silent when a Christian is personally assailed with insults, slander or curses, or is verbally disgraced or disparaged, reproached, harrassed, or provoked to reply in kind.

---

2. Clement of Alexandria, *To Newly Baptized*, 221–22.

Christian leaders even have a duty to urge silence on other people, such as insubordinate talkers, deceivers, speakers of empty things, and those who teach heresies, especially for money (Titus 1:10–11).

Chapter 46

Sloth

Early Christian Writers Tell Us
How to Avoid Spiritual Laziness

THE sin of sloth consists of sluggishness of soul to make the effort necessary to perform a good work, e.g., attend church on Sunday. The sin of laziness or sloth also occurs when a person is disinclined through inertia to make the exertion necessary to maintain a good relationship with God.

People in the First World today tend to overlook the sinfulness of sloth or laziness. So many labor-saving devices and service industries are available to perform so many kinds of tasks that Christians are tempted to assume that godliness or being a good Christian is an easy matter that can be attended to at our own convenience or delegated to service people, e.g., clergy, and machines.

This was not so for the earliest Christians. In the New Testament, the first generation of Christians clearly spoke against unwillingness to exert effort to maintain friendship with God through good works. The apostle Paul exhorted Christians to "not grow weary while doing good" (Gal 6:9; 2 Thess 3:13). The Letter to the Hebrews was written partly so that its readers would "not become sluggish, but imitate those who through faith and patience inherit the promises" (6:12). Hebrews also teaches that maturity in the Christian life is obtained by "those who have their faculties trained by practice" (5:14 RSV). Thus, Christian living requires practice and exercise, i.e., effort, and repeated effort.

The second generation of Christian writers, the first successors of the apostles and Bible writers, produced two long letters that touch on spiritual laziness. One of them, *The First Epistle of Clement*, was written toward the middle or end of the first century AD, when some apostles were still active. It condemns being "slothful in well-doing and ceas[ing] in the practice of love."[1] On the contrary, "let us hasten with all energy and readiness of mind to every good work" (33:10). The next chapter exhorts readers to "be prompt in the practice of well-doing," (34:2) and "be not lazy or slothful in any good work" (34:4). Note again that "practice" is necessary: Christians must exercise themselves repeatedly to gain virtue and godliness.

The other ancient writing, *The Letter of Barnabas*, contains a passage on what is necessary for progressing in or maintaining a Christian life:

> Thou shalt love, as the apple of thine eye, every one that speaketh to thee the word of the Lord. Thou shalt remember the day of judgment, night and day. Thou shalt seek out every day the faces of the saints, either by word examining them, and going to exhort them, and meditating on how to save a soul by the word . . .[2]

We are thus to pursue godliness or the Christian life in community with our clergy and local church, always remembering that God will one day judge us. Sometimes requiring help from other Christians, godliness or a healthy spiritual life was not regarded as easy or to be attended to at leisure, but was seen as entailing strenuous and constant practice. Because this letter is sometimes dated as early as AD 70, it might have been written by the apostle Barnabas, frequently mentioned in the Acts of the Apostles.

In the early third century came the church scholar and teacher Origen. His knowledge of our faith was so great that he was consulted by pastor-bishops throughout the eastern Mediterranean. Origen taught that hard, positive effort is necessary to maintain progress in the Christian life. He told his audience to exert themselves to be free from sinfulness, exerting hard work and sweat.[3] The sincere Christian must engage in constant practice and vigilance because progress in the spiritual life does not come to the slothful or inactive or negligent.[4] He warned that favor from God can be lost through negligence of mind and laziness of life.[5]

In the same vein, Origen touched on the natural inclination to spiritual inertia. Progress in Christian commitment and overcoming sin do not

---

1. *1 Clement* 23.1 (ANF 1:13).
2. *Letter of Barnabas* 19.9–10 (ANF 1:148).
3. Origen, *Commentary on Romans* 6.11.2; Origen *Homilies on Luke* 6.6.
4. Origen, *Commentary on Romans* 6.11.2.
5. Origen, *Commentary on Romans* 9.3.4.

come if we are lazy or drowsy.⁶ Weak Christians are slack and sluggish; they should stir up their idle and neglectful spirits in order to practice godliness and the other precepts of the gospel.⁷ He preached against laziness of mind and sluggishness of soul accompanied by bodily lusts and pleasures.⁸

These early authors were at one in affirming that exertion is necessary for the performance of good works and maintaining friendship with God, and that constant practice is necessary in the Christian life, like constant exercise is necessary for an athlete. Another term for these is "godliness," of which 1 Timothy 4:7–8 says: "exercise yourself toward godliness. For bodily exercise profits a little, but godliness is profitable for all things, having promise of the life that now is and of that which is to come."

---

6. Origen, *Commentary on Romans* 10.5.4; Origen, *Homilies on Joshua* 1.6.
7. Origen, *Homilies on Joshua* 1.6, 9.9.
8. Origen, *Homilies on Genesis* 4.4, 16.2.

Chapter 47

Suicide and Assisted Suicide

THIS chapter is directed to people who are contemplating suicide or helping other people commit suicide, whether on a broad basis as part of some "right to dignified death" movement, or out of personal compassion in a single individual case to spare a loved one from physical or mental pain or disability. To ascertain whether suicide and assisting suicide conform to Jesus' way of love for all humankind, this article surveys the teachings of the earliest Christians, Christians removed at most only a few generations from Christ and who preserved his spirit and words and Bible interpretations. This article is therefore relevant to all people interested in Christian ethics, and to people who believe that if they kill themselves they will be mercifully welcomed into a better existence in heaven.

First of all, we have the case of the jailer in Philippi in Macedonia who was exercising custody over the apostles Paul and Silas. Just as the jailer was about to kill himself with his own sword, Paul shouted to him, "Do yourself no harm" (Acts 16:28)! As a result of the turnkey sparing himself and listening to Paul's subsequent presentation of the gospel, he discovered his life to be much more worthwhile than he had thought and was soon rejoicing (Acts 16:34).

This same apostle Paul, who had witnessed many lives turn around for the happier, instructed his readers to "abide in faith, hope and love" (1 Cor 13:13). This is an absolute command for all Christians; it does not allow for circumstances to water it down. Nothing indicates a lack of the virtue of hope more than suicide.

Dating from the first half of the second century AD, the *Sentences of Sextus* is a collection of sayings on points of Christian ethics. It was so popular that it was widely distributed and translated into many languages. It rephrases the teachings of the Bible on disdaining the desires of the body, and reminds us that we are to treat it to the glory of God. Saying 321 specifically forbids causing one's own death; although a Christian must be ready to submit to martyrdom imposed by lawful authority, s/he must not take their own life.

Later authors went into more detail. Justin was a widely traveled student of philosophy who later converted to Christianity and became a Christian teacher at Rome. He wrote whole books explaining Christians and their practices to pagan or Jewish readers. In the middle of the second century he gave reasons why suicide is forbidden to Christians:

> We have been taught that God did not make the world aimlessly, but for the sake of the human race; and we have before stated that He takes pleasure in those who imitate His properties, and is displeased with those that embrace what is worthless either in word or deed. If, then, we all kill ourselves, we shall become the cause, as far as in us lies, why no one should be born, or instructed in the divine doctrines, or even why the human race should not exist; and we shall, if we so act, be ourselves acting in opposition to the will of God.[1]

In the Middle East about the time of Justin some believers collected memories of the apostle John and his teachings. One of them relates to murder-suicide. A young man had murdered his father because the father often tried to dissuade him from adultery with a particular married woman. Fearing the death penalty for this murder, and out of possessiveness for the woman, he resolved to kill her and her husband and then take his own life. John counseled him not to do so, took him to right the accomplished murder, rebuked him for his wicked deed and thoughts, and led him to repentance.[2]

In discussing other topics relevant to religion, Irenaeus cites as a given that Christians do not choose suicide.[3] Irenaeus had associated in his youth with Christians who had personally interacted with the apostles, including a man who was probably the "angel of the church in Smyrna" in Revelation 2:8. Irenaeus became a bishop in southern France and wrote in the 180s AD. Throughout his books he emphasized carrying on the teachings that

---

1. Justin Martyr, 2 *Apology* 4 (ANF 1:189).
2. *Acts of John* 48–54.
3. Irenaeus, *Against Heresies* 5.12.3, last sentence.

he and other men of his generation received from older Christians in a line back to the apostles.

Clement of Alexandria was dean of Christendom's leading educational institution in the 190s AD. In the category of "children of darkness" and "children of wrath" he included the lustful, people without sexual self-restraint, idolaters, robbers, murderers of neighbors, and those who commit suicide.[4]

Does a person sin by helping someone commit suicide or by consenting to another person desire to engage in such a sin? Does a person sin by knowingly providing a gun or poison to a person intent on killing themselves or another? Is a mere conspirator as culpable as the actual perpetrator? The answer is "yes" according to the Bible and its first interpreters who preserved Jesus' interpretations of it and his oral teachings.

First and oldest is Proverbs 1:10: "if sinners entice thee, consent thou not." In the New Testament, Paul appears to consider himself in some way guilty of the death of Stephen by stoning because he consented to the execution and minimally assisted by guarding the clothing of those who actually threw the stones (Acts 22:20). First Timothy 5:22 warns the reader not to "be partaker in other men's sins." The Bible applies this to seemingly minor matters: 2 John 11 forbids even wishing God's blessing on a heretic, "For he that biddeth him God's speed is a partaker of his evil deeds."

Christian writers of the first half of the second century concurred. According to *The Sentences of Sextus* 150, approving or sanctioning a sin renders it unbearable. *The Revelation of Peter*, which some in very early times would have included in the New Testament, describes the place and torments in hell for "murderers and those who conspired with them."[5] *The Traditions of Matthias* were even stricter as to the culpability of a person who in any way contributed to a given sin without actually perpetrating it:

> They say in the Traditions that Matthew the apostle constantly said, that "if the neighbor of an elect man sin, the elect man has sinned. For had he conducted himself as the Word prescribes, his neighbor also would have been filled with such reverence for the life he led as not to sin."[6]

---

4. Clement of Alexandria, *Stromata* 3.18 (106), 90.
5. *Revelation of Peter* 25, 509.
6. Quoted in Clement of Alexandria, *Stromata* 7.13 (ANF 2:547).

In the AD 180s, Irenaeus forbade consenting "to those who act wickedly."[7] Clement of Alexandria counseled praying only with people of the most sinless character, "For it is a dangerous thing to take part in others' sins."[8] Clement also alluded to 1 Corinthians 5:11, forbidding so much as eating with an unrepentant Christian sinner.[9]

In the late second or early third century, Tertullian, a former lawyer and the founder of Latin Christian literature, maintained that we must abstain not only from actual sin but also from the means by which other people can sin:

> For although the fault be done by others, it makes no difference if it be by my means. In no case ought I to be necessary to another, while he is doing what to me is unlawful. Hence I ought to understand that care must be taken by me, lest what I am forbidden to do be done by my means. In short, in another cause of no lighter guilt I observe that fore-judgment.[10]

Giving examples, Tertullian wrote that (1) because fornication is forbidden to Christians, so also is keeping a brothel or pimping or otherwise promoting prostitution, (2) because murder is against God's law, so is training people to kill, and (3) just as idolatry is forbidden, so also is providing sacrificial victims and incense.[11] Thus, contributing to another person's suicide is as sinful as the deed itself. As a prominent lawyer, Tertullian must have been acquainted with wrongful-death cases.

Clement's successor, Origen, preached that a person can be polluted not only by his own sin but also by associating with an actual malefactor, e.g., by being a friend of someone who is malicious, idolatrous, or given to rages, without personally practicing the wickedness. To avoid sharing in another's sin, it is necessary to separate oneself from a seducer of wives, one who hates his brother, and the sacrilegious.[12] In support of his position, Origen quoted Paul's instruction in 1 Corinthians 5:9–11 that Christians are not to eat with or otherwise associate with a Christian who is a fornicator, idolater, slanderer, drunkard, or extortionist.[13] Tertullian wrote in a

---

7. Irenaeus, *Against Heresies* 4.30.3 (ANF 1:504).
8. Clement of Alexandria, *Stromata* 7.7 (ANF 2:537).
9. Clement of Alexandria, *Stromata* 3.18(106) 90.
10. Tertullian, *On Idolatry* 11 (ANF 3:67, italics Romanized).
11. Tertullian, *On Idolatry* 11.
12. Origen, *Homilies on Leviticus* 5.10.5.
13. Origen, *Homilies on Leviticus* 3.3.3, 5.10.5.

similar vein after detailing some sins: "It is not enough that we do no such things ourselves, unless we break all connection also with those who do."[14]

Of course, some people bent on doing what Christian ethics considers evil try to quibble that their particular case constitutes an implied exception and that the "spirit" of Christian morality justifies such an act, e.g., killing oneself or another. But the authorities from the church's foundational period do not contemplate exceptions in any circumstances.[15] Indeed, the purpose of the present book in consulting the near-biblical sources is to find any such "spirit" and whether the early hearers of the message of Jesus and the apostles understood him and them in the full force of their words, which would indicate how the New Testament writers meant themselves to be understood.

One reason for suicide, or assisting in it, is that disease, affliction, or disability will render a person useless or a burden to others, such as family or society at large. The Christian view was stated in a description of Christian morals and doctrines by Bardesanes in early third-century Syria, who reiterated the worth of all human lives and their value to society. The infirmities of old age or disease or bodily defects do not render a potential suicide victim totally useless. After writing of wrongdoing, particularly stealing, lying, acts of profligacy, hatred, and deception, Bardesanes pointed out:

> even if a man be poor, and sick, and old, and disabled in his limbs, he is able to avoid doing all these things. And, as he is able to avoid doing these things, so is he able to love, and to bless, and to speak the truth, and to pray for what is good for everyone with whom he is acquainted.[16]

Lastly, we have the teaching and example of Jesus himself. First, whoever inflicts death through suicide on the least of Christ's brothers or sisters inflicts it on Jesus (Matt 25:35–45). Down through the centuries, the killing of Jesus has been regarded as a particularly heinous outrage. Secondly, when Jesus encountered people who were diseased, handicapped, or suffering, he always did his best to relieve their afflictions for the rest of their natural lives; he never put them out of their misery by helping them kill themselves or recommending that they do so.

---

14. Tertullian, *De Spectaculis* 15 (ANF 3:86).
15. Tertullian, *De Corona* 11; Origen, *Commentary on Romans* 6.3.5.
16. Bardesanes, *On Fate* (ANF 8:725).

Chapter 48

Taxes

"Taxes are what we pay for civilized society"[1] said Associate Justice Oliver Wendell Holmes of the United States Supreme Court. It is also what we pay for the privilege of being disciples of Jesus Christ. Starting with Jesus himself, the Christian faith commands us to pay all taxes levied by secular governments and to not evade them by such tricks as underreporting the value of a commercial transaction or the value of landed property, accepting cash in order to report a lesser monetary amount than would change hands (underground market), or fabricating fictitious deductions from income.

The first injunction to pay secular taxes appears in the Gospels. In Matthew 22:17–21, Mark 12:14–17, and Luke 20:22–25 the Pharisees asked Jesus "Is it lawful [i.e., under Jewish religious law] to pay taxes to Caesar or not?" Christ then pointed to a coin which bore a portrait and inscription, and asked whose they were. Being informed that they were Caesar's, the Roman head of state, he replied with the now-famous "Render to Caesar the things that are Caesar's." In other words, give back to the creator of secular money their due portion of it, whether that person is the Roman emperor, the United States government, or Queen Elizabeth as representative of the authorities of British Commonwealth countries. In Matthew 17:27, Jesus instructed Simon Peter to pay the Jewish Temple poll tax as well.

A little later, but still in Bible times, the apostle Paul commanded:

> pay taxes, for the authorities are ministers of God, attending to this very thing. Pay all of them their dues, taxes to whom taxes are

---

[1]. *Compañia General de Tabacos de Filipinas v. Collector of Internal Revenue*, 275 U.S. 87, 100 (1927).

due, revenue to whom revenue is due, honour to whom honour is due. Owe no one anything, except to love one another. (Rom 13:6–8)

The earliest generations of Christians interpreted this literally, not figuratively or spiritually. Their witness is valuable to us today because they lived in an era when the oral teachings and Bible interpretations of Jesus and the apostles were still fresh in Christian memories, and they remembered the sense and nuances in which the above words were written. These ancient postbiblical authors also operated in the same mental world and culture as the New Testament authors and their first hearers and readers, and shared their presuppositions and context, and thus more fully disclose the interpretations and lessons that the biblical authors intended their first audience to draw from the New Testament.

Justin, called "Martyr" because he died for the faith at government hands around AD 165, composed a description of Christianity and its teachings for the Roman emperor. Where "we" means Christians, Justin wrote: "everywhere we, more readily than all men, endeavour to pay to those appointed by you the taxes both ordinary and extraordinary, as we have been taught by Him."[2] Justin then summarized Matthew 22:17–21, and continued: "to God alone we render worship, but in other things we gladly serve you, acknowledging you as kings and rulers of men."[3]

On 17 July AD 180, one of a group of Christian martyrs also described Christian practices and attitudes toward the state. He said they refrain from murder, false witness, and theft; Christians honor Caesar as Caesar, and when they buy anything they always pay the sales tax out of a religious duty.[4]

Theophilus, as bishop, taught the Christian faith at Antioch in Syria in the third quarter of the second century. In a passage on Christians' relations with secular government, he narrated that "the divine word" instructs Christians to "lead a quiet and peaceable life. And it teaches us to render all things to all, honour to whom honour, fear to whom fear, tribute to whom tribute; to owe no many anything but to love all."[5]

After serving as dean of the world's foremost Christian educational institution of the era, Origen established his own in Palestine. He was the

2. Justin Martyr, *1 Apology* 17 (ANF 1:168).
3. Justin Martyr, *1 Apology* 17 (ANF 1:168).
4. *Acts of the Scillitan Martyrs* (ANF 10:[285]).
5. Theophilus, *To Autolycus* 3.14 (ANF 2:115).

most influential preacher and Bible scholar of his own day and for centuries to come, so much so that he was consulted by pastor-bishops throughout the eastern Mediterranean. Until the Reformation, he was the Christian who lived most in the Scriptures and was the most prolific Christian author. In his *Homilies on Luke* 23.6 (about AD 233), he told his audience "to pay what is due to other people: tribute to whom tribute is due, taxes to whom taxes, and honour to whom honour." At 39.4 he indicated that no believer of his day disagreed that Christians must pay taxes to the Roman government.

A year or two later, in discussing "forgive us our debts" in the Lord's Prayer, Origen repeated Romans 13:7–8, and added that taxes to whom taxes, revenue to whom revenue, etc., are debts due to other people because Christians have an obligation to render them, just as we are also to render "gentle speech" and other kinds of Christian deeds and dispositions.[6]

Origen said that taxes as taxes, revenue as revenue, etc., are among duties that are to be rendered to the other people, in the same category as duties to parents as parents, sons as sons, siblings as siblings, clergy as clergy, church elders as church elders, deacons as deacons, and laypeople as laypeople.[7] To Origen, payment of government levies was on a par with other conduct we associate with the Christian life, and just as binding and integral to it.

Ancient Christian sources give seven reasons for paying taxes, i.e., seven rationales behind the commandment:

First, to avoid giving offense. When Peter, in Matthew 17:24, asked Jesus about paying the temple poll tax, there followed a discussion to the effect that rulers demand taxes from people in general but never from their own sons, i.e., "the sons are free." However, Christ, in verse 27, instructed Peter to pay the tax anyway, in order "not to give offense to them" (the collectors of the religious tax).

Second, taxes are a debt rather than one's own property, which a Christian can give away or withhold at will. Origen considered taxes, revenues, etc., to constitute an account payable that Christians have no choice but to discharge. If we do not follow this commandment of the divine law to pay the tax in full, we despise the word of God and remain in debt.[8]

Third, remember Theophilus and Origen's categorizing payment of government taxes with other Christian traits and behaviors: payment allows

---

6. Origen, *On Prayer* 28.1.
7. Origen, *Homilies on Jeremiah* 14.4.1.
8. Origen, *On Prayer* 28.1.

us to "lead a quiet and peaceable life" and is in the same class as our duties as parents, sons, siblings, church office-bearers, etc. Origen's *Commentary on the Epistle to the Romans* 9.29 (between AD 239 and 245) considered it part of Christians' "living a quiet and tranquil life" and practicing justice and piety.

The *Commentary on the Epistle to the Romans* brings us to a fourth and purely practical reason to pay. Origen wrote it at a time when the church was intermittently persecuted by the state and when many Christians (such as Justin and the Scillitans) urged tolerance of it because Christians were conscientiously obedient to the state except on the sole matter of worship. Origen refuted the argument that Christians are not obliged to pay taxes. In an exegesis of Romans 13:5-6, he wrote that such refusal would "deservedly" bring the government's forces against Christians. Failing to pay taxes and revenues would constitute rebellion against the Roman Empire, depriving it of finances essential for its administration. Government officials would then be "justified persecutors"[9] of Christians who would be plainly guilty of repeatedly breaking a law which applied to all Roman subjects and which had nothing to do with religion. Instead of persecution for their beliefs, the government would attack Christians for pure rebelliousness. After all, widespread evasion or refusal to pay taxes can soon destroy the tax system and with it the very concept of any government.

A further reason against dishonest tax avoidance is that it cheats honest taxpayers. When the total tax revenues of a government decline, the rates go up to raise the same amount of money, with a disproportionately higher burden thrust onto honest taxpayers who report the full value of a transaction, benefit, or property, and without dishonestly padding deductions.

There is another reason for Christians to pay the full amount of taxes, which is more relevant to twenty-first-century democracies than when Christians in ancient times were disenfranchised and persecuted by governments. Religion aside, the obligation to pay taxes is morally stronger now than in Bible or early Christian times. In those days taxes were collected for despots who either inherited the government or imposed it by force of arms, with the people having no say in the matter. These despots often spent tax money to more efficiently oppress their subjects or on building projects that glorified themselves, again with taxpayers having no say in the matter. In the United States and British Commonwealth today, it is the people, mostly taxpayers, who have the right to elect representatives to levy

---

9. Origen, *Commentary on Romans* 9.29, 226.

and spend taxes, and to vote them out of office if they think taxes too high or misspent. Today, tax money is used however the people's representatives decide, and these representatives spend it on whatever they say is for the voters' good. Therefore, the obligation to pay is logically and morally more binding now than in early Christian times. Modern democratic governments finance far more services for the benefit of the common people than did those in that era, e.g., the post office, health care, child and family benefits, universal education, consumer protection, and protection of labor and the environment.

Lastly, illegal tax evasion is particularly oppressive of the poor because there will be less money for social programs intended to provide the needy with a more bearable level of existence.

On the other hand, a Christian need not comply with exaggerated demands from an overzealous tax collector who is not authorized by the taxing statutes or a court of law, nor need a Christian forego legitimate deductions. We are to render to Caesar only what is rightfully Caesar's. This was put another way by Tertullian in discussing "Render to Caesar the things that are Caesar's, and to God the things that are God's" in Matthew 24:21, Mark 12:17, and Luke 20:25, when Tertullian rhetorically asked "what will be God's, if all things are Caesar's?"[10] We live in free and democratic countries where the excessive use of power by tax collectors can be appealed, where no tax is valid unless authorized by a congress, parliament, or legislature, and where the courts interpret every taxing statute narrowly so that it applies to as few citizens as possible under the terms of the statute, and for the least amount of tax.

It is well known that Christ associated with tax collectors, but he also did so with prostitutes. His purpose was to seek and save the lost, not approve of their ways—certainly not levying higher taxes than was authorized by legitimate authority. Jesus was on a soul-saving mission like John the Baptist, who when asked by tax collectors what they should do as part of their repentance, replied "Collect no more than is appointed to you" (Luke 3:13). Similarly, Jesus befriended the chief collector Zacchaeus, but pronounced salvation on him only when Zacchaeus said he amply reimbursed any taxpayers he overcharged (Luke 19:2–10).

In *Homilies on Luke* 23.5, Origen also taught that tax collectors must take no more than the law allows. The *Didascalia*, a church manual of the first third of the third century, classes "dishonest tax-gatherers" in the same

---

10. Tertullian, *On Idolatry* 15 (ANF 3:70).

category as thieves, forgers, usurers, extortionists, cheaters of the poor, "hypocritical lawyers," and other reprobates.

Nor are good Christians debarred from relying on statutory limitation periods. Usually in a taxing statute itself, they provide that after so many years and under the right circumstances, the obligation to pay is extinguished. This provision is built into some laws whereby the Queen, on behalf of Commonwealth governments, forgives the obligation to pay all or part of taxes for a particular year. Forgiveness is at the heart of the gospel; although it usually applies to a Christian pardoning the lapses of someone else, there is also the element of graciously accepting forgiveness extended by another and so restoring peace with them. It would be un-Christian to spurn Her Majesty's grace and Christian indulgence by refusing to accept her forgiveness.

Chapter 49

Temptation and 1 Corinthians 10:13

THERE is a great reward for resisting and overcoming temptation to sin:

> My brethren, count it all joy when ye fall into diverse temptations; Knowing this, that the trying of your faith worketh patience. But let patience have her perfect work, that ye may be perfect and entire, wanting nothing. Blessed is the man that endureth temptation: for when he is tried, he shall receive the crown of life, which the Lord hath promised to them that love him. (James 1:2-4, 12)

How can we gain this reward? How can we withstand temptation? Unlike the purpose of temptation, the answer can be found in the writings of Origen. The dean of schools of Christian higher learning, he was the foremost Bible scholar, teacher, and preacher of his own time and for centuries afterwards. Traveling extensively throughout the eastern Mediterranean, he was well positioned to ascertain and relate the consensus of Christian ethics and faith in the first half of the third century.

Origen gave practical advice on how to resist and overcome temptation. In preaching to mixed congregations of clergy and laypeople, he advised imitating Christ when the devil had tempted him in the wilderness (Matt 4:1–10; Luke 4:1–12), even down to the point of speaking directly to Satan in rebuke. Origen encouraged his listeners to remember their individual progress in the Christian life, and to confront the devil head-on with statements that they belong to Christ and as such are forbidden to engage in immorality. He wrote that every Christian ought to rebuke Satan with

John 19:11: "You could have no power at all against me unless it were given you from above."

But Origen recognized that prevention is better than the best cure. Accordingly, he exhorted that his listeners be watchful and on guard as to where temptations come from, i.e., the places and manner in which the devil might creep in and invade a soul. Elaborating on such vigilance, Origen rhetorically asked how people who attend public worship only on holy days and church festivals thought they could escape temptation, when resisting it is difficult enough for regular attendees who constantly watch, pray, and hold fast to the word of God. Regular attendance at church is the first step in warding off temptation. Origen preached that Christians should always be prepared for enticements to sin and for abandoning friends and associates who would lead them into sin.

Christians should not interpret 1 Corinthians 10:13 to mean that all temptations are easily overcome and only the very lax will fall into sin, certainly not themselves. It reads: "There hath no temptation taken you but such as is common to man: but God is faithful, who will not suffer you to be tempted above that ye are able; but will with the temptation also make a way to escape, that ye may be able to bear it." Origen wrote that we must not think this means that a Christian who is tempted to sin will always win in their struggle against it, no matter how little resistance they offer. To this end, his *On First Principles* 3.2.3 compared Christian struggles against temptation and sin with those of athletes. The people who organize sports events do not permit a contestant to enter any competition indiscriminantly or at any level s/he chooses. Only in accord with preset categories as to size, weight, or age, do the organizers pair off contestants who are in the same category as to height, sex, etc., to compete against each other. God likewise

> arranges on most impartial principles all who descend into the struggles of this human life, according to each individual's power, which is known only to Him who alone beholds the hearts of men: so that one individual fights against one temptation of the flesh, and another against a second. One is exposed to its influence for so long a period of time, another only for so long.[1]

God allows each Christian to be tempted only in proportion to the amount of his/her strength, i.e., ability to resist temptation. Further in the analogy, Origen cautioned:

---

1. Origen, *On First Principles* (ANF 4:331).

> Now although we have said that it is by the just judgment of God that everyone is tempted according to the amount of his strength, we are not thereby to suppose that he who is tempted will by all means prove victorious in the struggle; in like manner as he who contends in sports—paired with his adversary on a just principle of arrangement—will nevertheless not necessarily be the winner. But unless the powers of the combatants are equal, the victor's prize will not be justly won; nor will blame justly attach to the vanquished, because He indeed allows us to be tempted, but not "beyond what we are able." For it is in proportion to our strength that we are tempted; and it is not written that He will make a way of escape from temptation such that we *will* bear it, but a way of escape such that we *will be able* to bear it. But it depends on ourselves to use either with energy or unenthusiastically the power that He has given us. Under every temptation we have a power of endurance, if we employ the strength that is granted us.[2]

This explains why Christians are not always successful in resisting temptation, and harmonizes 1 Corinthians 10:13 with free will. Like Jesus in the wilderness, we always have the capability to resist, but it is up to each tempted individual to use God's power and his/her own free will, either half-heartedly (and be defeated by the particular temptation), or diligently (and be successful and entitled to the reward the Epistle of James promises: the crown of life).

---

2. Origen, *On First Principles* (ANF 4:331).

Chapter 50

Tithing

Giving one-tenth of a believer's income for the support of God's ministers and work is a time-honored practice among God's people. Called "giving a tithe" or "tithing," it has very ancient origins, was required and practiced in the Old Testament, was commended by Jesus, and was one method by which the church financed ministers, worship, and charitable works until the sixteenth century. The binding nature of tithing may still continue into the twenty-first century.

Although most information about tithing comes from the law of Moses given around 1450 BC, the practice was ancient even then. According to Genesis 14:20 and the Letter to the Hebrews 7:2–9, Abraham, around 2000 BC, gave a tenth of all he gained to the high priest Melchizedek as the representative of God. As stated in Hebrews 7:9–10, the (hereditary) Israelite priests were themselves deemed to have tithed because they were represented in this by their ancestor Abraham.

Through Moses, God commanded the Israelites to tithe. Leviticus 27:30 and 32, Numbers 18:24, and Deuteronomy 14:22 state that one-tenth of all grain, fruit, and livestock was holy to the Lord and to be dedicated to God. Numbers 18:8, 11–19, and 24–28 specify that this tithe was to be given to the Aaronic priests and the Levites, who were God's ministers under the Mosaic covenant. Even the Levites were to pay a tithe to the Aaronic priests (18.26 and 28).

Although the Aaronic priesthood was rendered redundant by Christ, it was not so for the tithe to ministers, for Numbers 18:8, 11, and 19 declare that the tenth to God and God's ministers is "a perpetual due." Early Christians certainly regarded it as such.

In actual practice, the Israelites followed the law as regards tithing. Second Chronicles 31:4–6 and 31:12 record that the people in the reign of King Hezekiah gave "the tithe of everything" in addition to first fruits and other offerings. They gave them "abundantly" to the clergy as their due. Centuries later, exiles returning from Babylon were to give the clergy tithes and other gifts (Neh 10:38, 12:44). Note that, as in Moses' and Hezekiah's days, tithes were in addition to other gifts to God, God's work, and God's ministers.

Although generally overlooked, there are biblical passages in which Christ himself commended tithing. In commenting on the practice of the scribes and Pharisees in tithing tiny amounts of herbs and spices, Jesus declared "these you ought to have done" and encouraged them to go further by also observing more important precepts (Matt 23:23; Luke 11:42).

The earliest postbiblical Christians believed that the commandment to tithe was still binding on God's people, i.e., that it survived Christ's fulfilling of the law. Origen traveled much and was thus familiar with Christian practice in many lands. In an extended discussion on giving a tenth to God in his *Homilies on Genesis*, Origen drew comparisons between it and what the Egyptians had to pay to their government in return for being saved from starvation by pharaoh's prime minister, the patriarch Joseph. They were obliged to pay one part in five, or *20* percent, of their crops (Gen 47:24). This contrasts with the Israelites' (and Christians') *10* percent, or one part in ten. Origen saw symbolism in the numbers five and ten. Five is the number of bodily senses (sight, hearing, etc.), which indicates that the Egyptians served the bodily or carnal nature, which is forbidden for the people of God. Ten is the proper number for us because it represents the Ten Commandments and the ten virtues or fruits of the Spirit in Galatians 5:22–23: love, joy, peace, etc. Origen also said that in the gospel parable, ten also represents the ten pounds the good servant earned for his master and the ten cities over which he was given authority as a reward (Luke 19:12–17). In this sermon, Origen made it clear that Christians were obliged to give 10 percent to their church and its officers.[1]

About the same time as Origen, a church manual and guide for Christian life also spoke of tithing as a Christian obligation. It commanded people to devote tithes and other offerings to Christ and his ministers. They

---

1. Origen, *Homilies on Genesis* 16.6. Origen appears to have counted "purity" within the ten, which Galatians 5:22–23 does not include. See Origen, *Homilies on Genesis* 12.3, 179.

were to be presented to the pastor, either directly by the laity or through the deacons, for him to sustain himself and distribute to others.[2]

This church manual drew parallels between payments to Christian ministers and the tithes to Levitical and Aaronic priests: the law of Moses placed burdens on the Israelites by demanding sacrifices, oblations, sin offerings, vows, tithes, gifts of the first fruits of farm produce, and burnt offerings, but Christians are free from these heavy burdens. However, because Jesus commanded that our righteousness exceed that of the Jewish scribes and Pharisees (Matt 5:20), Christians are still to give abundantly to our office-bearers, especially the pastor. Under Moses, the manual said, the people were commanded to give tithes and gifts to the descendants of Levi and Aaron; under Christ, the priests and Levites are the pastor and other officers of the local church, so that tithes and other gifts are to be offered to God through them.[3]

Much earlier, the church father Irenaeus, in France, put forth a similar reason for Christian tithing. In the 180s AD, he wrote that Christians show our freedom in Christ by voluntarily giving a greater proportion to God than did Israelites, who gave only 10 percent, and then only because the Mosaic law compelled them.[4]

Apparently tithing continued in the church until the Reformation. Early Protestant Reformers asserted that the authority of Roman Catholic bishops over tithes was theirs only by human convention, by agreement of church members, rather than having been given them by God. These Reformers asserted that when bishops are negligent in their administration of tithes or do not apply them to proper purposes, it is the duty of Christian governments to take them over in the interests of justice and peace.[5] This was partly foreshadowed in 1 Samuel 8:10–17, where it was said that the king would take a tenth of the vineyards, grain, and livestock when rule by the judges was inefficient and unpopular. Thus, today governments take 10 percent and more of our incomes for justice, peacekeeping, charitable works, and other commendable purposes including many—but not all—that were performed by the priests and Levites.

However, state, provincial, and federal governments do not spend anywhere near the proportion that the Old Testament Israelites and early

2. Connolly, *Didascalia apostolorum* 9.
3. Connolly, *Didascalia apostolorum* 9.
4. Irenaeus, *Against Heresies* 4.18.1–2.
5. *Augsburg Confession* Article 28.29.

Christians did in relieving the poor, caring for widows and orphans, financing public worship, and supporting our spiritual lives and ministers. They have even reduced public assistance payments to the point that the poor must now depend on food banks—usually maintained by churches. Even taking 40 percent of our incomes, governments do not finance many aspects of Christian life. This means that we need to give directly to the church and its ministers—hopefully another 10 percent—as their "perpetual due."

Under the New Testament regime, Christians are not bound by arbitrary laws or fixed percentages like the Israelites, but are under grace. However, grace should motivate Christians to do as much or more than the law of Moses demanded. Again, our righteousness must exceed "that of the scribes and Pharisees" (Matt 5:20). The apostle Paul commanded us to give "bountifully . . . not reluctantly or under compulsion, for God loves a cheerful giver" (2 Cor 9:6–7). Further, "God is able to provide you with every blessing in abundance, so that you may always have enough of everything and may provide in abundance for every good work" (2 Cor 9:8).

Christians! If we fail to provide finances whereby the church can care for the poor, widows, orphans, strangers, homeless, and pastors, we are robbing God and God's agencies of their "perpetual due." Such a failing is not new: as early as 500 BC the prophet Malachi asked and answered the question "Will man rob God? Yet you are robbing me . . . [i]n your tithes and offerings" (Mal 3:8 RSV). Two verses later, the prophet invited God's people to put the Lord to the test by bringing all their tithes to God's house so that his ministers would have enough to eat. If we do so, God will pour on his people "an overflowing blessing" (Mal 3:10 RSV).

Chapter 51

Trust and Distrust

"Jesus Did Not Trust"

THERE is no obligation for a Christian to naively trust just anyone, in all circumstances. In fact, a healthy distrust—especially in religious matters—is encouraged by the earliest Christian literature, written at a time when the oral teachings and Bible interpretations of Jesus and the apostles were still fresh in Christian memories.

Jesus himself warned others to "beware of false prophets, who come to you in sheep's clothing but inwardly are ravenous wolves" (Matt 7:15), and that "false Christs and false prophets will arise" (Matt 24:24). The apostle John added: "do not believe every spirit, but test the spirits to see whether they are of God; for many false prophets have gone out into the world" (1 John 4:1). As Paul's letters show, his ministry was constantly beset by such frauds. Having become resigned to the phenomenon, in Acts 20:29–30 he told local church leaders: "I know that after my departure fierce wolves will come in among you, not sparing the flock; and from among your own selves will arise men speaking perverse things, to draw away the disciples after them."

Around AD 233, Origen advised:

> Be careful of immediately trusting just anyone that quotes the Scriptures. Examine the sort of life he leads, the religious beliefs he holds, and his intentions. He may pretend to be holy when he is not really holy. He may be a false teacher and wolf in sheep's

clothing. He may even be the mouthpiece of the devil, who quotes Scripture for a purpose.[1]

Whom, then, can we trust, particularly in religious matters? One apostle wrote "every spirit which confesses that Jesus Christ has come in the flesh is of God, and every spirit which does not confess Jesus is not of God" (1 John 4:2–3). However, as Origen noted, even some people that assert they are good Christians nevertheless ought to be investigated further.

In the middle of the second century came a book of Christian moral teaching that proved very popular and influential. It concisely states: "Trust you the righteous, but put no trust in the unrighteous,"[2] and then provided criteria by which to tell the two apart, and thus a guide as to a person's life, beliefs, intentions, and spirit. Mandate 6.2 states that the messenger of righteousness is "gentle and modest, meek and peaceful . . . he talks to you of righteousness, purity, chastity, contentment, and every righteous deed and glorious virtue. Trust him, then, and his works." On the other hand, "the messenger of iniquity . . . is wrathful, and bitter, and foolish, and his works are evil . . . . drunken revels, divers[e] luxuries, and things improper, . . . hankering after women . . . overreaching, and pride, and blustering."[3] In the same vein is Mandate 11:

> He who has the Divine Spirit proceeding from above is meek, and peaceable, and humble, and refrains from all iniquity and vain desire of this world, and contents himself with fewer wants than those of other men[4] . . . the spirit which is earthly, and empty[5] . . . exalts itself, and wishes to have the first seat, and is bold, and impudent, and talkative, and lives in the midst of many luxuries[6] . . . it never approaches an assembly of righteous men but shuns them.[7] . . .Try by his deeds and his life the man who says he is inspired. But as for you, trust the Spirit which comes from God, and has power; but the spirit which is earthly and empty trust not at all.[8]

---

1. Origen, *Homilies on Luke*, 31.
2. Herm. Mand. 6.1.2.
3. Herm. Mand. 6.2. (ANF 2:24).
4. Herm. Mand. 11.8 (ANF 2:27).
5. Herm. Mand. 11.11 (ANF 2:28).
6. Herm. Mand. 11.12 (ANF 2:28).
7. Herm. Mand. 11.13 (ANF 2:28).
8. Herm. Mand. 11.16 (ANF 2:28).

If readers think the foregoing article is too negative and cynical, remember that Christ himself took the same course of action:

> many believed in his name when they saw the signs which he did; but Jesus did not trust himself to them, because he knew all men and needed no one to bear witness of man; for he himself knew what was in man. (John 2:23–25)

We who do not possess Jesus' powers of knowing other people's inner thoughts and intentions must fall back on our usual, limited, human methods of finding out whom to trust and whom not to trust. These methods are outlined above in 1 John, Origen, and *Hermas*.

Chapter 52

Usury

WOULD you like to spend an eternity knee-deep in a lake of puss, blood, and boiling muck? Or spend your earthly life held in the same contempt as forgers, dishonest lawyers, thieves, murderers, oppressors of the poor, and idol-makers? You will if you practice usury. The first sentence above describes the place in hell for usurers according to the *Revelation of Peter*, a Christian book of the first half of the second century which once strongly contended for inclusion in the New Testament. The contempt in the second sentence is from a list of types of sinners from whom the church should not accept donations. It is from the Christian manual *Didascalia*, compiled in the first three decades of the third century.

In condemning dishonest sect leaders, Bishop Apollonius, around AD 211, implied that it was inconsistent with the character of a holy person to stain one's eyelids, demand money for prophesying, or lend on usury.

In ancient times, usury was the practice of charging interest on loans instead of being content with repayment of the principal. In modern Christianity, it means charging unjust and excessively high rates of interest, especially from borrowers with no other access to credit. The older view reflects the background and static economy of ancient Israel and early Christian times: little or no new money entered into circulation, financing was essential from planting to harvest, and money was considered unable to reproduce itself or grow.

In early Israel, charging interest was heinous because any borrower was already poor, which meant his Jewish neighbor had a duty to help a brother Israelite instead of impoverishing him further, which could lead to total destitution and starvation. Nehemiah 5 describes an example of God's law being disobeyed. Ordinary Jews had to borrow at interest for the necessities of life and taxes. Eventually they were reduced to selling their children into slavery to pay their mortgages and the interest.

All scriptural prohibitions on usury are in the Old Testament (e.g., Exod 22:25; Lev 23:36; Deut 23:19; Ezek 18:8, 13; 22:12). The silence of the New Testament about the ethics of usury is made up for by church tradition as recorded in the *Revelation of Peter* 31, the *Didascalia* 18, and the following authors before the middle of the third century AD.

The aspect of fraternity and help were uppermost in the mind of Clement of Alexandria, dean of the foremost Christian school in the 190s AD:

> The law prohibits a brother from taking usury: designating as a brother not only him who is born of the same parents, but also one of the same race and sentiments, and a participator in the same word; deeming it right not to take usury for money, but with open hands and heart to bestow on those who need. For God, the author and dispenser of such grace, takes as suitable usury the most precious things to be found among men—mildness, gentleness, magnanimity, reputation, renown.[1]

In the 220s AD, Clement's former student Origen mentioned the deleterious effect on usurers themselves, saying:

> It is absurd to suppose that the holy man will be a money lender, . . . distracted over payments and receipts, following a prohibited business; for the righteous man putteth not out his money to usury, and taketh not rewards against the innocent.[2]

Written shortly before AD 249, a massive compendium of Christian practice quoted various Old Testament (but not New Testament) passages as a summary of God's law that still forbade his people to lend at interest.[3]

Although not commenting specifically on the ethics of usury, Jesus taught an antimaterialism inconsistent with it:

> Matthew 5:42—Give to him that asketh thee, and from him that would borrow of thee turn not thou away.
>
> Luke 6:34–35—And if ye lend to them of whom ye hope to receive, what thank have ye? For sinners also lend to sinners, to receive

---

1. Clement of Alexandria, *Stromata* 2.18 (ANF 2:366).
2. *Commentary on Psalm 4* (my paraphrase).
3. *Testimonies against the Jews*, 48.

as much again. But love ye your enemies, and do good, and lend, hoping for nothing again.

In AD 213, the church father Tertullian elaborated on these sentiments of Jesus when discussing the compatibility of the law of Moses with that of Christ:

> The first step was to eradicate the fruit of the money lent [interest], the more easily to accustom a man to the loss, should it happen, of the money itself [principal], the interest of which he had learnt to lose. Now this, we affirm, was the function of the law as preparatory to the gospel. It was engaged in forming the faith of such as would learn, by gradual stages, for the perfect light of the Christian discipline, through the best precepts of which it was capable, inculcating a benevolence which as yet expressed itself but falteringly . . . . what else does He teach than that we should lend to those of whom we cannot receive again, inasmuch as He has imposed so great a loss on lending?[4]

In other words, foregoing interest is training for forgiving the entire debt. Before conversion and ordination, Tertullian had been a prominent lawyer and was thus probably very familiar with debts bearing interest and the consequent ruin of debtors. In his other books, Tertullian inculcated forgiveness particularly to debtors who are unable to pay, but did not limit the principle only to them.

Christ's teaching to lend without thought of return of the capital (let alone interest) and to be unmotivated about possession of wealth (especially not at the expense of another person), are exercises in detaching oneself from materialism. The common theme of the Jewish and Christian sentiments is: do not be greedy/avaricious or consumed by making money, especially not on the backs of other people.

---

4. Tertullian, *Against Marcion* 4.17 (ANF 3:372–73).

Chapter 53

Veiling of Christian Women

WHEN the gospel was new and pure, Christian women were to cover themselves with long robes and to veil themselves in public, just like Muslim women today. This was no chance remark by a single author, but was the unanimous judgment of all early Christian writers that commented on the subject. There was a controversy whether the forerunners of nuns needed to veil themselves during church services, but there was no dispute that Christian women, especially married women, ought to conceal their eyes and other bodily features when in other public places. All sources took for granted that they actually did so. Even proto-nuns covered themselves in the street.

The earliest reference is Paul the apostle in 1 Corinthians 11:5–6:

> But every woman that prayeth or prophesieth with her head uncovered dishonoureth her head: for that is even all one as if she were shaven. For if the woman be not covered, let her also be shorn: but if it be a shame for a woman to be shorn or shaven, let her be covered.

To emphasize the aspects of intuitive decency and the repugnant nature of an uncovered female head, Paul added "Judge in yourselves: is it comely that a woman pray unto God uncovered" (v. 13)? In verse 16 he also drew from the universal practice and tradition of the whole Christian church: "But if any man seem to be contentious, we have no such custom, neither the churches of God." Although considering it highly improper for a woman to be bareheaded in church, Paul did not record why some Christian sisters would do so, or whether they should be covered in the outside world. Subsequent Christian authors left no doubt.

How was 1 Corinthians 11 interpreted by the first heirs of the gospel? They had the benefit of the oral teachings and Scripture interpretations of Christ and the apostles, and could observe firsthand the actual practice of earlier Christians. The way they applied this Scripture is an indication of how first-century Christians judged themselves, and what was the custom of the churches of God.

The next reference is from Clement of Alexandria, who wrote while he was dean or president between AD 192 and 202 of Christianity's foremost institution of learning. He wrote that it is unseemly for clothes to end above the knee, "nor is it becoming for any part of a woman to be exposed."[1] A Christian woman must be

> entirely covered, unless she happen to be at home. For that style of dress is grave, and protects from being gazed at. And she will never fall, who puts before her eyes modesty, and her shawl; nor will she invite another to fall into sin by uncovering her face.[2]

Clement also pointed out that "it is prohibited to expose the ankle . . . it has also been enjoined that the head should be veiled and the face covered; for it is a wicked thing for beauty to be a snare to men."[3] He considered as no proper clothing for women anything that did not cover the eyes,[4] nor hide the shape of the body.[5]

Shortly after Clement, in the opening decades of the third century, the *Didascalia* mentioned modesty in female attire, particularly as it applied to married women. Produced in Syria or Palestine, the *Didascalia* was a comprehensive manual of Christian corporate and private life in the genre of Christian literature known as "church orders." As such, it drew from wider traditions than did individual authors, and possessed a broader influence and applicability than they did.

After discountenancing otherwise-honorable women that even then adopted the clothing, footwear, and hairstyles of streetwalkers, the *Didascalia* instructed:

> Thou therefore that art a Christian, do not imitate such women; but if thou wouldst be a faithful woman, please thy husband only.

---

1. Clement of Alexandria, *Paedagogus* 2.11 (ANF 2:266).
2. Clement of Alexandria, *Paedagogus* 3.12 (ANF 2.290).
3. Clement of Alexandria, *Paedagogus* 3.12 (ANF 2.266).
4. Clement of Alexandria, *Paedagogus* 2.11 (ANF 264–65).
5. Clement of Alexandria, *Paedagogus* 2.11 (ANF 2.265).

And when thou walkest in the street, cover thy head with thy robe, that by reason of thy veil thy great beauty may be hidden. And adorn not thy natural face; but walk with downcast looks, being veiled.[6]

In reference to the ubiquitous Roman practice of public nude bathing of both sexes together, the same chapter asked Christian women how they could appear naked in such circumstances even though they took pains to cover their faces and bodies in the street, and added "For it behoves women by a veil of modesty and humility to shew (their) fear of God."[7]

Between the times of Clement and the *Didascalia* came the church father Tertullian, although his *On Prayer* may be as early as AD 198. In what was supposed to be an exposition on prayer, it presents a comparatively long dissertation on whether the forerunners of nuns were free to be unveiled in church when all Christian women wore veils outside it. There was a controversy in the Carthaginian church over whether "woman" in 1 Corinthians 11:5–16 applied to (1) every post-pubescent female, or (2) only an adult female who was sexually experienced, i.e., not a virgin. The founder of Christian literature in the Latin language, he was a prominent Roman lawyer before converting and being ordained, and championed the cause that "woman" included sexually inexperienced adult females.

At more than one point in chapter 22, Tertullian spoke of hiding the face in public as universal among Christian females. As part of his argument, he called on proto-nuns to be consistent by veiling at public worship as well, and spoke of outdoor veiling as a law of nature.[8] He rhetorically queried: "Why do you denude before God what you cover before men? Will you be more modest in public than in the church?"[9] Part of his reasoning was that, as brides of Christ, the sisters ought to be veiled because "He bids the brides of others to be veiled, His own, of course, much more."[10]

Tertullian was consistent in his views on the topic after he left the mainline church in the middle of his writing ministry and joined the Montantists, an apocalyptic denomination that enjoined a more rigorous and committed mode of Christian practice, as witness here: "For it is *they* which must be subjected, for the sake of which 'power' ought to be 'had on

6. Connolly, *Didascalia apostolorum* 3, 26.
7. Connolly, *Didascalia apostolorum*, 28.
8. Tertullian, *On Prayer* 22 (ANF 3:688).
9. Tertullian, *On Prayer* 22 (ANF 3:688–89).
10. Tertullian, *On Prayer* 22 (ANF 3:689).

the head:' the veil is their yoke."[11] Again, he asked why the forerunners of nuns adopted full dress and veiled their heads in public, in the presence of heathen men, but did not do so in church,[12] with the implication that all adult Christian females wore burkas, or at least ample veils, outside home and church.

Not one extant author in the first two centuries of the Christian church was barefaced enough to dispute that married women must be veiled in church or that all believing adult females must cover their features when outside it or their home.

Addressing the virgins, Tertullian incidentally indicated that what Muhammad did centuries later was actually to *liberalize* the rules on veiling among his people: "Arabia's heathen *females* will be your judges, who cover not only the head, but the face also, so entirely, that they are content, with one eye free, to enjoy rather half the light than to prostitute the entire face."[13]

---

11. Tertullian, *On the Veiling of Virgins* 17 (ANF 4:37; italics translator's).
12. Tertullian, *On the Veiling of Virgins* 13 (ANF 4:35).
13. Tertullian, *On the Veiling of Virgins* 17 (ANF 4:37; italics translator's).

Chapter 54

Wifely Submission

"Be Subject to One Another"

Parameters

Some Bible verses are quoted to drive women to submit to and obey their husbands unconditionally: "Wives, submit yourselves unto your own husbands, as unto the Lord" (Eph 5:22), "as the church is subject unto Christ, so let the wives be to their own husbands in everything" (Eph 5:24), "Wives, submit yourselves unto your own husbands, as it is fit in the Lord" (Col 3:18), "The aged women [are to be] . . . teachers of good things that they may teach the young women to be . . . obedient to their own husbands" (Titus 2:3–5), and "ye wives, be in subjection to your own husbands" (1 Pet 3:1).

The readers addressed in these passages were expected to interpret them in the same milieu and culture as the New Testament writers, that is, in the context of all Christian literature of the day. Some early readers interpreted and paraphrased them for generations of Christians. The dean of Christendom's foremost educational institution in the 190s AD repeated Ephesians 5:22 in his own writings. Origen expanded on Ephesians 5:24 by urging that wives be subject to husbands "in a passionless, sinless and holy manner."[1] Commenting on Romans 16, Origen wrote that women, and not just older women, labor well in the church when they teach young women to be submissive to their husbands. Dating from the same time as Origen,

---

1. Origen, *Commentary on Ephesians* 5.24, 234.

a Syrian manual of organizational and individual Christian life lays down that a woman must not only be subject to her husband, but must revere him, fear him, honor only him, please only him, and be ready to serve him.

But what do "submission" and "obedience" entail? Did the apostles and church fathers really intend abject subservience and prostrate subjugation? No, the earliest Christian authors envisaged limits and conditions on them, and allowed wives room for judgment and flexibility. Not only wives were enjoined to be submissive; early Christians, including male Christians, were commanded to submit to other persons in their society. The present chapter will examine what constituted the submission mandated for the first Christians to see how they would have understood what submission entailed, and therefore how it was meant to be understood and how much leeway and independence of action are permitted to wives.

Submission to Clergy

A twenty-first century woman can learn the full ramifications of wifely submission by observing how her husband submits to the pastor and other church authorities. The ancient sources demanded that all Christians submit to church leaders. First is Hebrews 13:17—Christians are to obey and submit to those who have rule over us in the church, that their jobs may be easier and happier. Indeed, one of the qualifications for a bishop was "having his children in subjection with all gravity; For if a man know not how to rule his own house, how shall he take care of the church of God" (1 Tim 3:4–5)?

Next comes *1 Clement*, a writing so old and so influential that it was included in some early editions of the New Testament. Written in the first century AD when many apostles were still alive, it is usually attributed to Paul's fellow worker in Philippians 4:3. *First Clement* addressed a situation where malcontents in the congregation at Corinth had deposed clergy in succession from the apostles and had appointed their own. Throughout sixty-five chapters, *1 Clement* exhorts obedience to the true leaders of the church. Chapter 57.1 summarizes: "Ye, therefore, who laid the foundation of this sedition, submit yourselves to the presbyters [church elders], and receive correction so as to repent, bending the knees of your hearts."

The main early proponent of submission to clergy was Ignatius, a bishop of Antioch martyred around AD 107. According to legend (as distinct from the known history related in the rest of this chapter), he was the little child Jesus pointed to when teaching in Matthew 18:2–6 and Luke 9:47–48 what we all must be like to enter the kingdom of heaven.

Ignatius praised the Christians at Tralles because "ye are subject to the bishop as to Jesus Christ"[2] and exhorted them to similarly treat the presbyters as well. To those at Magnesia he wrote "Be ye subject to the bishop, and to one another, as Jesus Christ to the Father, according to the flesh, and the apostles to Christ, and to the Father, and to the Spirit."[3] Another of his letters tells the Ephesians to "be subject to the bishop and presbyters that you may be sanctified, perfectly joined together, in the same mind and judgment, and that you may all speak the same thing."[4] Last of all, Ignatius encouraged Bishop Polycarp of the city of Smyrna to see to it that Polycarp's parishioners heeded him as bishop and submitted themselves to him and other local clergy.[5] Polycarp, in turn, wrote to the young men in Philippi that they must be "subject to the presbyters and deacons, as unto God and Christ."[6]

About a century later, Origen preached that various categories of Christians should be subject to those in other categories: children to parents, citizens to secular rulers, laypersons to clergy, and lower church officers to higher office-bearers. Preachers or presbyters must submit to the bishop because God has placed him above them as a father to them. Likewise, there must be subjection to presbyters because they are the Lord's choice set over laypeople. The rule operates notwithstanding that a particular office-bearer is a lesser man, or not as intelligent, said Origen, for Jesus subjected himself to Joseph and Mary notwithstanding his true superiority.

Given that a clergyperson might be less worthy or less intelligent than a particular layman who happens to be married, a wife need show no more deference and no more enthusiasm in her submission to her husband than he displays toward "that dumb pastor." Like his teacher, Origen also advised sinners deficient in methods of self-discipline not to put trust in themselves but to become servants to saintly Christians, with the latter performing in the role of spiritual director.

---

2. Ignatius of Antioch, *Letter to Trallians* 2 (ANF 1:66).
3. Ignatius of Antioch, *Letter to Magnesians* 13 (ANF 1:64–65).
4. Ignatius of Antioch, *Letter to the Ephesians* 2 (ANF 1:50; my translation).
5. Ignatius of Antioch, *Letter to Polycarp* 6.
6. Polycarp, *Letter to the Philippians* 5 (ANF 1:34).

Submission to Government

Peter, Paul, and other Christians before AD 250 stressed submission and obedience to secular governments. Their writings show what these meant in their original context, which was the same context that promotes submission and obedience by wives. They show this, first, by indicating that the deference a wife is to render her husband need be no greater than what she, he, or Christians in general, render to the state, for early authors used the same descriptors for both relationships. Second, just as there are limits and leeway in Christian compliance with government, so also are there for wives. The fact that Christians enjoy certain liberties and room for judgment and discretion toward the state, so the ancient literature implies a degree of freedom of action as wives toward their husbands.

Origen quoted Romans as the rule for church members not to oppose secular authorities:

> Let every soul be subject unto the higher powers. For there is no power but of God: the powers that be are ordained of God. Whosoever therefore resisteth the power, resisteth the ordinance of God: and they that resist shall receive to themselves damnation.... Wherefore ye must needs be subject, not only for wrath, but also for conscience sake. For for this cause pay ye tribute also: for they are God's ministers, attending continually upon this very thing. Render therefore to all their dues: tribute to whom tribute is due; custom to whom custom; fear to whom fear; honor to whom honor. (Rom 13:1–2, 5–7)

Submission to the head of state "as supreme" is mandated in 1 Peter 2:13 "for the Lord's sake," while the following verse extends compliance "unto governors, as unto them that are sent by him for the punishment of evildoers."

In *Commentary on the Epistle to the Romans*, Origen stressed that submission and obedience to Caesar must be rendered especially by Christians who possess money, which is stamped with Caesar's image (now with Queen Elizabeth or an American president).

This may sound like absolute authoritarianism, but Acts 4:19–20 and Acts 5:29 teach that we must obey God rather than men, thus indicating that there is an exemption from the rule, and thus hinting that there are other exceptions to other rules about obedience and submission. In America and the Commonwealth, obedience and submission do not prevent Christians—including Christian husbands—from signing petitions, complaining about politicians, voting against the party in power, or running for office themselves. Because the words "submit," "submission," etc. are used for both wives and citizens, without the early authors drawing distinctions or differences between the extent of duties to the husband or government, it would appear that they meant wives to have similar choices and to be able to exercise a degree of liberty in their submissions.

Submission to Yet Others

Christians are commanded to submit in a variety of ways to a variety of other people, which indicates both that wives were not singled out and also that there are degrees of submission and liberty for independent action and discretion.

First Corinthians 16:16 commands submission not only to local clergy, but to every fellow worker that helps and labors in the gospel. *First Clement* 38.1 mandates: "let everyone be subject to his neighbor." More widely, Ephesians 5:21 encourages "submitting yourselves to one another in the fear of God." First Peter 5:5 says not only "ye younger, submit yourselves to the elder," but also "Yea, all of you be subject to one another." Besides submission to the bishop, Ignatius, a generation later, phrased it thusly: "to one another, as Jesus Christ to the Father, according to the flesh, and the apostles to Christ, and to the Father, and to the Spirit,"[7] as noted above. More concisely, Polycarp exhorted the Philippian Christians, "Be all of you subject to one another."[8] Nor can anything be more comprehensive than "Submit yourselves to every ordinance of man for the Lord's sake" (1 Pet 2:13).

If everybody is to be subject to everyone else, especially other Christians, are not husbands in some way to submit to their wives? Does not such subjection reduce the rigor and degree of deference demanded when interpreting the passages quoted in the first paragraph of this chapter? Moreover, *1 Clement* 38.1 implies that submission to one's neighbor is a spiritual gift, a charism, bestowed by the grace of God, which indicates that any submitting is a matter of degree and only to the extent the Lord gives ability.

---

7. Ignatius of Antioch, *Letter to Magnesians* 13 (ANF 1:64–65).
8. Polycarp, *Letter to the Philippians* 10.2 (ANF 1:35).

Husbands's Countervailing Duties

Nor is marriage one-sided for the husband. Verses near the main ones cited in this chapter's first two paragraphs lay duties on husbands toward their wives. Besides submitting themselves to their wife as another Christian, Paul commanded: "Husbands, love your wives, even as Christ also loved the church, and gave himself for it" (Eph 5:25), "So ought men to love their wives as their own bodies; he that loveth his wife loveth himself" (Eph 5:28), "let every one of you in particular so love his wife even as himself; and the wife see that she reverence her husband" (Eph 5:33), and "Husbands, love your wives, and be not bitter against them" (Col 3:19). First Peter 3:7 mandates that husbands live considerately with their wives and honor them. Ignatius requested Polycarp "to exhort my brethren, in the name of Jesus Christ, that they love their wives, even as the Lord the Church."[9] In the 190s AD, Origen's teacher exhorted: "let husbands love their wives as Christ also hath loved the Church."[10] In fact, according to Origen's teacher, a husband's trustworthiness, reliability, self-control, and love of others—all of which are to characterize a Christian's relations with outsiders—are also to be exhibited to his wife. Indeed, he said, marriage should be the training ground for developing and practicing love of neighbor.

No loving husband turns his beloved wife into a subservient, robotic drudge. The husband's obligations and the wife's leeway for action and independent judgment make Christian marriage less a dictatorship than a partnership.

---

9. Ignatius of Antioch, *Letter to Polycarp* 5.1 (ANF 1:95).
10. Clement of Alexandria, *Paedagogus* 3.12 (ANF 2:294).

Bibliography

Acts of John. In *New Testament Apocrypha*, edited by Wilhelm Schneemelcher, 2:172–204. Translated by R. McL. Wilson. Rev. ed. Louisville: Westminster/John Knox, 1991.
Acts of Paul (includes *Acts of Paul and Thecla*). In *The Apocryphal New Testament*, edited by Montague Rhodes James, 270–99 and 570–78. Oxford: Clarendon, 1953.
Acts of the Scillitan Martyrs. In ANF 10:[285].
Ambrose the Deacon. *Hypomnemata.* In ANF 8:739–41.
Apocalypse of Zephaniah. In *The Old Testament Pseudepigrapha*, translated by O. S. Wintermute, edited by James H. Charlesworth, 1:[508]–15. 2 vols. Garden City, NY: Doubleday, 1983–85.
Apollonius. *Against the Montanists.* In *Church History*, by Eusebius, translated by Arthur Cushman McGiffert, 235–36. 1890. Reprint. Grand Rapids, MI: Eerdmans, 1997.
Apostolic Constitutions, or *Constitutions of the Holy Apostles.* In ANF 7:391–505.
Aristides. *Apology.* In ANF 10:[263]–79,
Athenagoras. *Legatio = A Plea for the Christians.* In ANF 2:129–48.
Augsburg Confession. In *Triglot Concordia: The Symbolical Books of the Evangelical Lutheran Church: German-Latin-English*, translated by W. H. T. Dau and F. Bente, 42–95. St. Louis: Concordia, 1921.
Bardesanes. *De Fato*, or *On Fate*, or *Book of the Laws of Regions.* In ANF 8:723–34.
Carroll, Scott T., trans. *De Aleatoribus,* or "An Early Church Sermon Against Gambling (CPL 60)." *Second Century* 8.2 (1991) 83–95.
Clement of Alexandria. *Eclogae propheticae; or, Selections from the Prophetic Scriptures.* In ANF 8:43-50.
———. *Paedagogus*, or *The Instructor.* In ANF 2:209–96.
———. *Quis Dives Salvetur.* In ANF 2:591–604.
———. *Stromata, or Miscellanies.* In ANF 2:299–567
———. *To Newly Baptized, or Exhortation to Endurance.* In *Clement of Alexandria With an English Translation*, edited by G. W. Butterworth, 221–23. New York: G. P. Putnam's Sons, 1919.
Collins, J. J., trans. *Sibylline Oracles.* In *The Old Testament Pseudepigrapha*, edited by James H. Charlesworth, 1:[327]–472. 2 vols. Garden City, NY: Doubleday, 1983.
Connolly, R. Hugh, trans. *Didascalia apostolorum; The Syriac Version Translated and Accompanied by the Verona Latin Fragments.* Oxford: Clarendon, 1929.
Council of Elvira. "Canons." In *Morality and Ethics in Early Christianity,* translated and edited by Jan Womer, 75–82. Philadelphia: Fortress, 1987.

BIBLIOGRAPHY

Cyprian of Carthage. *Ad Demetrianum*. Edited by Wilhelm August Hartel. Vienna: Geroldi, 1871.

———. *De opere et eleemosynmis*, or *On Works and Alms*. In ANF 5:476–84.

———. *Epistle 61*. In ANF 5:356–58.

Diatessaron. In ANF 10:43–129.

Didache. In ANF 7:377–82.

Epistle of the Apostles. trans Montague Rhodes James in *The Apocryphal New Testament* 485–503. Oxford: Clarendon, 1953.

The First Epistle of Clement to the Corinthians. In ANF 1:[5]–21, 10:[229]–48.

Gaylord, H. E., Jr. *Greek Apocalypse of Baruch*. In *The Old Testament Pseudepigrapha*, edited by James H. Charlesworth, 1:662–79. 2 vols. Garden City, NY: Doubleday, 1983–85.

Gospel of Judas. Translated by Randolphe Kasser, et al. Washington, DC: National Geographic, 2006.

Gregory. *Metaphrase of the Book of Ecclesiastes*. In ANF 6:9–17.

Hippolytus. *The Apostolic Tradition of Hippolytus*. Translated by Scott Easton Burton. New York: Macmillan, 1934.

———. *Blessings of Moses, Levi*. Translated by Maurice Brière, et al. *Patrologia orientalis* 27.1 (1954) 148–49, 155–57.

———. *Commentary on Daniel*. Translated by Thomas Coffman Schmidt. Charleston, SC: privately printed, 2011.

Ignatius of Antioch. *Letter to Polycarp*. In ANF 1:93–96.

———. *Letter to the Ephesians*. In ANF 1:49–58.

———. *Letter to the Magnesians*. In ANF 1:59–65.

———. *Letter to the Philadelphians*. In ANF 1:79–85.

———. *Letter to the Romans*. In ANF 1:73–78.

———. *Letter to the Smyrnaeans*. In ANF 1:86–92.

———. *Letter to the Trallians*. In ANF 1:66–72.

Irenaeus of Lyons. *Against Heresies*. In ANF 1:315–567.

Justin Martyr. *1 Apology*. In ANF 1:163–87.

———. *2 Apology*. In ANF 1:188–93.

———. *Dialogue with Trypho*. In ANF 1:194–270.

Letter of Barnabas. In ANF 1:137–49.

Letter to Diognetus. In ANF 1:25–30.

Lucian of Samosata. "The Passing of Perigrinus." In *Lucian with an English Translation*, edited by Austin M. Harmon, 5:2–51. 8 vols. Cambridge, MA: Harvard University Press, 1936.

Martyrdom of Potamiaena and Basilides. In *Church History*, by Eusebius, translated by Arthur Cushman McGiffert, *Nicene and Post-Nicene Fathers 2d*, 1:253. 1890. Reprint, Grand Rapids: Eerdmans, 1997.

McGuckin, John Anthony. *The Westminster Handbook to Origen*. Louisville: Westminster John Knox, 2004.

Melito of Sardis. *On Pascha*. In *Melito of Sardis: On Pascha and Fragments*, edited by Stuart George Hall, 2–61. Oxford: Clarendon, 1979.

Minucius Felix. *Octavius*. In ANF 4:173–98.

Origen. *Against Celsus*. In ANF 4:395–669.

———. *Commentary on Ephesians.* In *The Commentaries of Origen and Jerome on St. Paul's Epistle to the Ephesians,* translated by Ronald E. Heine. Oxford: Oxford University Press, 2002.

———. *Commentary on Matthew.* Books 1 and 2 [fragment], 10–14: In ANF 10:413–512.

———. *Commentary on the Epistle to the Romans.* Translated by Thomas P. Scheck. 2 vols. Washington, DC: Catholic University of America Press, 2001–02.

———. *Commentary on the Song of Songs.* In *Origen: The Song of Songs: Commentary and Homilies,* translated and annotated by R. P. Lawson, 21–263. New York: Newman, 1957.

———. *Commentary on Titus.* In *Apology for Origen St. Pamphilus; with the Letter of Rufinus on the Falsification of the Books of Origen,* translated by Thomas P. Scheck, 54–60, 110–11. Washington, DC: Catholic University of America Press, 2010.

———. *Homilies on Exodus.* In *Origen: Homilies on Genesis and Exodus,* translated by Ronald E. Heine, 227–387. Washington, DC: Catholic University of America Press, 1982.

———. *Homilies on Ezekiel,* translated by Thomas P. Scheck. New York: Newman, 2010.

———. *Homilies on Genesis.* In *Origen: Homilies on Genesis and Exodus,* translated by Ronald E. Heine, 47–224. Washington, DC: Catholic University of America Press, 1982.

———. *Homilies on Jeremiah* In *Origen: Homilies on Jeremiah, Homily on 1 Kings 28,* translated by John Clark Smith, 3–316. Washington, DC: Catholic University of America Press, 1998.

———. *Homilies on Joshua.* Edited by Cynthia White. Translated by Barbara J. Bruce. Washington, DC: Catholic University of America Press, 2002.

———. *Homilies on Leviticus,* translated by Gary Wayne Barkley. Washington, DC: Catholic University of America Press, 1990.

———. *Homilies on Luke; Fragments on Luke.* Translated by Joseph T. Lienhard. Washington, DC: Catholic University of America Press, 1996.

———. *Homilies on Numbers.* Translated by Thomas P. Scheck. Edited by Christopher A. Hall. Downers Grove, IL: IVP Academic, 2009.

———. *Homilies on Psalm 36.* In *Homélies sur les Psaumes 36 à 38,* translated by Henri Crouzel and Luc Brésard, [49]–255. Paris: Cerf, 1995.

———. *Homilies on Psalm 37.* In *Homélies sur les Psaumes 36 à 38,* translated by Henri Crouzel and Luc Brésard, [257]–327. Paris: Cerf, 1995.

———. *Homilies on Samuel.* Translated by Pierre Nautin and Marie-Thérèse Nautin. Paris: Cerf, 1986.

———. *Homilies on the Song of Songs.* In *Origen: The Song of Songs: Commentary and Homilies,* translated by R. P. Lawson, 265–305. New York: Newman, 1957.

———. *Letter to Friends in Alexandria.* In *The Heritage of the Early Church: Essays in Honor of the Very Rev. George Visilievich Florovsky,* edited by David Neiman and Margaret Shatkin, 135–50. Rome: Pont. Institutum Studiorum Orientalium, 1973.

———. *On Prayer.* In *Origen: An Exhortation to Martyrdom, Prayer, First Principles,* translated by Rowan A. Greer, 81–170. London: SPCK, 1979.

———. *On First Principles, or De principiis.* In ANF 4:239–382.

Oulton, John Ernest Leonard, and Henry Chadwick, eds. *Alexandrian Christianity: Selected Translations,* Philadelphia: Westminster, 1954.

Passion of Perpetua and Felicitas. In ANF 3:[699]–706.

Pliny the Younger, *Letter 10.96*. In *Selections from Early Writers Illustrative of Church History to the Time of Constantine*, edited by Henry Melvill Gwatkin, 29–31. London: Macmillan, 1914.

Polycarp. *Letter to the Philippians*. In ANF 1:33–36.

Ptolemy the Gnostic. *Letter to Flora*. In *Biblical Interpretation in the Early Church*, translated by Karlfried Froehlich, 37–43. Philadelphia: Fortress, 1985.

Revelation of Peter. In *The Apocryphal New Testament*, edited by Montague Rhodes James, 506–24. Oxford: Clarendon, 1953.

Roberts, Alexander, and James Donaldson. *The Ante-Nicene Fathers: Translations of the Writings of the Fathers Down to A.D. 325*. Buffalo, NY: Christian Literature, 1885–96.

Schmidt, Carl, ed. *The Books of Jeu and the Untitled Text in the Bruce Codex*. Translated by Violet MacDermot. Leiden: Brill, 1978.

The Second Epistle of Clement to the Corinthians. In ANF 10:[251]–56.

Sentences of Sextus. Translated by Richard A. Edwards and Robert A. Wild. Chico, CA: Scholars, 1981.

Tatian. *Address to the Greeks* In ANF 2:65–83.

Tertullian. *Ad Nationes*, or *To the Nations*. In ANF 3:[109]–47.

———. *Against Marcion*. In ANF 3:[271]–474.

———. *Apology*. In ANF 3:[17]–55.

———. *De cultu feminarum*, or, *On the Apparel of Women*. In ANF 4:14–25.

———. *De pallio*, or *On the Pallium*. In ANF 4:5–12.

———. *De Spectaculis*. In ANF 3:[79]–91.

———. *On Fasting*. In ANF 4:102–14.

———. *On Flight in Persecution: AD 211/212*. In ANF 4:116–25.

———. *On Garlands*, or *On Crowns*, or *De corona*. In ANF 3:[93]–103.

———. *On Idolatry*. In ANF 3:[61]–76.

———. *On Modesty*. In ANF 4:74–101.

———. *On Monogamy*. In ANF 4:59–72.

———. *On Patience*. In ANF 3:[707]–17.

———. *On Prayer*. In ANF 3:[681]–91.

———. *On the Soul*. In ANF 3:[181]–235.

———. *On the Veiling of Virgins*. In ANF 4:27–37.

———. *To His Wife*. In ANF 4:39–49.

Testimonies against the Jews. In ANF 5:507–57.

Theophilus. *To Autolycus*. In ANF 2:89–121.

To Abercius Marcellus. In *Church History*, by Eusebius, translated by Arthur Cushman McGiffert, 230–33. 1890. Reprint. Grand Rapids, MI: Eerdmans, 1997.

Traditions of Matthias. In *The Apocryphal New Testament*, edited by Montague Rhodes James, 12–13. Oxford: Clarendon, 1953.

Two Letters on Virginity. In ANF 8:55–66.

Urbanus, Asterius. "The Extant Writings of Asterisus Urbanus." In ANF 7:335–37.

Vienne and Lyons Churches, *Letter of the Churches of Vienne and Lyons to the Churches of Asia and Phrygia*. In ANF 8:778–84.

Walzer, Richard. *Galen on Jews and Christians*. Oxford: Oxford University Press, 1949

Wood, Simon P., trans. *Clement of Alexandria: Christ the Educator*. New York: Fathers of the Church, 1954.

www.ingramcontent.com/pod-product-compliance
Lightning Source LLC
Chambersburg PA
CBHW070250230426
43664CB00014B/2481